For
Abraham and Sarah Terian
With love,
Vahan H. Tootikian

Sept. 18, '94

UNDERSTANDING THE NEW TESTAMENT

Vahan H. Tootikian

Armenian Heritage Committee
P.O. Box 531
Southfield, Michigan

1991

Dedicated to
My Granddaughter
Talia Juliette Zartarian

UNDERSTANDING THE NEW TESTAMENT

ORDER FROM
ARMENIAN HERITAGE COMMITTEE
P.O. BOX 531
SOUTHFIELD, MICHIGAN 48037

PRICE: $25.00

Shipping and Handling add $2.50
(plus $.75 per book for orders of 2 or more)

ISBN: 0-8187-0137-4
Library of Congress Catalog Card Nunmber: 91-71070

Tootikian, H. Vahan
    Understanding the New Testament

    Bibliography.
    Includes Index.

Library of Congress Catalog Card Number:

Published in the United States of America 1991

Copyright © 1991 Vahan H. Tootikian. All rights reserved.

This book may not be reproduced, in whole or in part, in any form (except by reviewers for the public press), without written permission from the author.

CONTENTS

PREFACE 7
PART 1   A SURVEY OF THE NEW TESTAMENT 9
   The Formation of the New Testament Canon 9
   How the New Testament Was Handed Down to Us 12
   The World Into Which Jesus Was Born 21
   The Jewish Community in Which Jesus Lived 23
   The Impact of the Intertestimental Hebrew Literature
      & Greek Language and Culture 27
   The Synagogue: Platform for Early Christian
      Missionaries 32

PART 2   THE GOSPELS 35
   An Overview of the Gospels: The Rise of the Christian Faith—the Historical Jesus; the Nature of the Gospels; the "How," "Why," and "When" of the Gospels
   The Gospel of Matthew 42
   The Gospel of Mark 59
   The Gospel of Luke 78
   The Gospel of John 105

PART 3   THE ACTS OF THE APOSTLES 129

PART 4   THE EPISTLES 157
A. Major Pauline Epistles 157
      Romans 158
      I Corinthians 167
      II Corinthians 179
      Galatians 185
      Ephesians 191
      Philippians 196
      Colossians 202
      I Thessalonians 208
      II Thessalonians 212
      Philemon 215

B. The Pastoral Epistles 222
       I Timothy 225
       II Timothy 227
       Titus 229
C. Hebrews and General (Catholic) Epistles 233
       Hebrews 234
       James 240
       I Peter 245
       II Peter 248
       I John 252
       II John 254
       III John 256
       Jude 257
PART 5   THE BOOK OF REVELATION 263
EPILOGUE 282
BIBLIOGRAPHY 285
INDEX 291

Preface

Understanding the New Testament, a survey of the New Testament, is designed to provide college undergraduate students with a working understanding of the New Testament books. In addition, it is intended to be a study tool for adult education and Bible study groups and for those who have neither the time nor guidance for serious study of the New Testament but desire to grasp the central thrust of the foundation document of Christianity.

The purpose of this volume is to acquaint the reader with the content of each of the twenty-seven books of the New Testament and to supply sufficient information concerning their historical, theological, and literary backgrounds.

Discussions in *Understanding the New Testament* include data about each book's date, historical context, authorship, and theological content. A general outline and summary commentary follow the introductory data for each of the books. Each book is examined as a self-contained entity, following the classification order of the New Testament. I have attempted to deal candidly with major problems of biblical research, present opposite positions, and give a balanced account. Because this volume is not written for biblical scholars and experts, I have employed a minimum of technical phraseology.

Understanding the New Testament is divided into five parts:

Part One places the New Testament in the context of its relationship to the older Hebrew Bible. It presents a survey of the process by which the New Testament canon was formed. It summarizes the political events that brought Jesus' homeland under Roman domination, and it describes the world of first-century Judaism.

Part Two examines the various approaches of studying the Gospels—the literary *genre* the early Christians invented to relate the teachings and deeds of Jesus. Since the four Gospels are the foundation documents of Christianity and comprise forty percent of the New Testament, a relatively larger space is given to them in this volume.

Part Three contains the Acts of Apostles which narrates a

series of crucial events dealing with the genesis and development of the early church. Covering a span of thirty years (33-63 A.D.), this narrative traces the spread of Christianity from its Jewish birthplace through the eastern Mediterranean to the center of Gentile power, Rome itself.

Part Four deals with the twenty-one epistles (another distinct literary *genre*), most of which were written by Paul, and Pauline disciples who later wrote them in his name and spirit. These epistles fall under three major categories: the Major Pauline Letters, the Pastoral Letters, and the General (Catholic) Letters.

Part Five is a presentation of the Book of Revelation, which represents another unique literary category in Christian Scriptures: *apocalypse* (a disclosure, vision, of spiritual realities or truths hidden in the future).

All Scripture quotations in this volume are from the New International Version.

I am grateful to the following: Armenian Heritage Committee for publishing this volume; Mrs. Louise Monacelli for typing and re-typing the manuscript; Mrs. Ann Marie Nickel for her editorial help; Mr. Robert Monacelli for his artistic work to prepare the maps and outside cover of the book; Dr. John Peterson for his proof-reading the final draft; and my students of the past fifteen years at Lawrence Technological University, whose probing questions and deep interest provided the inspiration for this book.

January 6, 1991　　　　　　　　　　　　　　Vahan H. Tootikian
Southfield, Michigan

PART 1

A SURVEY OF THE NEW TESTAMENT

1. The Formation of the New Testament Canon

The twenty-seven books which constitute the second part of the two portions into which the Bible is divided are called the New Testament.

The very term *NEW* Testament obviously implies an OLD, and came into being when Christianity found the need to have its own *canon* in addition to the Hebrew Bible. "Canon" describes the body of biblical literature recognized as uniquely authoritative for a given religious community. It comes from a Greek term used to express the idea of a standard or a norm of measurement. Thus, the Christian canon of scripture contains the entire Hebrew Bible (parenthetically, of all major world religions, Christianity is the only one that has adopted the scriptures of another religion) and those additional books which in the judgment of the early Christian community measured up to a divinely given rule or standard of authority.

The term *New Testament* or "the new covenant" (in biblical terms, *testament* is a synonym for *covenant*) first occurs in the New Testament in connection with Jesus' institution of the Lord's Supper on the night before his crucifixion (Luke 22:20; I Cor. 11:25; Matt. 26:28; Mark 14:24). Believing themselves to be people of the new covenant with God, Christians eventually called their sacred writings the New Testament.[1]

The Christian canon of scriptures is, in some respects, closely related to the Hebrew Bible. Throughout its pages are references to persons and events of Hebrew history and quotes from the Hebrew Scriptures. Moreover, the Hebrew Bible was the Bible of Jesus Christ, the apostles, and the early Church. The first Christian community in Palestine primarily consisted of Jews whose Scripture was the Hebrew Bible.

The early Christians, however, viewed the Hebrew scriptures differently than Jews. They insisted that what had been accomplished in the life, death, and resurrection of Jesus had happened "according to the scriptures" (I Cor. 15:3-4). In other words, the early Church reinterpreted those scriptures in the light of its faith in the Person of Jesus Christ. For the early Christians the supreme authority was not the Hebrew Bible but Jesus Christ, their Master and risen Lord.

It is not surprising, therefore, that in the early Church the words of Jesus were treasured and quoted, and considered superior to the authority of the Hebrew Bible (Acts 20:35; I Cor. 7:10; 9:14; I Tim. 5:18). Parallel with the oral circulation of Jesus' teaching were apostolic interpretations of the significance of his person and work for the life of the Church.[2]

Exactly when the New Testament writings began to be generally accepted as of equal authority with the Hebrew Bible (the Old Testament) is not known.

In the same way, just how the New Testament writings were assembled in one volume is unknown to us. Each of the twenty-seven books originated as a separate document and at first circulated independently of the others. The list of New Testament books known or accepted by individual churches may be deduced from the quotations and statements that appear in the works of the early Church Fathers. Such lists, however, were unofficial.

The first known canon to be adopted consciously was the Canon of Marcion, which appeared in 140 A.D. Marcion, a Gnostic, established a Christian Scripture distinct from the Jewish Bible, which he rejected. Measured by his own theological premises, he selected Luke for his Gospel and used ten of Paul's epistles in the following order: Galatians, I and II Corinthians, Romans, I and II Thessalonians, Ephesians (which he called Laodiceans), Colossians, Philippians, and Philemon.

The Canon of Marcion produced a violent reaction in the

Church. Marcion was excommunicated from the Church at Rome in 140 A.D. Christian leaders now were forced to come to grips with the problem. At that point the church fathers began to publish lists of sacred Christian writings which were acceptable by the masses at large. These lists became the foundation for the official New Testament Canon.

The earliest surviving list is the so-called Muratorian Canon. This Latin fragment, contained in an eighth-century manuscript, was discovered in the library at Milan in 1740 by the librarian Muratori. The fragment is to be dated ca. 200 A.D. and probably originated in Rome.[3] Since the manuscript is only a fragment of a larger work, it is not complete. It begins in a middle of a sentence, and the first book mentioned is Luke, which the fragment calls the third Gospel. Probably Matthew and Mark preceded Luke in this list. It also contained thirteen letters of Paul (but excluding Hebrews); Jude; I (but not II) Peter; I and II (but not III) John; the Wisdom of Solomon, Revelation, and the Apocalypse of Peter.[4]

Other lists, such as Codex Claromontanus, included much noncanonical material: the Epistle of Barnabas, the Shepherd of Hermas, the Acts of Paul, and the Revelation of Peter. Another Greek manuscript known as the Codex Alexandrinus included both I and II Clement as part of the New Testament.[5]

By the end of the second century the basic shape of the Christian Canon had emerged. The essential core consisted of the four Gospels, the Pauline epistles, the catholic epistles, and less certainly the Book of Revelation. Some writings, accepted later, were not yet included or even mentioned: Hebrews, James, I and II Peter, and one of the Johannine letters. Other writings (which were later considered noncanonical) were accepted by some and rejected by others.

Through the third century the debate continued on the acceptance or rejection of some of the "fringe" writings. In the meantime, the Church was in the process of developing certain criteria for admitting writings to canonical status. The primary criterion, of course, was the divine inspiration of the individual books. But since divine inspiration is something intangible, the Church adopted four secondary criteria:

a. *Apostolicity*: the books should have been written by an apostle or a person having close contact with an apostle;
 b. *Spirituality*: the contents of the individual books had to bear witness of that divine inspiration;
 c. *Orthodoxy*: the contents of the books had to be in line with right belief as defined by the accepted officials of the Church;
 d. *General Acceptance*: Each book had to be accepted by the greatest possible majority of the churches.

The first official listing of the twenty-seven books that accords with the present New Testament contents was not issued unto 367 A.D., more than three centuries after the deaths of Jesus' original disciples. This historic list appeared in the Easter Letter of Athanasius, bishop of Alexandria.[6]

The Synod of Laodicea in 363 A.D. was the first ecclesiastical council to deal with the question of the Canon. Its 59th rule ordered that only the canonical books of the Old and New should be read in the Church. The 60th rule gave the list of the New Testament Canon composed of twenty-six books, excluding the Book of Revelation.

The Synod of Rome in 382 and the African Councils of Hippo (393) and Carthage (397), one after the other, accepted all the twenty-seven books of the New Testament as canonical.[7] Thus, by the end of the fourth century, the New Testament stood with the Hebrew Bible as the official scripture of Christianity.

2. How the New Testament Was Handed Down to Us

A. *Transmission of the New Testament Text*

The New Testament was written in *Koine* Greek, the international language of the first-century workaday world. This does not necessarily mean that all of the twenty-seven books were originally composed in that language. There are some scholars who believe that at least Mark and Matthew, and perhaps other parts of the New Testament, were first written in Aramaic and later translated into Greek.[8] Aramaic was the mother tongue of the Palestinian Jews during the time of the New Testament. It was the language of Arameans (ancient Syrians), a Semitic tongue used in parts of Mesopotamia about 1000 B.C. After the Babylonian Captivity (538 B.C.), it became the common language of Palestinian Jews. It was the language spoken by Jesus.

An Aramaic New Testament, however, would have had comparatively few readers outside Palestine. Greek was then spoken by so large a percentage of the population that it communicated far more effectively than any other language. Thus, the *Koine* Greek, as a powerful medium of communication, became the language of the New Testament to a Greek-speaking and Greek-reading world.

The Christian Church continued to use Greek for several centuries. In 313, when Christianity became the favorite religion of the Empire under Constantine, the Church had the resources to produce fine manuscripts, which were written in Greek. Greek continued to be the official language of a major branch of the Christian Church in the East, and manuscripts of the New Testament continued to be produced in Greek until the invention of printing.[9]

These manuscripts may be classified as follows:

a. *Papyrus Codices* - manuscripts which are on sheets of papyrus bound together as a *codex*. A *codex* is a manuscript book of an ancient biblical text, a form pioneered by Christians to replace the unwieldy scrolls, rolled around a stick, on which the Scriptures were recorded.

b. *The Great Uncial Codices* - Manuscripts of the complete New Testament written in continuous script written on parchment in uncial characters (large or capital letters). They are written without spaces between words; also called "manuscules."

Although there are no complete New Testament texts earlier than the fourth century A.D., the oldest manuscript fragments date from the second century and include versions in Greek, Syriac, Latin, and other languages. These, however, do not present a total picture of the New Testament.

The most important manuscripts are the following uncial codices:

a. *Codex Vatincanus* - an early fourth-century manuscript, containing the whole Greek Bible (the Septuagint), is the earliest of the great uncials. It has been in the Vatican Library in Rome since 1475.

   b. *Codex Sinaiticus* - a mid-fourth-century manuscript discovered by Konstantin Von Tischendorf in the monastery of St. Catherine at the foot of Mount Sinai in the mid-1800's. Besides the entire New Testament it contains most of the Greek Old Testament and a few noncanonical books.

   c. *Codex Alexandrinus* - an early fifth century manuscript which contained the Old and the New Testament and a collection of noncanonical Jewish psalms. Originally kept in Alexandria, now it is in the British Museum.

   d. *Codex Bezae* - a fifth or sixth century manuscript written in both Greek and Latin, having a Greek text and a Latin translation on facing pages. It is at Cambridge University.

Of these and numerous other manuscripts, no two are precisely alike, which present the translators and biblical scholars with a formidable challenge. They have to compare variations among thousands of manuscripts and try to determine the most reliable ones.[10] Scribal errors of all kinds have crept into these manuscripts.

Through the centuries many attempts have been made to establish a reliable Greek text from which translations could be made. In the sixteenth century (1516), for example, Dutch humanist Desiderius Erasmus made such an attempt. In 1522 the Catholic Bishop Ximenes published a Greek New Testament with Hebrew, Aramaic, Latin, and Greek in parallel columns. In 1546, the Protestant printer-editor Robert Estiene (Stephanus) began to publish a Greek New Testament.[11] Many other efforts in this realm were put forth by many Christian churches.

One of the most successful attempts was that of B.F. Wescott and F.J. Hort in 1881-82, when they published their monumental work entitled *New Testament in the Original Greek.*

Wescott and Hort recognized that the ancient manuscripts could be sorted into various groups, each representing the text of a given area of the ancient Church, and they went on to claim that one of these groups did in fact represent almost the original text of the New Testament transmitted in a comparatively uncorrupted form. This was for them the "Neutral Text," essentially the great uncial Vaticanus and Sinaiticus. Their *New Testament in the Original Greek* was based on these manuscripts.[12]

Since the publication of the Westcott and Hort text, the scholarly process of refining and improving the text has continued. Because no original copy of the New Testament has survived, and because all manuscripts differ from one another to some degree, enhancing the quality and reliability of the biblical text will be an ongoing process and challenge.

B. *English Translations*

The Bible is by far the most translated book in the world. The Jews translated their scriptures into Greek and other languages. The Christian Church also translated its scriptures in order to accommodate its multi-racial and multi-lingual members as well as reach out to masses in their own language.[13] Thus the Bible was translated into many tongues.

One of the earliest and most important translations of the New Testament in the early centuries was St. Jerome's Latin Vulgate translation. Jerome was commissoned by the bishop of Rome to translate the Bible into the common tongue for the Latin-speaking Catholic Church between 385 to 405 A.D. This version became the official Bible of the Roman Catholic Church for many centuries, while the New Testament continued to circulate in its original *Koine* Greek throughout the eastern half of the Roman Empire (later known as the Byzantine Empire).

In the eighth century an attempt was made to translate the Bible into English. In 730 Venerable Bede, a Benedictine monk and historian of Anglo-Saxon England, rendered part of Jerome's Latin Vulgate into Old English. He was the first person in history to do so. Similar attempts were made during the tenth and eleventh centuries, but it was not until during the fourteenth century that the entire Bible was translated into English. The pioneering translation was the work of John Wycliffe, an English priest. To make the Scriptures accessible to his countrymen in their own language, Wycliffe translated both Old and New Testaments from the Vulgate. He completed his translation around 1384. But the Catholic Church, fearing the consequences of the Bible's availability to and interpretation by the average layperson, condemned Wycliffe's translation in 1408. Further attempts were suppressed by the Church for at least a century and a half.[14]

By the sixteenth century some historical events on the continent of Europe ensured that the Bible would find a larger reading in English. The Renaissance, Johann Gutenberg's invention of movable type, and the Protestant Reformation brought about tremendous upheaval in the realm of religion, along with cultural, political, and social spheres. In Germany, the Protestant Reformer Martin Luther rendered the German translation of the Bible in the years 1522-34. This was the first version in a modern European language based not on the official Latin Vulgate Bible but on the original Hebrew and Greek.

In 1525, William Tyndale completed the first translation of the New Testament from Greek manuscripts. Tyndale's translation aroused great controversy in England. Intense hostility and persecution prevented him from completing his translation of the Old Testament, and in 1535 he was betrayed, tried for heresy, and burned at the stake.

The next major English translator, Myles Coverdale, published the first complete printed Bible in English in 1535. Matthew's Bible (1537) which contained additional sections of the Old Testament, was revised by Coverdale, and the result was called the Great Bible (1539). The Bishop's Bible (1568) was a revision of the Great Bible, and the King James was commissioned as a scholarly revision of the Bishop's Bible. The Geneva Bible (1560), which the English Puritans had produced in Switzerland, also influenced the King James Version.[15]

Meanwhile, the Roman Catholic Church rendered its first English Bible known as Reims Douay Bible. The translation was made by two Oxfordians, Gregory Martin and Allen. The New Testament appeared in 1582, and the Old Testament was delayed until 1609. It also had its influence upon the King James Version.

One of the most popular English translations has been the King James (KJV) or Authorized Version. It was authorized by James I of England, who appointed fifty-four scholars to make a new version of the Bishop's Bible for official use by the Church of England. After seven years of painstaking labor, during which the oldest available manuscripts were consulted, these scholars produced in 1611 the Authorized or King James Version. This translation became a landmark in the religious history of the English-speaking people and one of the masterpieces of English literature.

Although the King James remains unsurpassed in literary excellence, and although it phrases the Scriptures in beautiful, memorable fashion, later discovered manuscripts and language changes over the years necessitated revisions, updating, and reediting. In 1881, after more than two and a half centuries, a revision of KJV was undertaken. The result was the English Revised Version (RV or ERV) of the New Testament. A modification of this edition, the American Revised Version, was published in 1901.

In the course of time, translators have developed three basic theories of translation: *Literal, Free*, and *Dynamic Equivalence*.

a. *Literal Translation* is concerned with transferring words and phrases into the receptor language exactly as they appear in the original.

b. *Free Translation*, or paraphrase, is less concerned with maintaining the exact words of the original, attempting instead to transfer the ideas from one language to another.

c. *Dynamic Equivalence Translation* is a blend of the most up-to-date scholarship concerning the meaning and use of the ancient words and grammatical constructions in order to produce precise equivalents in the receptor language.

In the twentieth century alone, more than eighty translations of the New Testament have been rendered. The shortcomings of the Literal Translations like that of King James, English Revised, and American Standard Revised led the American Standard Bible Committee to appoint a committee of over thirty competent biblical scholars to undertake a new translation of the Bible. Between 1946 and 1952 the Revised Standard Version (RSV) appeared.

A number of private translations were produced in the twentieth century. They are essentially Free Translations. The three most important are probably those by James Moffatt, Edgar J. Goodspeed, and J.B. Phillips.

Moffat, a Scottish New Testament scholar, published in

1928 in one volume his two separate translations of the New and Old Testaments entitled *The Bible: A New Translation*. In 1927, Goodspeed, an American New Testament scholar, published his version called *The Bible: An American Translation*. Phillips, an Anglican vicar, published in one volume his translation of the New Testament (originally in four volumes) as *The New Testament in Modern English,* in 1958.

Until the 1930s, Roman Catholic translations of the New Testament have been translations of the Latin Vulgate. A change came, however, beginning in 1935 with the publication of the Westminister Version in England, and the Kleist-Lilly New Testament in America in 1954. These were free translations of the Greek manuscripts.

Two of the most important new translations by the Roman Catholics are the Jerusalem Bible (1966) and the New American Bible (1970; revised in 1987). The latter was translated from the Greek into modern English.

An excellent international version is the New English Bible (NEB) produced by Protestant, Catholic, and Jewish biblical scholars in 1970.

Another outstanding translation rendered in 1973 is the New International Version (NIV), which closely parallels the Revised Standard Version, and is a good example of Dynamic Equivalence translation.

Among the modern popular versions are the Good News and the Living Bible, both of which are free translations.

Major Events in New Testament History

63 B.C.	General Pompey's legions occupy Palestine, annexing it as part of the Roman Empire.
40 B.C.	Herod (Herod the Great) is appointed king of Judea by the Roman Senate; he rules from 40-4 B.C.
30 B.C.-14 A.D.	Augustus Caesar rules as emperor of Rome.
4 B.C. (?)	Jesus is born to Mary and Joseph in Bethlehem (Matt. 2; Luke 2); King Herod dies and his kingdom is divided among his three sons.
14-37 A.D.	Tiberius, stepson of Augustus, rules Rome (Luke 3:1).
27-29 A.D. or 30-32 A.D.	John the Baptist conducts his ministry (Mark 1:2-11; 6:17-29; John 1:19-36; 3:22-36).
27-30 A.D. or 29-33 A.D. (?)	Jesus' public ministry, recorded in the Gospels of Matthew, Mark, Luke, and John.
30 or 33 A.D.	Crucifixion and Resurrection of Jesus, in the four Gospels.
30 or 35 A.D.	Conversion of Apostle Paul (Acts 9:1-19; 22:1-21; 26:1-23; Gal. 1:11-16).
50-62 A.D.	Paul writes his epistles; about 47-56 he embarks upon three missionary journeys among the Gentiles.
62 A.D.	Martyrdom of James, brother of Jesus
64-65 A.D.	Following a major fire in Rome, the emperor Nero persecutes Christians there.
66-70 A.D.	Jewish revolt against Rome begins in 66 A.D.; in 70 A.D. Titus captures and destroys Jerusalem and its Temple.
68-100 A.D.	The Four Gospels and the Book of Acts are written.
85-95 A.D.	Hebrews, I Peter, and James are written.
95 A.D.	Persecutions by emperor Domitian cause John of Patmos to write the Book of Revelation.
95-110 A.D.	I, II, and III John are written.
110-135 A.D.	I and II Timothy, Titus, Jude, and II Peter are written.
367 A.D.	Bishop Athanasius of Alexandria publishes list of twenty-seven New Testament books corresponding to present New Testament canon.

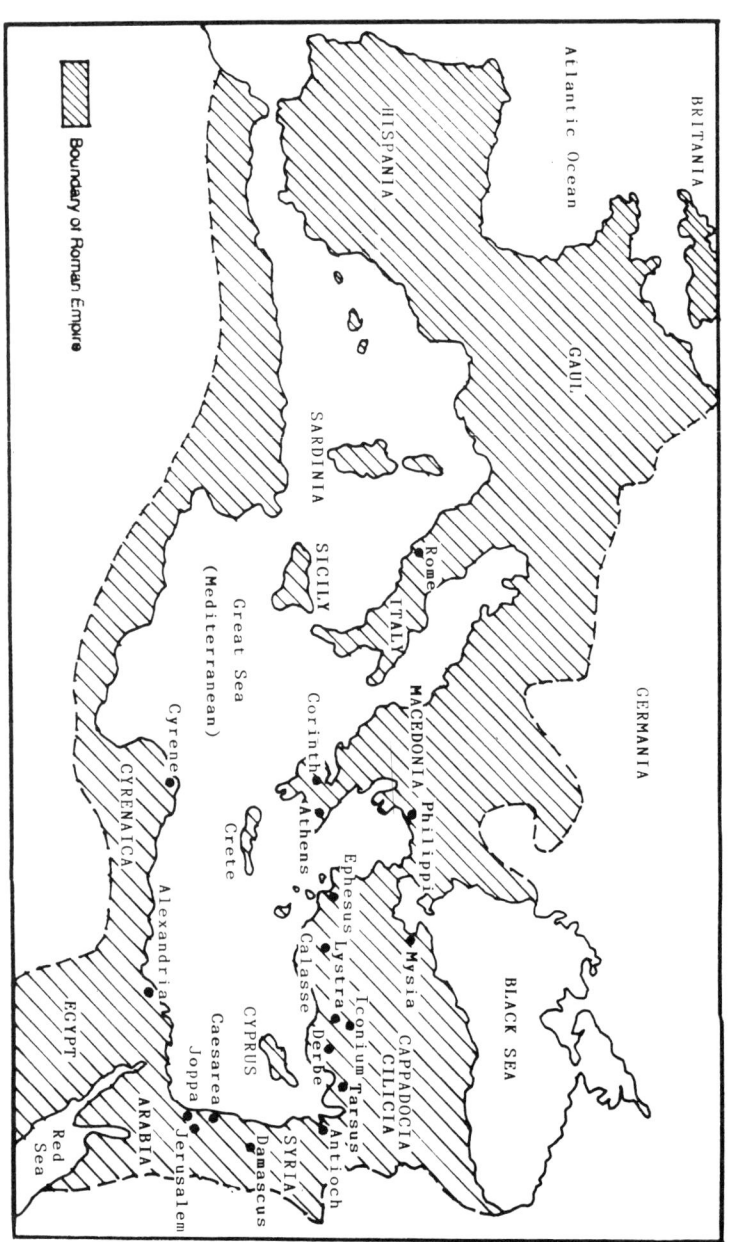

3. The World Into Which Jesus Was Born

The New Testament contains the primary source material on the life of Jesus Christ, and provides the earliest account of the spread of Christianity from Palestine. To understand Jesus, his early followers, and their time, it is necessary to study the intertestamental period—the period between the end of the Old and the beginning of the New Testaments. When Jesus was born, Israel was a land of approximately two million people occupying six thousand square miles.[16] It was ruled by Rome, but before becoming part of the Roman Empire it had been under the rule of other foreign nations.

In 922 B.C., the Hebrew kingdom divided into the ten-tribe northern state of Israel and the two-tribe southern state of Judah (I Kings 12). In 721 B.C., Assyria conquered Israel, destroying its capital Samaria and deporting the population (II Kings 17). In 586 B.C., King Nebuchadnezzar of Babylon occupied Judah, destroyed its capital Jerusalem, burned Solomon's Temple, and took Jews captive to Babylon (II Kings 24). In 539 B.C., Cyrus the Great of Persia defeated the Babylonians, and the following year, in 538 B.C., allowed the Jewish exiles to return to their homeland (Ezra 1-6). In 333 B.C., Alexander the Great of Macedonia became a world conqueror, and in about 332 B.C., he occupied Palestine (I Maccabees 1). He planted Greek cities all over his conquered domains and enforced Greek culture and language in all the occupied territories.[17]

Upon Alexander's death in 323 B.C. his empire was divided among four generals. Of the two eastern sections, Syria went to the Seleucids and Egypt to Ptolemy. Palestine, lying between Syria and Egypt, at first went to Ptolemy from 323-197 B.C. and then, from 197-142, to the Seleucid dynasty of Syria.

The most infamous ruler of the Seleucid dynasty that governed Palestine was Antiochus Epiphanes IV (175-163 B.C.). He pursued an energetic policy of Hellenization in Palestine and ruthlessly persecuted Jews who objected. In the year 168 B.C., Antiochus IV erected in the Jewish temple in Jerusalem an altar to the Olympian god Zeus. He practically outlawed Judaism by forbidding temple sacrifices, ritual circumcision, Sabbath observance, and reading of the Hebrew Scriptures. Thousands who refused to yield were slaughtered, or were sold into slavery, or fled the country. Such brutality eventually led to the Maccabean revolt.[18]

The Apocryphal books I and II Maccabees provide information of this revolt and the ensuing period of independence. The Maccabean revolution was organized by a Hasmonean priest named Mattathias and carried through to success by his five sons Judas, Jonathan, Simon, John, and Eleazar. So courageous a fighter was Mattathias' eldest son Judas that he was given the title "Maccabeus," a word meaning "The Hammer," in the recognition of his hard-hitting blows against the enemy. Judas and his band of loyal freedom fighters won a great victory over Antiochus' forces, despite overwhelming odds against them. Judas Maccabeus rebuilt the altar of the temple and reestablished the worship services, inaugurating the Feast of Hanukkah (Rededication), which Jews still celebrate in the month of December. Thus the Maccabean revolt grew from a resistance movement to a full-scale war of independence. The Jews enjoyed one century of autonomy and religious freedom under the rule of Hasmonean priest-kings until Pompey's Roman armies invaded Jerusalem in 63 B.C. and captured the city, ending the Hasmonean dynasty.

After General Pompey's victorious march on Jerusalem, Herod Antipater, an Idumean (Edomite) was appointed ruler of Judea. He was succeeded by his son, Herod the Great, who became king of Judea from 40-4 B.C.[19]

In spite of his long and politically successful reign, and in spite of his elaborate building program and the reconstruction of the Jewish temple in Jerusalem, Herod was not popular with the Jews. They resented his heavy taxes, royal extravagances, tyranny, cruelties, and appeasement of Rome. It was during his reign when Jesus was born, and the familiar story of the "Slaughter of the Innocents," in Matthew 2, is typical of acts attributed to Herod the Great.[20]

After Herod's death in 4 B.C., his kingdom was divided among his three sons. The eldest surviving son Archelaus (4 B.C. - 6 A.D.), whose name is mentioned in Matthew 2:22, received

Judea and Samaria; Antipas (4 B.C. - 39 A.D.), the crafty ruler whom Jesus called "that fox" (Luke 13:32) and whose name is frequently mentioned in the Gospels, became tetrarch of Galilee and Perea (Trans-Jordan); and the third son Philip (4 B.C. - 34 A.D.), the most able of Herod's heirs, ruled over the territories northeast of the lake of Galilee.[21]

In 6 A.D., Archelaus was deposed by Emperor Augustus for his misrule, following which Judea was made an empirical province and was administered by seven Roman procurators until 41 A.D. The best known of these procurators was Pontius Pilate, 26-36 A.D., during whose administration Jesus' ministry took place. It was he who was finally responsible for Jesus' crucifixion.

4. The Jewish Community in Which Jesus Lived

By Jesus' time Palestinian Jews were divided among several religious factions. These sectarian divisions took place in the late Hellenistic and early Roman periods (c. 200 B.C. to 100 A.D.). First century Jewish historian Flavius Josephus gives a description of the leading religious groups of Judaism in his *Wars of the Jews*.[22] Some of these competing groups set Jew against Jew.

a. The *Pharisees* derived their name from the Hebrew term *Perushim*, meaning the "Separatists" or "Puritans." They constituted the nucleus of the religious and academic leadership. They made out of traditional Judaism a vast system of minute laws to regulate life in Israel. They developed as a movement from the *Hasadim* (the loyalists for the Torah) who had supported Judas Maccabeus in his revolt against the Syrians. In other words, the Pharisees emerged as a religious-political party during the Hasmonean period in opposition to the prevailing rule of the priesthood over daily affairs.[23]

The Pharisees coordinated tradition and the written law as joint rules of faith and practice. In addition to the Hebrew Bible (TaNaK), they accepted the "oral law" or the "tradition of the elders," which passed on by word of mouth from teacher to pupil. In about 200 A.D. these were codified in the *Mishnah* and preserved in the Talmud, a vast written collection of Jewish religious interpretations. The Pharisees separated themselves from the priestly interpretations of the Law and also from all ritual and social impurity. They developed an elaborate system of legal traditions which "built a fence around the Law," setting the boundaries whereby the Law would never be intentionally or accidentally transgressed.

Despite their rigorous devotion to the Law, the Pharisees were quite open to new ideas, some apparently of Greek origin, that later became part of Christian doctrine. They believed in (1) the immortality of the human soul, the bodily resurrection of people, and rewards of righteousness and punishment of sinners; (2) the existence of angels, demons, and other spirits; (3) God's providential governance of history; (4) salvation by good works, which externalized their whole religious life; (5) a coming Messiah who would deliver Israel from its enemies and restore it to its former glory.[24]

In the Gospels several conflicts are recorded between Jesus and the Pharisees, particularly in regards to the observance of Sabbath and ceremonial cleanness (Matt. 12:10, 15:11). Jesus primarily criticized their emphasis on ritualism and legalism. Jesus repudiated their man-made rules of daily behavior, their blind adherance to outward forms unmindful of the motive behind them, their being slaves to the letter of the law rather than to the spirit.

b. The *Sadducees* were the priestly, aristocratic party in Judaism which controlled the Temple and thus exercised great authority over the people. They came into existence following the Maccabean revolt in the second century B.C. and constituted the nucleus of the political and social aristocracy. Their name (Greek *Saddoukaiai* from the Hebrew *Zaddukim*) is derived from Zadok who was a high priest in King Solomon's time. The Sadducees claimed that as descendants of Zadok they were the sole custodians of the temple.[25] They based this claim on Prophet Ezekiel's words that only the "sons of Zadok could approach Yahweh in the temple service" (Ezek. 30:46).

Being the official custodians of organized religion, the

Sadducees held the Torah to be God's only revelation and thus rejected the oral "tradition of the elders," cherished by the Pharisees. They also rejected the existence of angels and spirits and taught that there is no resurrection, no future reward or punishment. They repudiated the teaching that the Messiah would shortly come to destroy Israel's enemies. On the contrary, as the officiating priests of the temple in Jerusalem and a powerful religio-political group, they played a mediating role between the Jewish people and their foreign rulers. Their conciliatory relationship with the Syrians and their close association with Rome earned them the contempt of the other groups.

In Jesus' day, Sadducees dominated the Sanhedrin, the Supreme Council of Judaism. Their adoption of Hellenistic customs and their collaboration with Rome helped them to manipulate political affairs. They were determined to preserve the status quo and to accommodate Rome for the sake of political stability in their land. That was reflected in their eagerness to get rid of Jesus as a "potential revolutionary and a threat to Judah's security."[26]

c. The *Essenes* were one of a number of radical monastic groups which often withdrew into the desert to live and prepare for the imminent apocalyptic end of history. The most notable among these sects was the Qumran community whose library of scrolls was discovered in caves near the Dead Sea in 1947. The scrolls found in the Qumran caves include copies and fragments of the canonical books of the Hebrew Bible, parts of apocryphal and pseudepigraphic works, and a number of original works pertaining to the teachings of the Essenes. From the biblical perspective, the significance of the Dead Sea Scrolls is that they are the oldest surviving texts and provide us a standard to determine which manuscripts are the closest to the supposed original.[27]

These "Dead Sea Scrolls" also reveal a great deal about the communal life of the Essenes. They followed a strict regimen of Torah study, purificatory baths, ritual meals, and daily prayers. For their extreme expression of piety they were called "emphatic

Pharisees."[28] But they differed from Pharisees in their asceticism and their isolation. Some scholars have speculated that John the Baptist and Jesus had been associated with the Essenes.[29]

  d. The *Zealots* were the ultra-patriots in the Palestinian Jewry who advocated the violent overthrow of the Roman occupiers. They emerged as a party around the turn of the Christian era. They sought a Messiah who through brute force would restore the one-time glorious kingdom of David. They envisaged Israel as a theocracy, and thought that "God's Nation" might be governed by God-appointed priests and kings.

  The founder of the Zealots was Judas of Gamala. Inspired by the example of Mattathias Maccabeus, Judas gathered around him a considerable following and, in 7 A.D., he organized a revolt which was very short-lived. Later, in 66 A.D., the Zealots made a second attempt to drive the Romans from Palestine.[30] This fatal clash with the Roman army under Titus compelled the Romans to destroy Jerusalem and the temple and to kill thousands of Jews.

  Jesus saw the problem of conflict between Israel and Rome. He was aware of the fact that some of his disciples may have had sympathetic feelings toward the aspirations of the Zealots (Luke 6:15; Acts 1:13). One of his disciples must have been a party regular—Simon "the Zealot." There are some scholars who speculate that Judas' betrayal may have been a "misguided attempt to force Jesus to lead a revolt against Rome."[31]

  Outside of the four groups, Pharisees, Sadducees, Essenes, and Zealots, there were other elements in the Jewish community of Palestine, two of which were noteworthy:

  e. *"The People of the Land"* (Am Haaretz). These common folk, who did not belong to any organized religious group or political group or political party, constituted the bulk of the Jewish community. Because many of them were poor, the Sadducees looked down upon them. Many were not literate, so the Pharisees despised them. Because they were not militant, the Zealots hated their timidity. And the Essenes did not care for their secularity. This group included those on the "bottom of the social ladder."[32]

There were a variety of people in the Am Haaretz—the poor, the disinherited, the ignorant, even the publicans (tax-collectors). Jesus and his disciples were often criticized because they associated with them. Particularly Jesus was assaulted because he dared to "eat with publicans and sinners."

  f. The *Samaritans*, strictly speaking, were not a religious group within Judaism, but they did claim a common ancestry and shared many religious traditions with the Jews. The Samaritans were the native Israelites who were left behind during the Assyrian deportation which followed the defeat of the Northern Kingdom in 722 B.C. They intermarried with the colonists which Shalmaneser, King of Assyria, imported from other provinces to resettle in the land of Israel. The Samaritans extended a helping hand to the Babylonian Jewish repatriates to help rebuild the temple in Jerusalem, but they were rebuffed by the Jews because of their religious heterodoxy and racial impurity. This rebuff led to lasting animosity between these two "Israelite" traditions— a break that was permanently sealed when the Samaritans built their own temple on Mount Gerizim during the time of Alexander the Great (c. 330 B.C.). Separated from the rest of Judaism, the Samaritans had a Bible consisting of their own edition of the Torah. They were brought under the Jewish control for sixty years after John Hyrcanus destroyed the Gerizim temple in 128 B.C., but the Samaritans regained their political freedom from the Jews when Pompey took Jerusalem in 63 B.C.

  In spite of the animosity between the Jews and Samaritans, Jesus, as a Jew, had dealings with Samaritans. Jesus discussed the meaning of true worship with a Samaritan woman at Jacob's well in Samaria (John 4:5-42), and made a "good Samaritan" the hero of a famous parable (Luke 10:29-37).[33]

5. The Impact of the Intertestamental Hebrew Literature and Greek Language and Culture

  Beginning with the fourth century B.C., Jews, like other people in the Near East, faced the propects of Hellenization. One important carrier of Hellenism was the Greek language. The

Palestine at the time of Jesus

vernacular Greek, known as *Koine* became the *lingua franca* of Alexander the Great's empire and remained so even after the Roman conquests. The Hebrew language became a dead language, particularly for the Diasporan Jews. This necessitated the translation of the Hebrew Bible into Greek. This translation was called the Septuagint and was used not only by Greek-speaking Jews but also later by Christians. This Greek edition of the Jewish Bible contained all the books of the Hebrew Canon, as well as a number of popular apocryphal writings from the intertestamental period, such as supplements to the books of Esther, Jeremiah, and Daniel, and the independent books of I and II Esdras, Tobit, Judith, Wisdom, Sirach, and I and II Maccabees.[34]

There is no doubt the Greek language and literature greatly affected early Christian thought. For one thing, the New Testament was written in Koine Greek, the international language of Hellenistic civilization. The apocryphal books of the Old Testament also show a number of Greek ideas concerning resurrection and the immortality of the soul (II Macc. 7:9; 14-46).

The intertestamental period roughly covers the time between the third century B.C. and the first half of the first century A.D. During this period, the Jews created a large body of literature—works now preserved in three collections: the Apocrypha, the Pseudepigrapha, and the Dead Sea Scrolls. In addition to these, commentaries were written on numerous biblical and nonbiblical works. The early Christians who used the Septuagint as their "Old Testament" made full use of these disputed writings, although their canonical status was a matter of theological debate among the early church fathers.

In addition to the canonical and apocryphal books, Jewish writers produced a body of religious literature known collectively as the *Pseudepigrapha*. The majority of these books were inaccurately attributed to biblical figures, and many of them were found among the Dead Sea Scrolls.[35]

As for the *Dead Sea Scrolls*, they are thought to have been produced by a community of Essenes that flourished around Qumran from the second century B.C. to 70 A.D., when it was destroyed or dispersed by the Romans.[36]

The manuscripts found in the Qumran caves included:

a. fragments and whole books of copies of the Hebrew Bible;

b. fragments of copies of apocryphal or pseudepigraphal works;

c. fragments of commentaries on canoncial works;

d. new works, such as A *Manual of Discipline*, the Zadokite Document, Essene hymns, *The War of the Sons of Light Against the Sons of Darkness*;

e. a compendium of Messianic rules, and a description of a communal meal of bread and wine that resembles Jesus' Last Supper.[37]

In the a*pocryphal books* one can find apocalyptic and eschatological concerns—visions of "the end of time," divine judgment, heaven, hell, and resurrection (II Esd. 9-10). The promise of resurrection and "everlasting life" for the faithful (II Macc. 7:9,14,23,36) is one of the central tenets of II Maccabees—very important theological concept propagated before Christ's time.

The influence of Greek thought in the Book of Wisdom is conspicuous. There is a dualistic concept of good and evil. God and Satan battle over the minds and hearts of men—a battle that God will inevitably win. When God wins the battle, the righteous will enjoy eternal salvation and the unrighteous will suffer eternal damnation (Wisd. of Sol. 18). Thus, the book attributes the presence of evil and death to "the Devil's spite" (Wisd. of Sol. 2:23-24), an interpretation of the serpent's role in Genesis 3 that would culminate in the doctrine of Original Sin expounded by Paul (Romans 5).[38]

One of the most prominent topics in the apocryphal and pseudepigraphical books of the Old Testament is the Messianic theme. In these books various conceptions of the person and work of the Messiah can be discerned:

a. In some cases the Messiah is pictured as an ordinary human being, raised up by God to bring in the Kingdom. Although a Jew, no special ancestry, human or divine, is identified.

b. In other cases, the Messiah is presented as a human being with a special priestly ancestry. The idea is of a priestly Messiah who will establish a new age of true worship. We know the Qumran community of the Essenes looked forward to the coming of a Priest-Messiah.[39]

c. Another view is of a human Messiah of royal ancestry. Most of the great prophets looked forward to the Messianic age as a restored Davidic dynasty. The Son-of-David-Messiah was the most popular of all forms of Messianic expectations.

d. Still in other cases, the Messiah is expected to be a resurrected figure from the past—someone like Moses or Elijah. The Prophet-Messiah would proclaim the Law of God throughout the earth, writing His commandments on every heart.

e. Finally, there emerged in Hellenistic Judaism the idea of the Messiah as a heavenly being come to earth. This Being existed before the creation of the world and at the end of time will put down the kings of the world and will be a light to the Gentile and a deliverer of the righteous.[40]

These various ideas of the Messiah carried the common characteristic that the Messiah was to be God's agent doing God's work who would banish strife, punish wickedness, reward righteousness, and establish peace throughout the world.

The remarkable thing about the early Christian community is that they drew on all five of these Messianic traditions in giving their account of who Jesus was and what he did. Jesus was a man specifically chosen for the special Messianic work of God (Mark 1:1-11). Jesus was a descendant of David who brings in the true Kingdom of God as the Son of David-Messiah (Matthew 1:1-25; Luke 3:1-38). Jesus was the pre-existent Son of God who brings salvation to the world (John 1:1-14). Jesus was the prophet and priest-Messiah who finally fulfills the Law (Hebrews 7:1-8:13). According to the early Church, Jesus was all of these and more because he fulfilled these expectations by transforming and unifying them. The Messiah who came was not only the Messiah, but his coming fulfilled every Messianic hope beyond all expectation.[41]

6. The Synagogue: Platform for Early Christian Missionaries

The focal point of Judaism was, undoubtedly, the Temple. It was in the Jerusalem Temple that the Jews held their sacrificial worship. But since the Dispersion in the sixth century B.C. the Jews learned Yahweh could be worshipped not only in Palestine and in the Temple, but also away from the Holy City, even in foreign countries. The emergence of the synagogue was a religious necessity for those far away from Jerusalem and in time spread wherever there was a Jewish community. The synagogues multiplied so swiftly that in the time of Jesus there were many not only in the Jewish Diaspora but in the Holy Land and Jerusalem as well. They became the centers of Jewish religion, culture, social service, religious education, fellowship, and worship. After 70 A.D. (when the Temple was destroyed) the synagogues kept Judaism alive.[42]

The synagogues of the Dispersion, simple and democratic in organization, provided the pattern for the early Christian communities. They became platforms for the early Christian missionaries who, without necessarily ceasing to regard themselves as Jews, brought the good news of God's new salvation in Jesus Christ.

The Gospels tell us that Jesus was accustomed to go to the synagogue on the Sabbath (Luke 4:16). The custom may not only have been for the sake of worship but because the synagogue worship afforded him, as later on with Paul, an opportunity to give his message. In fact it was Paul's habit to go to the synagogue upon entering a new city. Most probably this was also the practice of the other apostles.

In short, no institution is connected more closely with the beginnings of Christianity than the synagogue.[43]

References

1   Stephen L. Harris, *The New Testament: A Student's Introduction* (Mountain Vew, California: Mayfield Publications Co., 1988), pp. 2-3.
2   Bruce Manning Metzger, *The New Testament: Its Background, Growth, and Content* (Nashville and New York: Abingdon Press, 1965), pp. 273-274.

3   Oscar Cullman, *The New Testament: An Introduction to the General Reader* (Philadelphia: Westminster Press, 1966), p. 128.
4   Richard L. Jeske, *New Testament: Toward a Historical Understanding* (Lawrence, Kansas: University of Kansas 1988), p. 190.
5   Harris, *The New Testament*, p. 9.
6   *Ibid.*
7   Merrill C. Tenney, *New Testament Survey* (Grand Rapids: William B. Eerdman's Publishing Co., 1967), p. 410.
8   Chamberlin and Feldman (Ed.), *The Dartmouth Bible* (Boston: Houghton Mifflin Co., 1961), p. XXXII.
9   Norman Perrin, *The New Testament: An Introduction* (New York: Harcourt Brace Jovanovich, 1974), pp. 18-20.
10 Stephen L. Harris, *Understanding the Bible* (Palo Alto and London: California State University, 1986), p. 7.
11 Jeskin p. 233.
12 Perrin, pp. 24-25.
13 Allen Wikgren, "The English Bible," *The Interpreter's Bible, Vol. I* (New York and Nashville: Abingdon Press, 1956), p. 84.
14 Chamberlin and Feldman, p. XXXV.
15 Wikgren, pp. 95-97.
16 William H. Marty, *The New Testament* (Dubuque: Kendall/Hunt Publishing Co., 1987), p. 1.
17 Harris, *Understanding the Bible*, pp. 246-247.
18 Solomon Nigosian, *Judaism: The Way of Holiness* (Great Britain: Crucible, The Aquarian Press, 1986), pp. 190-191.
19 T.W. Manson, "Background to the Ministry of Jesus," in *The Bible Today* (New York: Harper & Brothers, 1955), pp. 67-69.
20 Chamberlin and Feldman, p. 847.
21 Manson, p. 68.
22 Flavius Josephus, *The Jewish War*, Loeb Ed., trans. L.H. Felman (Cambridge, Massachusetts: Harvard University Press, 1965), pp. 33-52.
23 Jacob Neusner, *From Politics to Piety: The Emergence of Pharisaic Judaism* (Englewood Cliffs, New Jersey: Prentice-Hall, 1973), pp. 24-38.
24 Leo Baeck, "The Phariseeism," in *Pharisees and Other Essays* (New York: Schocken Books, 1966), pp. 1-50.
25 Marcel Simon, *Jewish Sects at the Time of Jesus* (Philadelphia: Fortress Press, 1967), pp. 45-58.
26 Harris, *Understanding the Bible*, p. 253.
27 O. Betz, "Dead Sea Scrolls," in *The Interpreter's Dictionary of the Bible*, Supplementary Volume. (Nashville: Abingdon Press, 1955), pp. 130-136.
28 Millar Burrows, *The Dead Sea Scrolls* (New York: Viking Press, 1955), pp. 5-7.
29 Helmer Ringren, *The Faith of Qumran* (Philadelphia: Fortress Press, 1961), pp. 35-46.
30 Chamberlin and Feldman, p. 852.
31 Harris, *Understanding the Bible*, p. 254.
32 Chamberlin and Feldman, p. 853.
33 Harris, *Understanding the Bible*, p. 417.
34 Vahan H. Tootikian, *A Survey of the Hebrew Bible* (Southfield, Michigan: Armenian Heritage Committee, 1990), p. 12.
35 James H. Charlesworth, Ed., *The Old Testament Pseudepigrapha* (Garden City, New York Doubleday, 1983) Vol. I, pp. 1-10.

36 Harris, *Understanding the Bible*, p. 243.
37 *Ibid.*, p. 243-244.
38 Lawrence E. Toombs, *The Threshold of Christianity* (Philadelphia: Westminster Press, 1960), pp. 33-44.
39 Ringren, pp. 38-46.
40 *The People of Promise: A Survey of the Old Testament* (Dallas: Gold Label Publications, 1982), pp. 180-181.
41 *Ibid.*, p. 182.
42 Manson, p. 74.
43 Harris Franklin Rall, *New Testament History* (New York: Abingdon-Cokesbury Press, 1914), p. 50.

PART 2

THE GOSPELS

AN OVERVIEW OF THE GOSPELS

The Rise of the Christian Faith: The Historical Jesus

The focal point and the *raison d'être* of the Christian faith is Jesus Christ himself. The Christian faith did not emerge from the New Testament; on the contrary, the New Testament sprang from the early Christian Church that proclaimed the good news of Jesus Christ. Thus, the New Testament is basically an anthology of writings about Jesus Christ and his Church. Unlike Judaism, Christianity is based on a Person, not on a book. Consequently, the starting point of the Christian faith and the New Testament is Jesus Christ.

Because the center of the Christian faith is Jesus, scholars throughout the ages, but particularly in the past two centuries, have been engaged in the quest of "the historical Jesus."

The main source of such a search is the New Testament, especially the four Gospels. Apart from the New Testament there are but a few literary sources from the ancient world that mention Jesus of Nazareth. They can be divided into three types: Roman authors, Jewish authors, and nonbiblical Christian sources.

Some Roman sources offer interesting information about the growing Christian movement and make references to its leader Jesus. For example, in 110 A.D. Pliny the Younger, a Roman Governor of Bithynia in Asia Minor, consulted emperor Trajan (reigned 98-117 A.D.) about the "depraved and extravagant superstition" and the followers of this rapidly growing movement who sang hymns "to Christ as to a god."[1] Also, Roman historian Suetonius (75-160 A.D.) mentioned that the emperor Claudius (reigned 41-54 A.D.) expelled the Jews from Rome (about 51 A.D.) because of a riot instigated by a certain "Christos."[2] Tacitus (60-120 A.D.), another Roman historian, reported that the Christians were blamed for the burning of Rome during the reign of the emperor Nero in 64 A.D., and, in passing, stated that the name of this "pernicious superstition" came from their leader, "Christus."[3]

From the Jewish authors, references about Jesus are found in the writings of historian Flavius Josephus (37-100) who, reporting the execution of Jesus' brother James, referred to him as "the brother of Jesus, who was called Christ."[4] In another passage (Antiquities 18:63-64), Josephus referred to Jesus as "a wise man, if needed one ought to call him a man . . . who was crucified . . . and on the third day he appeared to them restored to life . . . and the tribe of the Christians, so called after him, is still to this day not disappeared."[5]

Another major Jewish source for references to Jesus is the Hebrew Talmud, where Jesus is viewed very negatively. According to one of these references, Jesus was "hanged" because "he practiced sorcery and led Israel astray."[6] The Talmudic accounts, like the Roman ones, are of a polemical nature, but they confirm Jesus' existence.

In addition to non-Christian sources, there are a number of isolated sayings attributed to Jesus in Christian sources but not found in the four Gospels, such as in books of the New Testament Apocrypha.[7] These sources also offer very little information about historical Jesus, but they affirm the existence of Jesus.

The Nature of the Gospels

The New Testament canon begins with the Gospels, the four documents labeled with the names of their supposed authors: Matthew, Mark, Luke, and John.

The word "Gospel" comes from the Anglo-Saxon godspell, which is the translation of the Latin evangelism, from the Greek evangelion, meaning "good news."[8] The four documents were first called "Gospels" at about the middle of the second century A.D., and since then the word has carried two meanings: the message and the books.

The four Gospels form a unique literary genre. They are biographies of Jesus, but not in the historical sense. They do not provide a complete life of Jesus. They do not, for instance, relate the events of Jesus' life between the ages 12 to 30; they do not tell us about Jesus' education and the forces that shaped his intellectual and religious outlook. Although partly biographical, they are the memoirs of the apostles, concentrating primarily on Jesus' public life, his teaching and healing ministry, his death and resurrection. The Gospels are not day-by-day running accounts of the life of Jesus, but such events as recorded are to instruct Christians and others about Jesus as the Lord of life. The essence of the Gospels is the personality, the spirit of Jesus.

The four Gospels are not books *by* Jesus but *about* Jesus—books which contain both a narrative of Jesus' life and a large recollection of his teachings. These teachings (sayings) were originally spoken in Aramaic, because that was the vernacular language in Palestine at the time of Jesus, but were rendered in Greek. Why in Greek? By the time the Gospels were written, Christianity had moved into a Greek-speaking and reading world. Greek was the language of the Roman Empire. Even the Jews of the Dispersion were speaking Greek, and the version of the Old Testament they were reading was the Septuagint, a Greek version. If Christianity were to carry its mission to that world, then its documents had to be in the language that world used.

We do not know for sure why there are four Gospels instead of more or less. Probably different Christian communities each had need for a document about Jesus. The Christians in these communities had different needs and concerns for a book about Jesus besides knowing about who Christ was and what he said and did.

Further, the Gospels were not the earliest documents of the New Testament to be written. The first of these Gospels, Mark, was written more than three decades after the crucifixion and resurrection of Jesus.

There were at least five reasons for the delay:
a. The earliest Christians were not a literary group.
b. There was a very strong tradition for the custom of the oral transmission of religious teaching. Judaism, to a certain extent, had been passed on by word of mouth.
c. Writing materials were costly and the early Christians, for the most part, were poor people.
d. The church was scattered by persecution, and time was needed for the collection of materials.
e. The people were looking for the *Parousia* (Greek term, meaning "being near," used to denote the Second Coming of Christ), the early end of the world and the speedy return of the Lord—hence there was no need for written records. There was much more immediate and important work to be done.

The "How," "Why," and "When" of the Gospels

The early Church considered all four Gospels equally authoritative, but as early as the second century A.D. there were some who questioned the equal authority of them. Marcion, for example, accepted only a shortened form of the Gospel of Luke and discarded all the others. Tatian tried to combine the four Gospels into one. Neither attempt succeeded. Thus we have four separate documents which are different in content, arrangement, emphasis, and purpose.[9]

All four of the Gospels present Jesus as the unique Son of God, the Messiah, the Christ. Yet each approaches the matter from a different point of view, is written for a specific group, and presents a distinguishable portrait of the Person, Jesus.

While the Gospel of John is in a class by itself, the other three, Matthew, Mark and Luke, are closely related. They are referred to as the *Synoptics*, a Greek word meaning "seen with the same eyes."[10] These three parallel each other in both content and order, relating many of the same events and dialogues.

New Testament scholars are generally agreed that Mark was the earliest of the Gospels and that Matthew and Luke used Mark as a principle source. Matthew and Luke also apparently had access to a body of material independent of Mark which they incorporated in their Gospels. This hypothetical document is called *Q* (from the German *Quelle*) and was probably comprised largely of sayings and teachings of Jesus. Furthermore, Matthew and Luke each had access to materials the other did not have, so in each there is considerable unique material. This hypothesis assumes that there actually were writings in circulation before the composition of the Gospels.

Some scholars, however, believe that there was very little written in the first and second decades following Jesus' death and resurrection. The Christian testimony about him was oral as long as eye-witnesses of these events were alive. The disciples probably transmitted their recollections of Jesus' teachings and his life without writing. Stories circulated independently of one another as individual witnesses of Jesus' words and deeds preached or settled in different Christian centers—Jerusalem, Antioch, Caesarea, Ephesus—where "their particular Gospels took root and grew."[11]

Other biblical scholars advocate a new method of study, form criticism, known in German as *Formsgeschichte*. Form critics isolate and analyze individual units or characteristic forms contained in a literary text and identify the probable preliterary form of these units; in other words, they attempt to trace or reconstruct the process by which various traditions evolved from their original oral state to their final literary form.[12]

According to this study, the first form into which the Jesus-tradition was cast was the sermon—the evangelistic means of reaching out. For the immediate contemporaries of Jesus, there was no need to portray him as he was. They already knew him or knew of him through eye-witnesses. But as Christianity spread farther away from its birthplace, the preaching was gradually enriched by illustrative material, mainly by eye-witness recollections, such as paradigms (isolated short narratives usually ending in a saying of Jesus); "tales" which pictured Jesus as a miracle worker; and "myths" with which to further enhance his supernatural power.[13] This hypothesis, advocated by liberal scholars, is not popular. It is vehemently opposed by the majority of biblical authorities.

Why were the Gospels finally written? There were many reasons, but they may be reduced to four:

1. The *Parousia*, the Second Coming of Christ and the end of the world, did not occur. This was a major concept in apocalyptic Christianity (Mark 13; Matthew 24-25; Luke 21; I and II Thessalonians, II Peter 2-3, and the Book of Revelation). The early followers of Christ were eagerly expecting Christ's return to judge the world, punish the wicked, and redeem the saved. But as time passed, the early eye-witnesses died off. Some means had to be found to preserve their witness and get their evidence written down, lest by their death the facts about Jesus might be permanently lost.

2. There needed to be in the Church a body of normative written material for teaching purposes. Along with new generations emerging within the Church, there were Gentiles who were being converted into Christianity, and both of these groups needed Christian literature for instructional purposes.

3. There needed to be, in written form, the essentials of the Christian message as a defense against competing and attacking philosophies of life, and especially against the eroding effect of Gnosticism, a major heresy in the primitive Church, which attempted to drain away all the significance of the historical life of Jesus. The early Church's arguments about the divine and human natures of Christ and other theological doctrines necessitated the writing of the Gospels.

4. There was also a missionary motive. As more Gentiles and Jews became Christians and Christianity grew beyond Palestine, it was necessary to have definitive written records presenting the story of Christ and the essence of the Christian faith to the Graeco-Roman world. The infant Church needed authoritative Christian documents for circulation among would-be converts.

So the Gospels began to appear because there were very practical reasons and needs for them. Each of them was written at a particular time, for a particular purpose, and for a specific group of people. The Gospel according to Mark, for example, was written between 65 and 70 A.D. (according to a number of scholars about 68 A.D.) for the Christians in Rome, to present to them a picture of Christ as the heroic Son of Man in action and for the purpose of inspiring them in their time of trial and persecution. There is no absolute certainty about who the author was. The most commonly held view, and the most ancient, is that the author was John Mark, the son of a Jerusalem woman whose home was a gathering place for early Christians. According to the fourth-century Church father and historian, Eusebius, who in turn quotes from the second century churchman Papias, Mark had not known Jesus personally, but, as a companion and interpreter, he had recorded Peter's recollections.

The Gospel of Matthew was written sometime between 80-85 A.D., probably in Antioch, Syria. It was written specifically for the Jews with the purpose of convincing them that Jesus was the Christ, their long-looked-for Messiah. It cites about fifty passages from the Hebrew Bible to prove that Jesus was the Messiah of Jewish prophecy. The author uses most of Mark's account but also draws some additional material from the Q document with particular emphasis on Jesus' teaching ministry.[15] One of the major purposes of the Gospel was to preserve the teachings of Jesus which Mark had not fully recorded.

The Gospel according to Luke is the most precise and polished of the Synoptics, written by the Gentile physician and traveling companion of Paul (Col. 4:14; Philem. 1:24; II Tim. 4:11), between 85-90 A.D. Luke's purpose was to write a clear and orderly account of the life, work, and teachings of Jesus Christ. This purpose grew out of several factors. First, about sixty years had passed since the crucifixion and the resurrection of Jesus and the Christian Church was under dire attack by the Jewish religious leadership. Christians were regarded as apostates. There was a need for a clear picture of Jesus in the face of distorted and hostile views. Second, Christians were also under serious threat from Rome. Christianity was accused of being an underground and subversive movement. Luke wrote to clarify these misrepresentations. Third, there was need to present the "good news" to the Gentile world.[16] So, Luke wrote the longest Gospel as he reproduced about half of Mark along with considerable Q material, and added another source, designated "L" by the scholars.

John, the fourth Gospel, is different from the Synoptics in style and tone. It is a theological and philosophical Gospel. It is not a narrative of the life and teachings of Jesus in the sense that Matthew, Mark and Luke are. Rather, the Gospel of John is an interpretation of the meaning of the Person of Jesus in terms of certain concepts of Greek philosophy. Written sometime between 100 to 120 A.D., John presents "the evangel" in the thought forms of the Graeco-Roman world.[17] It was not that the message, the Gospel, had changed. It was that the audience had diversified and the categories of thought had changed. The unchanging truth of Christ had to be restated in new words to the Gentile world. John translated the story of Christ from Jewish categories into the concepts of Greek thought. As Matthew presented a Christianized Judaism, John presented a Hellenized Christianity.

A very important consideration in John's Gospel is to present Jesus as the God Incarnate, who appears on the scene as the incarnation of the eternal "Word" or *Logos*.[18] This is stated in the opening verses, and from there on, everything else is a witness to this.

Obviously, there are similarities and differences in the four Gospels. Scholars have calculated these similarities and differences on a percentage basis: 42% of Matthew is unique; only 7% of Mark is unique; 41% of Luke is unique; and 92% of John is unique.[19] Similarities are to be expected in the reporting of the same events. Differences are not necessarily contradictions. Rather, they represent the different purposes of different writers writing to different audiences.

1. *The Gospel of Matthew*

While it is not the oldest, nor the longest, nor the most literary of the Gospels, Matthew has been the most important Gospel and has been accepted in all periods of Christianity as a most fundamental document of Christianity. When the fourfold collection of the Christian Gospel emerged in the second century, the Gospel According to Matthew headed this collection, and nearly every second-century Christian writer quoted the book more frequently than any other Gospel.[20]

From its origin until now, it has been the most widely read and quoted Gospel. In various liturgies of the Church, in daily appointed readings from the New Testament, in various books of prayer, Matthew is listed more frequently than any other Gospel or any other New Testament source.

The popularity of Matthew arises from several things. It was the first Gospel to be accepted by the early Christian center, Antioch, where the followers of Christ were first called "Christians." It was a complete Gospel. Mark, which was the first Gospel written, began with Jesus as a grown man, while Matthew begins the story with a genealogy of Jesus going back to Abraham. The inclusion of the Sermon on the Mount guaranteed its wide appeal. Matthew also met the needs of an emerging church for a teaching document usable both in the training of people in Christianity and in the liturgy of the Church. [21]

Scholars are divided in the matters of the authorship and date of the book. According to early tradition, the author was Matthew, one of the twelve disciples of Jesus. Matthew's surname was Levi (Mark 2:14; Luke 5:27); Matthew (Hebrew, "gift") was his given name. He was a tax collector who responded to the call of Jesus (Matthew 9:9-13; Mark 2:15). Eusebius, the fourth-century Church historian, who quotes a second century Christian leader, Papius, states that "Matthew compiled the *Sayings* in the Aramaic language, and everyone translated them as well as he could."[22]

Modern scholars believe that the Gospel was not written by Matthew the disciple, but by an anonymous writer who put it together in Greek but was also well versed in Aramaic and Hebrew. They claim that there was a tendency of tradition to attach an apostolic name to a book, in this case Matthew Levi's name to the Gospel According to Matthew.[23]

Some scholars also argue that Matthew could not have been the work of an apostle because it drew so heavily on the earlier Gospel of Mark, itself a Greek work written by someone who was not an eyewitness of Jesus' career. The author of the Gospel of Matthew followed Mark's order of events and utilized a substantial part of his text, something a writer who knew Jesus personally was not likely to have done.[24] Matthew includes more than ninety percent of Mark's text, but also contains material not found in

Mark: extensive collections of Jesus' teachings from the Q document and some material unique to his Gospel, known as the "M" source. On the other hand, since one of Matthew's purposes may have been to supplement Mark from his own eyewitness memories, it is plausible that he wrote in response to and in addition to Mark.

Matthew was written to a Jewish audience to convince them that Jesus was the Messiah-King of the Jews; that He was the culmination of Jewish messianic expectations. Jesus was both the Son of God and the direct descendant of King David, and thus fulfilled in his person all the messianic prophecies of the Hebrew Scriptures.

There are some unique features that characterize the Gospel of Matthew:

First, Matthew, written for the Jewish people, is markedly a Jewish Gospel, and this is illustrated in a variety of ways.

    a. The Hebrew Bible (Old Testament) is quoted directly 43 times and there are more than eighty additional indirect allusions to it.[25]

    b. Matthew begins with a genealogy of Jesus, going through a list of 42 names, or generations, back to Abraham (Matthew 1). This long list of genealogy is included because the author knew that nothing was so significant to Jewish readers as a person's ancestors. To trace the lineage of Jesus back through David to Abraham, the father of the Hebrew people, was impressive indeed to the readers for whom the Gospel was intended. What may look like a dull beginning to us was a clever introduction geared to the interests of a specific audience.

    c. Matthew draws a parallel between the events in Jesus' life and the story of the Hebrew people. The journey of the Holy Family to Egypt (2:13-15) paralleled the journey of the Israelites into Egypt (Exodus 16-18). The slaughter of the children (Matt. 2:16-18) paralleled the massacre of Hebrew babies by the Egyptian pharaoh during Moses' time (Ex. 2). Jesus' Sermon on the Mount (Matt. 5:1-7:29) paralleled Moses' going to Mount Sinai to receive the Decalogue (Ex. 21:11-20). Moses gave the Torah; Jesus gave the new Torah.

d. Matthew ties many actions of Jesus' life to the Hebrew Scriptures in an effort to validate Jesus as the promised Messiah. In this context his key sentence is: "All this happened in order to fulfill what the Lord declared through the prophet . . . " (1:22). Repeatedly in Matthew we come across this formula. The following are but a few examples to illustrate the point:

Concerning the birth of Christ, "All this took place to fulfill what the Lord had said . . . the Virgin will be with child . . . "(1:22, ref. Isaiah 7:14).

About the escape to Egypt, "And so was fulfilled what the Lord had said through the prophet: 'Out of Egypt I called my Son' " (2:15, ref. Hos. 11:1).

Relative to the Triumphal Entry, "This took place to fulfill what was spoken through the prophet: 'Say to the Daughter of Zion, See, your king comes to you, gentle and riding on a donkey' " (21:4-5, ref. Zech. 9:9).

e. Matthew's great interest in the Law also shows how much the Gospel is Jewish-oriented. Other New Testament books seem to disregard the Law, while in Matthew Jesus is seen as the new Moses who brings a New Law which does not destroy the old Law but fulfills it.

The second characteristic of the Gospel According to Matthew is that it is the ecclesiastical, or "churchly" Gospel.

It is the only Gospel to use the word *ecclesia* (church). It is in Matthew's version of the confession of Peter at Caesarea Philippi that Jesus says, " . . . on this rock I will build my church . . . " (16:18).

The post-resurrection appearance of Jesus culminates in Jesus' commissioning the disciples in Galilee to go forth and make disciples of "all nations" (28:19-20). Here we see an ecclesia, a separate and new society, of which Jesus is the Head.[26] Matthew even gives detailed instructions and procedures for church discipline (Matt. 18).

Third, Matthew is the ecumenical Gospel. Although Matthew is written for Jewish readers, it is not an exclusive book to a particular people. Jesus' ministry begins among the Jewish people, but it does not stop there. That ministry extends to *all* people. So Jesus specifically states, "This gospel of the kingdom will be preached in the whole world as a testimony to all nations . . . " (24:14). Also, "Go and make disciples of all nations . . . " (28:19).

This ecumenicity is not only stated clearly, but also revealed in subtle ways:

a. It is revealed in the genealogy with which Matthew begins his Gospel. Normally, Jewish genealogies did not use women's names; the standard pedigree of a period was traced through the male ancestors. Matthew's list of the 42 ancestors of Jesus not only includes names of four women, but these women were of questionable reputation: Rahab was a prostitute in Jericho (Joshua 2); Tamar was a seducer and adulteress (Genesis 38); Ruth was a Moabite, (Ruth 1) (and Jewish law forbade a Moabite or an Ammonite from entering the Jewish congregation, even after ten generations (Deut. 23:3)); Bathsheba was the mother of King Solomon and was the woman King David seduced after having her husband, Uriah, killed. Four most incredible ancestors for Jesus Christ! What the author is saying by all this is that not only is Jesus the Messiah of the Jews, but of all people, and in him all barriers of race, sex, nation, and the barrier between the righteous and the sinner are overcome.

b. Matthew again signals its ecumenical character in a subtle way with the story of the Wise Men, the Gentile astrologers. Jesus, born a Jew, had the irresistible appeal to draw to his cradle the Gentiles of other nations.

Fourth, Matthew is the apocalyptic Gospel. Matthew emphasizes the *Parousia* or Second Coming of Christ more than the other Gospels. This is apparently the influence of the Antioch church which was a center of apocalyptic teachings and hopes.

Matthew tells many "signs" that will precede Jesus' return (mostly drawn from the books of the Hebrew Bible such as Joel, Daniel, and Zechariah)—signs including the occurrence of international wars, earthquakes, famines, persecution of believers, and appearances of false Messiahs (24).

Matthew emphasizes, however, that not even "the Son" knows the exact time of the Parousia (24:36).

In the Parables of the Second Coming (25), the author tells about the unannounced reappearance of Jesus when he will return to judge the world, separating the godly (sheep) from the wicked (goats) and assigning them rewards and punishments (25:31-46).

Fifth, Matthew is the regal Gospel and presents Jesus as the Messiah-King.

In a broad sense, the entire Gospel of Matthew is a presentation of Jesus as the Messiah-King. In the opening pages of the Gospel is the introduction of the Messiah-King. The emphasis here is on fulfilled prophecy. Seven times Matthew uses a prophetic fulfillment formula (1:22; 2:5, 17, 23; 3:3; 4:14).

In the Sermon on the Mount, the Messiah-King gives an account of what internal and spiritual righteousness is required for the Kingdom of God in contrast to an external and legislated righteousness (4:17-7:29).

Following the Sermon on the Mount, Matthew presents a series of miracles which are the authentication of the Messiah-King (8-10).

Then follows the opposition to the Messiah-King when the religious leaders refuse to acknowledge him as such (11-13). Later, in chapters 19-26, because of his royal entry into Jerusalem and the cleansing of the Temple, the Jewish leadership challenges Jesus' authority and refuses to recognize that he is the Son of David.

Matthew uses the phrase "Son of David," a royal appelation, repeatedly. From the beginning of his life to the end, Jesus is described as the king. The Wise Men look for him who is "born King of the Jews" (2:2). In the Triumphal Entry incident Jesus is presented as a king. The crowd shouts, "Hosanna to the Son of David! Blessed is he who comes in the name of the Lord!" (21:9). When governor Pontius Pilate asks Jesus, "Are you the king of the Jews?" "Yes, it is as you say," Jesus replies (27:37).

Throughout the Gospel, the author tries to convince his Jewish audience that Jesus is the Messiah-King of the Jews.

Sixth, Matthew is the teaching Gospel and presents Jesus as the Superlative Teacher.

One of the major purposes of the Gospel was to preserve the teachings of Jesus which the earliest Gospel, Mark, had not recorded. Only about one-third of Mark is devoted to the teachings of Jesus, with two-thirds to the action and events of Jesus' life. In Matthew, it is about the reverse. Matthew is skilled in writing about Jesus' teachings; he presents the moral and religious teachings of Jesus so effectively that his Gospel is regarded to this day as "the best compendium of Christian ethics."[27]

The instructional purpose of the Gospel is made clear by the insertion of five collections of teaching material: the Sermon on the Mount (5-7), the Charge to the Twelve Disciples (10), Parables on the Kingdom (13), Instructions for the Church (18), and the Denunciation of the scribes and Pharisees (23).

Furthermore, this teaching purpose and function of the Gospel can be seen in the way in which the materials of the Gospel are arranged and organized. Matthew is divided into five portions corresponding to the Five Books of Moses (Torah). With these arrangements, there is another notable teaching aspect designed to help in learning and memorization. To aid in the memory process, Matthew arranged things by threes and by sevens. There are three messages to Joseph, three denials by Peter, three questions of Pilate. There are seven woes to the scribes and Pharisees, seven parables of the kingdom. There are three sections in the genealogy; each section has twice seven names.

In short, Matthew, written to a Jewish audience, begins the story of Jesus by tracing his ancestry to Abraham. In Matthew there are few of the actions of Jesus, but much emphasis upon the teachings of Jesus. In addition to the five teaching discourses, Matthew also contains fifteen parables and twenty miracles. Three of the miracles—the healing of two blind men (9:27-31), the deliverance of a mute demoniac (9:32-33), and the finding of the Temple tax (17:14-18)—are only recorded in Matthew.

The Gospel of Matthew is divided into the following major parts:

    1. Birth and Infancy Narrative (1-2)
    2. Beginning of Jesus' Ministry (3-4)

3. First Discourse: Sermon on the Mount (5-7)
4. Jesus' Ministry of Mighty Works: Miracles (8:1-9:34)
5. Second Discourse: Missionary Work (9:35-10:42)
6. Opposition to Jesus' Ministry (11-12)
7. Third Discourse: Parables of the Kingdom (13)
8. Controversy and Conflict (14-17)
9. Fourth Discourse: Instructions for the Church (18)
10. The Beginning of the End of Jesus' Public Ministry (19-23)
11. Fifth Discourse: Jesus' Apocalyptic Predictions and Parables 24-25)
12. Jesus' Crucifixion (26-27)
13. Jesus' Resurrection (28)

1. Birth and Infancy Narrative (1-2). The Gospel According to Matthew begins with a genealogy of 42 names linking Jesus with major figures of the Old Testament history, culminating with Abraham, father of the Jews.[28] The only other gospel to include a genealogy is Luke and it differs from Matthew's. Matthew goes back to Abraham; Luke to Adam. Matthew gives Joseph's line (1), showing Jesus to be legal heir to the promises given Abraham and David. Luke gives Mary's line (Luke 1).

The genealogy is followed by the birth narrative. Neither the day, nor the season, nor even the year of Jesus' birth are certain. December 25 was designated as Christmas Day only at the end of the fourth century. This date was an arbitrary date coinciding with the popular pagan festival of Saturnalia. Most probably it was not even winter when Jesus was born. Likewise, the year of Jesus' birth has long been debated. Matthew 2:1 states that he was born under Herod the Great, who died sometime between 6 or 4 B.C. The calendar which most of Christendom observes is known as the Gregorian Calendar; it was established by Pope Gregory XIII in 1582, based on a calendar developed by Roman Abbot Dionysius Exiguus during the sixth century. Apparently the latter made an error, probably missing one of the four-year Olympiads, therefore dating the birth of Christ possibly 4 years later than actuality.[29]

Jesus was born in the ancient little town of Bethlehem which had been the home of Ruth and Naomi and King David.

Matthew tells us that Jesus was born of Mary, a virgin, who was engaged to a carpenter from Nazareth by the name of Joseph. Mary miraculously conceived (1:23), as a fulfillment of an Old Testament prophecy that "a virgin shall conceive" (Is. 7:14). Matthew also tells us through Joseph's genealogy that Jesus is the Messianic king, of the line of David, predicted in Isaiah 9:6-7.

"Wise Men" (astrologers) came from the east (probably from Persia or Babylonia), who apparently had concluded from a horoscope of Judah that a king was then due to appear. Led by a star, they stopped at Jerusalem to inquire about it from King Herod. The inquiry aroused Herod's suspicions, who ordered the slaying of the children in an attempt to eliminate a potential rival (2:16). Joseph, being forewarned by an angel of the Lord in a dream, took Mary and baby Jesus away to Egypt. The place in Egypt at which the Holy Family resided is not named. The traditions of the Egyptian Coptic Church says it was On, modern Heliopolis, six miles outside Cairo (the same place from which Joseph of the Old Testament had ruled Egypt many centuries before—Gen. 41:45).

The stay in Egypt could not have been for long, as Herod died at Jericho in 4 B.C. The angel of the Lord appeared once more to Joseph saying that he should take the child and his mother back to the land of Israel. Joseph was planning to return to Bethlehem, but God sent them back to their Galilean home (2:19-21). Matthew does not give any information about the boyhood of Jesus.

2. The Beginning of Jesus' Ministry (3-4). Jesus' first public appearance was at his baptism by John in the Jordan River, an event which is commonly regarded as the beginning of his ministry. His baptism is connected with John the Baptist's preaching. John, son of the priest Zechariah and Elizabeth, was an ascetic who preached the imminence of judgment and baptized converts in the Jordan River as a symbol of their repentance from sin (3:1-2).

If Jesus was sinless, why was he baptized? Matthew does not explain why the sinless Jesus underwent a baptism in token of repentance for the forgiveness of sins (Mark 1:4-5). Theologians have explained that Jesus' baptism was a symbolic gesture of taking "his stand by the side of sinners . . . making their shame his shame, their penitence his penitence, their burden his burden."[30]

Immediately following the act of baptism, a voice from heaven announced, "This is my Son, whom I love; with him I am well pleased" (3:17). Jesus, filled with the Holy Spirit, received his call as God's Anointed, the Messiah.

Jesus' baptism was followed by forty days' solitary withdrawal to the wilderness of Judea, just west of the Dead Sea. It was there that the Devil tried to tempt Jesus.

What was the nature of his temptations? They included the ordinary temptations succumbed to by worldly leaders throughout history. The first temptation, bread, was to win a following through material inducements (4:3-4); the second, to display his power by hurling himself from the pinnacle (tower) of the Temple, was to rely on showmanship and magic for popular support (4:5-7); the third, to rule "kingdoms of the world" was to gain earthly dominion through the worship of Satan (4:8-10). Jesus refuted these seductions with direct quotations from Jewish law (Deut. 8:3; 6:13; 6:16).

3. First Discourse: Sermon on the Mount (5-7). The first of the five discourses in Matthew is the Sermon on the Mount, which is meant to parallel the Mosaic Law revealed on Mount Sinai (Exodus 19-24).

The Sermon on the Mount begins with a list of "blessings" or "happinesses" called the beatitudes (5:3-12). Luke gives a variation of these pronouncements (Luke 6:20-23). Blessed or happy are the merciful, the pure in heart, the peacemakers, and those persecuted "for Jesus' sake." There are nine beatitudes in total contrasting present sufferings and duties with future joys.

In the Sermon on the Mount, Matthew also records Jesus' position in relation to the Law. Jesus came not to destroy the Law, but to fulfill it. Jesus' new standard of righteousness surpasses that of the old Law (5:17-20). The contrast between old and new is stressed in six antitheses, in each of which Jesus gives a new reinterpretation, for example: "You have heard that it was said, 'eye for eye, and tooth for tooth.' But I tell you, do not resist an evil person. If someone strikes you on the right cheek, turn to him the other also" (5:38-39).

Matthew proceeds to recall Jesus' lessons contrasting the old interpretation of the Law and the new. He illustrates this by citing five particulars: murder, adultery, oaths, retaliation, and hatred. Jesus goes beyond the Mosaic Law by condemning not only the actual act but also the inner force leading to these sins.[31] Thus, he prohibits not only the act of murder but the emotion, anger, that leads to it (5:21-26), not only adultery but lust (5:33-37), not only retaliation but nursing dark feelings in one's heart (5:38-42), not only hatred but any negative and unloving motive (5:43-48).

In chapter 6, Jesus contrasts the old practice of religion and the new. He deals with the secret motives of life. He illustrates this in two particulars: almsgiving and prayer. Almsgiving ought to be an act unto God, but not as ostentation (6:2-4). Prayer should not be lengthy, formal, and a display of piety, but rather simple and direct, as is the Lord's Prayer (6:9-13).

In the latter part of chapter 6 and in part of chapter 7 there are other teachings on the religious life such as the right use of property (6:25-34), anxiety and trust (6:25-34), and the censorious spirit (7:1-5). Then Jesus talks of a general rule of behavior, what is commonly known as the Golden Rule—"Do to others what you would have them do to you" (7:12). Many think that this is an implication of the Old Testament injunction "Love your neighbor as yourself" (Lev. 19:18). Others find similarities between the Golden Rule and Confucius' wisdom "What I do not wish men to do to me, I also wish not to do to them," or as Aristotle taught, "Men should act toward their friends as we would that they should act toward us."[32]

4. Jesus' Ministry of Mighty Works: Miracles (8:1-9:34). Following the Sermon on the Mount, Matthew presents a series of miracles. Each group contains three specific miracles. The first series of miracles includes the healing of a leper (8:2-4), the healing of a centurion's servant (8:5-13), and the healing of Peter's mother-in-law and others (8:14-17). The second group of miracles contains the tempest stilled (8:23-27), the Gadarene demoniacs (8:28-34), and a paralytic healed (9:1-18). The third group of miracles includes the healing of Jairus' daughter (9:18-26), the healing of the two blind men and the dumb (9:27-33).

5. Second Discourse: Missionary Work (9:35-11:1). The second major collection of teaching material begins with Jesus' call of and instructions to the Twelve (listed by name in Matthew 10:2-4). The choosing and training of the twelve disciples was an extremely important part of Jesus' earthly mission. To each of the Twelve the call came quite suddenly and decisively. They were to preach the imminent coming of the Kingdom of God, heal the sick, cleanse the lepers, and cast out demons.

The disciples' first mission was to "the lost sheep of the house of Israel" (10:5, 6). They were to be absolutely loyal to their Master, forsaking their families and taking up their crosses and following him. Discipleship was costly, causing suffering, rejection, and even death (10:30-38). But risking their lives and handing them over to God would give them a share in the life of the world to come.

6. Opposition to Jesus' Ministry (11-12). In spite of Jesus' preaching and miracles, the religious leaders refused to acknowledge him as the Messiah. This section reveals the progressive opposition of the Pharisees, and Jesus' response to that opposition. Examples of opposition and rejection are the controversy over the plucking of grain on the Sabbath (12:1-8) and the controversy over healing on the Sabbath (12:9-14). The climax in the controversy between Jesus and the Pharisees comes when the Pharisees attribute Christ's miraculous power to Beelzebub, the prince of demons (12:22-24). In response to this blasphemous accusation, Christ accuses the Pharisees of committing the unpardonable sin (12:25-30). Christ's statement is startling in view of the New Testament teaching on the extent of divine forgiveness. Probably what he implied was that unpardonable sin is one's willful blindness and stubborn disobedience.

7. Third Discourse: Parables of the Kingdom (13). As opposition intensified Jesus began to teach in parables. Matthew 13 is remarkable because it contains the largest grouping of parables in the four Gospels. A parable (Greek: *parabole* meaning "a placing beside" or "a comparison") is a short story that compares something familiar to a spiritual value. It is usually a story from everyday life to illustrate and teach spiritual truth. Jesus declared that parables were intended to both reveal and conceal truth (13:11-17). The seven kingdom of heaven parables in this chapter are the soils, the wheat and the tares, the mustard seed, the leaven, the hidden treasure, the pearl, and the net. The first four are public; the remaining three private, for the inner circle of disciples. An Old Testament passage is cited to explain Jesus' use of parables (13:10-17; Isa. 6:9-10).

Two out of these seven parables, the wheat and the tares (13:24-30), and the net (13:47-50), are unique to the Gospel of Matthew.

8. Controversy and Conflict (14:17). This period of Christ's life is marked by withdrawals. He withdrew from opposition and the crowds to teach his disciples. The pattern is opposition, withdrawal, and ministry.

The highlight of this section is Peter's testimony that Jesus is the Christ, the Son of the living God (16:13-17). In response to Peter's declaration, Christ prophesied the establishment of the Church (16:18-20). Perhaps one of the most debated verses in the New Testament is Matthew 16:18—"You are Peter (Rock), and on this rock I will build my church." It has been debated what Jesus was referring to by the "rock." Was it Peter the man? Or was it Peter's confession of faith? The Roman Catholic Church claims that the Church was founded upon Peter. Non-Catholic Christians insist that it was founded upon Peter's confession of faith, "You are the Christ, the Son of the Living God."[33]

9. Fourth Discourse: Instructions for the Church (18). In this chapter the author reflects on the life of the Christian community. This Gospel is the only Gospel which speaks of the "Church" (from Greek *ecclesia*, "assembly"—Matt. 18:15-20; 16:18). Indeed, the author is the only Gospel writer who defines what the church is (two or three believers gathered in Jesus' name) and what its role is; he speaks of a rule for church discipline and of the church's spiritual power (18:15-35).[34] Although the Church has the prerogative to excommunicate the unrepentant (18:15-17), it must also be ready to forgive others' offenses as its members themselves have been forgiven. The parable of the unmerciful servant eloquently stresses that truth (18:23-35).

10. The Beginning of the End of Jesus' Public Ministry (19-23). In this section, Matthew relates Jesus' going to Jerusalem and facing intensifying opposition. The main attack upon the life and character of Jesus was launched by the Pharisees. They believed Jesus to be an imposter, and they resented Jesus' attitude to the Law and to tradition.

After Jesus' royal entry into Jerusalem (21:1-11) and the cleansing of the Temple (21:12-17), the Jewish leaders challenged Jesus' authority and refused to recognize that he was the Son of David. Christ responded by pronouncing judgment on the nation. He also denounced the scribes and the Pharisees (23:1-39); he condemned their deeds and heartlessness (23:1-4) and their ostentation (23:5-12). Jesus pronounced seven woes (a solemn pronouncement of judgment) upon them: a) their locking up of the kingdom (23:13); b) the character of their proselytes (23:15); c) their rulings on oaths (23:16-22), d) their rulings about trifles (23:23-64), e) their rulings on cleanliness (23:25-26), f) their external righteousness (23:27-28), and g) their hypocritical honor of the prophets (23:29-33). In turn, the Jewish leaders wanted to end Jesus' public ministry.

11. Fifth Discourse: Jesus' Apocalyptic Predictions and Parables (24-25). In this last discourse, addressed to the disciples, Jesus discusses the end of the age and makes a detailed prophecy (24:1-36).

Somewhat puzzled by his denouncement of the nation, Jesus' disciples pointed out to him the magnificent temple buildings. To their surprise, he predicted that the Temple would be destroyed. This prompted two questions by his disciples: when? and what? (24:1-3).

Jesus gave the signs of the end. Before the *Parousia*, the end of the world and his Second Coming, there will be persecution and apostasy (24:9-14), famines, earthquakes, loss of faith, and international wars (24:23-31). But the exact time of the Parousia not even "the Son" would know. According to Matthew, Jesus' Second Coming will be unexpected and without warning.

Chapter 25 contains three parables of Jesus' unannounced reappearance:

a. *The parable of the ten virgins* (25:1-13), in which five foolish virgins fail to provide their lamps with oil, so that when the bridegroom (Messiah) appears they are absent and therefore denied entrance to the marriage feast (Messianic kingdom). This is a parable on preparedness.

b. *The parable of the talents* (25:14-30), along with constant preparedness, emphasizes the use of capabilities.

c. *The parable of the sheep and the goats* (25:31-46) is a parable on the last judgment. Matthew describes Jesus as a judge who comes at the close of the age to separate the righteous from the wicked.

12. Jesus' Crucifixion (26-27). In this section of Matthew, Jesus' death is dealt with in two parts: the preliminary events leading up to his death, and the Crucifixion.

A. *Matthew records ten events leading up to the crucifixion (26:3-27:66):*

a. *The "chief priests and scribes" plotted to kill Jesus* (26:3-5).

b. *Jesus was anointed in the house of Simon the leper at Bethany by an anonymous woman* (26:6-13). Jesus called her action "beautiful" and accepted it as preparation for his burial.

c. *Judas betrayed Jesus with thirty pieces of silver* (26:20-25) and then, overcome with remorse, he returned the blood money and hanged himself. The priests then used this money to buy "a burying place for foreigners" (27:3-10), which Matthew sees as fulfillment of Jeremiah 32:6-13 and Zechariah 11:12-13.[35]

d. *Jesus ate the Passover with his disciples,* substituting in its place his own Supper, a new covenant (26:17-29).

e. *Peter promised that he would never forsake Jesus.* Jesus predicted that Peter would deny him three times that night (26:31-35).

f. *Jesus prayed in the Garden of Gethsemane*, where as fully man he expressed dread over his coming ordeal yet, as fully God, he accepted "the cup" placed before him (26:36-46).

g. *Jesus was arrested by a great crowd sent by the chief priests and elders of the people.* They came at night with swords and clubs because they regarded Jesus as a "revolutionist who may offer resistance" (26:47-56).[36]

h. *Jesus had a hearing before the Sanhedrin, where he was charged with blasphemy* (26:57-68). Jesus' appearance before the Sanhedrin, the supreme judicial council of the Jews, was not a legal trial, for it was held before dawn, an illegal hour, and with only a part of the membership present. Also, capital punishment could be decreed only by Rome, after a trial in a Roman court.[37]

i. *Peter cowardly denied Jesus in the courtyard* (26:69-75).

j. *Jesus had a hearing before the Roman governor, Pilate* (27:11-25), whose effort to avoid crucifying Jesus is a pitiful story. Pilate's wife, tormented by a dream, urged him to have nothing to do with the accused (27:19). Pilate publicly washed his hands of responsibility for Jesus' death and reluctantly delivered him over for crucifixion.

B. *The Crucifixion (27:27-56)* covers the four stages through which Jesus went: mistreatment by the Roman soldiers, his journey to the Cross, his ordeal on the Cross, and his death.

a. *Jesus was mistreated by the Roman soldiers* (27:27-31). He was scourged. Scourging usually preceded capital punishment. It was done with a whip, which was made of a number of thongs weighted with pieces of lead or sharp metal.[38] Then Jesus was mocked by Pilate's soldiers, priests, elders, and scribes.

b. *Jesus' journey to the Cross* (27:32) was not only humiliating but also torturous. Exhausted by his night of agony and the scourging, he had not gone far before he became too weak to bear his cross. Simon of Cyrene was drafted to help him carry it.

c. *Jesus was crucified on the hill of Golgotha* (the Aramaic word *galgata* means skull or head) (27:33-44). On the Cross he was given gall (this was a pious Jewish custom intended to render the victim unconscious). They divided his garments (the garments of a condemned man belonged to his executioners). Two robbers, who might have been revolutionaries, were crucified with him.

   d. *Jesus' death took place on Friday at the ninth hour (3:00 p.m.)* (27:45-56), Matthew cites a number of phenomena attending Jesus' death—darkness gripped all the land, an earthquake shook the earth, and the tombs opened. The veil of the temple was rent, a symbol that the barrier between God and man had disappeared (Heb. 9:8). The Roman centurion who crucified Jesus was convinced that Jesus was indeed the Son of God.

   Following his death, Jesus' body was delivered to one of his influential sympathizers, Joseph of Arimathea, and was laid in a new tomb (27:57-61). And the next day, on the Jewish Sabbath, the Pharisees asked governor Pilate to have Jesus' tomb guarded, "Lest his disciples go and steal him and tell the people, 'He has risen from the dead' " (27:64).

   13. Jesus' Resurrection (28). This section is divided into four parts: the angel and the women, Jesus' appearance to the women, the false witness of the guards, and the final appearance to the Eleven.

   a. *The angel appeared to Mary Magdalene and the other Mary* who went to see the sepulcher toward the dawn of the first day of the week (28:1-8). The angel heralded Jesus' resurrection. This was the greatest news! Christ, who was wrestling with our sin upon the Cross, had been victorious; God had raised him from the dead!

   b. *Jesus' appearance to the women* (28:9-10) first caused fear, but the fear was quickly replaced with great joy, bringing them to their knees in worship. Then their joy was translated into action; "they ran to tell his disciples"(28:10).

   c. *Guards had been put at the tomb at the request of the Sanhedrin* as a precaution against the possibility of Jesus' body being stolen (28:11-15). Terrified at the earthquake, the angel, and the absence of Jesus' body from the tomb, the guards fled to report to the Sanhedrin. The Sanhedrin bribed them to say that they had fallen asleep.

   d. *The final appearance of Jesus to the eleven* (28:16-20) and his "Great Commission" to them to proclaim the Gospel to all nations and make disciples is the culmination of the Gospel. His last words, "I am with you always" (28:20) is a reassuring promise. The disciples then and the followers of Christ afterwards are assured that he is still with them as a living presence.

2. THE GOSPEL OF MARK

The Gospel According to Mark is a very important sourcebook for the life of Jesus. New Testament biblical commentator William Barclay called it "the most important book in the world."[39] Like many scholars, Barclay believed Mark was the earliest of all the Gospels, and the first "life" of Jesus that has come down to us. It initiated the whole Gospel-writing movement. It had enormous influence on both Matthew and Luke who drew heavily upon it. It is the nearest approach to an eyewitness account of Jesus we have and brings us nearer to the "immediate circle of Jesus' followers than any other record of him we possess."[40]

There has been much discussion about who the author of Mark was. There are some scholars who believe that the author is anonymous, perhaps a Gentile Christian writing to other Christians in a difficult time of turmoil, persecution, and uncertainty, to undergird their faith.[41] The most ancient and commonly held view, however, is that the author was John Mark, the son of a well-to-do Jerusalem lady named Mary (perhaps the widow of a Roman citizen), whose home was a meeting place for the disciples of Jesus (Acts 12:12).

Mark was also a nephew of Barnabas, a prominent leader of the early Church in Jerusalem and one of Paul's traveling companions in the preaching of the Gospel. When Paul and Barnabas set out on their first missionary journey they took Mark along with them as secretary (Acts 12:25). This journey was most unfortunate for young Mark, for when they reached Perga, Paul proposed that they travel inland, and for some reason Mark left the expedition and went home (Acts 13:13). This caused Paul and Barnabas to disagree about taking Mark on the next trip.

We next read about Mark in the epistles of Paul to the Colossians (Col. 4:10), Philemon (vs. 24), and Timothy (II Tim. 4:11). A testament to the ability to recover, Mark's early failure and rejection by Paul was replaced by a firm relationship between the two men. In later years, he became one of Paul's intimate and beloved helpers.

It is assumed that Mark got his information about the life of Jesus Christ from his close associations with the Christian community and from listening to the preaching of the Apostle Peter. Eusebius, the fourth-century Church historian, reports, and also quotes Papias, bishop of Hierapolis (about 140 A.D.), as stating that Mark became the companion and interpreter of Peter and wrote down what Peter remembered of his experiences with Jesus.[42]

The Gospels were written, each at a particular time, for a particular purpose, and for a specific group of people. In the case of Mark, the Gospel was written probably between 65-70 A.D. (about 68 A.D.), for the Christians in Rome, to present to them a picture of Christ as the Heroic Man of Action and for the purpose of inspiring them in their time of trial and persecution.

In 64 A.D. a great fire destroyed most of Rome. Emperor Nero was suspected. He found a convenient scapegoat in the Christians on whom he placed the blame and against whom he embarked upon a campaign of persecution. Christians in Rome were persecuted for their faith and many died as martyrs. Since Mark's readers had already believed the "good news," his primary purpose was to encourage them to follow Jesus in spite of the danger of persecution. He is writing for a martyr church, for Christians who may soon pay the ultimate price. The purpose of the Gospel is not just to give the facts about Jesus, but to indicate the significance of Jesus, and, by his example of heroism, to call the Christians of Rome to fidelity and heroism. It was written for their inspiration and undergirding in time of gravest peril and suffering.

To help his audience identify with the persecution of Jesus, Mark cites a number of controversies which led to the death of Jesus. Mark believes that Jesus died because:

a. The religious leaders suspected and hated him;

    b. He chose to die, and give his life "for many";
    c. God used his death for the changing of human life.[43]

The chief characteristics of the Gospel According to Mark are the following:

    A. *Mark is not only the earliest but also the shortest of the Gospels.* It is half as long as Luke, and two-thirds as long as Matthew. Mark does not include nativity stories such as Matthew and Luke later produced. Instead, he begins with the announcement of Jesus Christ as the Son of God, followed by a messianic prophecy involving John the Baptist and a brief account of Jesus' baptism and temptation, and then, in 1:14, he launches into Jesus' Galilean ministry. The style of the Gospel is marked by abruptness. Mark is a writer in a hurry. In the first chapter there are only 45 verses. In them he covers in rapid succession John the Baptist, the baptism of Jesus, the temptation of Jesus, the call of the first disciples, the synagogue incident in Capernaum, the healing of the leper, the healing of the paralytic, and the rising popularity of Jesus so that he had to flee to the desert for rest. There are no smooth transitions in these topics. The author is not interested in tying things with ribbons. He has an existential concern: in Rome people are dying for their faith; he wants to strengthen their faith and courage in the face of martyrdom.

    B. *Mark's style is not polished, but is very vivid.* The style is marked by ruggedness, directness, and simplicity. He has almost a religious devotion to the conjunction "and." In the third chapter alone he connects 34 clauses and sentences with "and." He is fond of such words as "forthwith," and "immediately." The latter occurs in the Gospel 36 times. Mark was in a hurry and Mark's Jesus was always in a hurry. He "races by, scattering miracles like rice at a wedding."[44] Mark's disciples are in a hurry to respond to Jesus. Immediately they leave their nets and follow him! Mark rushes on with a breathless attempt to make the story as real and alive to his readers as it is to him.

    The Gospel of Mark is filled with the verbs of faith: Come! Repent! Go! "Come, follow," says the Jesus of St. Mark. The author ends his book, as he begins it, almost in the middle of a sentence. One gets the feeling that there was not time to gather up all the loose ends.[45]

C. *Mark is much more interested in events and actions than in the teachings and discourses of Jesus.* Mark contains little of the teachings in which the other Synoptic Gospels abound. The Christians in Rome knew the teachings of Jesus. Mark is telling them the events and actions of Jesus. Only about one-third of the Gospel deals with teachings, the rest deals with actions. Thus, Mark is a Gospel of action. It records 18 of Jesus' miracles but only 4 parables and one major discourse.

Four Greek words are employed in the four Gospels to describe the works of Jesus: *teras*, wonder (Mark 13:22); *dunamis*, power.(Mark 6:2, 5, 14; 9:3); *semeion*, sign (Mark 1:11, 12; 16:17, 20); *ergon*, miraculous deed (John 7:3, 21). The first three are used by Mark.[46]

From the beginning to the end of Mark's Gospel, Jesus is the Christ, the Son of God. However, Mark's perspective of Jesus is unique, in that he portrays Jesus as a Servant (10:45). He is not so much the teacher or the prophet, but the Man of Action, the Doer of Deeds. Mere action, however, is not the important thing. In Mark, Jesus is not important because he is an austere man of action, but the actions are important because Jesus does them. In Mark, the Gospel—the good news—is Jesus himself. The deeds and the teaching are important because of the doer and the speaker, Jesus. The Doer, the Man of Action, the Son of God—Jesus Christ—*is* the Gospel.

D. *Mark emphasizes the humanity of Jesus.* No other Gospel portrays so realistically and vividly the intense humanity of Jesus as does Mark. One of Mark's favorite titles for Jesus was "Son of Man." No other Gospel tells us so much about the emotions of Jesus as does Mark. Jesus sighs, gets angry, gets weary, is moved with compassion, feels the pangs of hunger. For Mark the real Jesus, the real Lord of mankind, was very much of flesh and blood, of emotion and feeling. In Mark, the humanity of Jesus shines through. But so does the divinity! Mark begins his Gospel by clearly stating, "The beginning of the Gospel of Jesus Christ, the Son of God" (1:1). In other words, to Mark he was not merely a man among men, but God among humankind, who had taken human flesh upon himself.

E. *Mark portrays Jesus Christ as God's Son who passes through the world largely unrecognized.* Mark presents Jesus as one who works to keep his true nature secret from everyone save a few intimates. Scholars call this the "Messianic Secret."[47] Jesus gives his apocalyptic discourse about the end of the world only to his disciples. He forbids those whom he miraculously heals or cleanses from telling his identity (1:23-24, 34; 3:11-12; 8:30; 9:2-9). Some scholars think that this "secret" was the writer's way of explaining why Jesus was not recognized as a divine being during his lifetime.[48] Others point out that the reason Jesus did not disclose his true role was that his concept of Messiahship differed from those of his contemporaries. The Jews of Jesus' day believed in a warrior-king type of a Messiah who would restore the one-time glorious Kingdom of David, while "Mark's Jesus is a Messiah revealed only through suffering and death."[49] In this Gospel, Jesus publicly acknowledged his identity only once: before the Sanhedrin when the High Priest asked him, "Are you the Christ, the Son of the Blessed One?" To which Jesus replied, "I am."

Mark also implies that even Jesus' faithful followers did not fully understand their Master. For instance, when Jesus stilled the storm on the Sea of Galilee, the disciples were impressed but were unaware of the meaning of this miraculous act (4:35-41). After the feeding of the five thousand, the disciples "were completely amazed," but did not understand "the intent of the loaves" (6:51-52). After hearing the parable of the sower, the disciples did not understand the point. Jesus told them, "If you don't understand this parable, how then will you understand any parable?" (4:13). After the Transfiguration of Jesus, the Master tells his three loyal disciples "not to tell anyone what they had seen until the Son of Man had risen from the dead." The disciples were apparently puzzled as to what Jesus meant by "rising from the dead." (9:9-10).

Moreover, even when Jesus "explained everything" to his

disciples (4:34) and "spoke plainly" to them, and his leading disciple Peter proclaimed him "the Christ" (8:29), the disciples deserted him after his arrest (14:50) and Peter denied him three times (14:66-72).

The Gospel According to Mark is divided into five major parts:
1. Introduction (1:1-13)
2. Jesus' Galilean Ministry (1:14-9:50)
3. Jesus' Perean Ministry (10:1-10:52)
4. Jesus' Last Week in and around Jerusalem (11:1-15:47)
5. Jesus' Empty Tomb (16)

1. Introduction (1:1-13). In his typical style, Mark begins abruptly with the announcement of "Jesus Christ, the Son of God" (1:1), followed by a messianic prophecy involving John the Baptist preparing a path for the Lord. Without reference to the birth story, such as Luke and Matthew later produced, Mark launches at once into the public ministry of his hero by presenting the adult Jesus at the River Jordan for baptism. The Spirit of God descended upon Jesus and a voice from heaven pronounced him as the "beloved Son" of God (1:9-11), after which he retreated to the wilderness for forty days and was tempted by Satan (1:12-13). The temptation is told in fuller detail in Matthew and Luke.

2. Jesus' Galilean Ministry (1:14-9:50). According to Mark, Jesus' ministry began in Galilee after John's ministry was ended by Herod Antipas, ruler of the Galilean region of Palestine. Jesus' Galilean ministry is divided into two parts:

A. Jesus' Ministry around the Sea of Galilee (1:14-5:43)
B. Jesus' Ministry beyond the Sea of Galilee (6:1-9:50)

A. *Jesus' Ministry Around the Sea of Galilee.* Soon after his baptism, Jesus went to Galilee "proclaiming the good news of God" (1:14). His first proclamation was, "The kingdom of God is near. Repent and believe in the good news" (1:15).
  a. "The kingdom of God" is a phrase that we read throughout

the Gospel as a watchword or master thought in Jesus' preaching ministry. This was the subject of his first sermon in Mark. This was also the theme of his last discourse, as he spoke to his disciples "of the things pertaining to the kingdom of God" recorded in Acts 1:3.

What was "the kingdom of God"? For Jesus the kingdom of God was the rule of God in the heart. It was moral not nationalistic. Although his fellow countrymen considered Rome the enemy, Jesus told them that the enemy whom they ought to fight was Satan and the evil forces.[50] Jesus made this very clear when he told Pilate, "My kingdom is not of this world . . . if my kingdom were of this world, then would my servants fight" (John 18:36). It was not the earthly kingdom on which the Jews had set their hearts; it was a spiritual kingdom in the hearts of the people. It was the rule of God in the world—a family fellowship of the children of God. It was a universal kingdom, not a local one. In Jesus' words, "People will come from east and west and north and south, and will take their place at the feast in the kingdom of God" (Luke 13:29). Furthermore, the kingdom of God awaits a final consummation and is not yet complete. This is paradoxical in the sense that the Kingdom is both present and future—present because it exists now wherever there is a fully surrendered heart, but also future because the crowning glory is still to come, "when the Son of Man shall come in his glory" (Matt. 25:31), breaking in triumphantly at his Second Advent. In short, there will be a new earth in which the rule of God will prevail in all the world; this rule, or kingdom will be ethical and spiritual, not political, where people will live together as the family of God.[51]

b. <u>The Disciples</u>. After this important proclamation about the kingdom, Jesus began his recruiting of his disciples, calling Simon Peter and his brother Andrew, and James and John (the sons of Zebedee) to leave their fishing trade and follow him (1:16-20). Later, Jesus chose another eight men to complete the Twelve, a number symbolic of the twelve tribes of Israel.[52] What was Jesus' purpose in selecting these men for special discipleship? Mark states, "He appointed twelve—designating them apostles—that they might be with him and that he might send them out to preach" (3:14).

Of the Twelve, four were fishermen, one was a tax-collector, one a Zealot. We do not know what the others were. All were Galileans, except Judas Iscariot. There are four listings of the names of the disciples. The order of these listings varies from Gospel to Gospel.

Here are the names of the disciples in the following four books:

Mt. 10:2-4	Mk 3:16-19	Lk 6:12-19	Acts 1:13
Simon	Simon	Simon	Peter
Andrew	James	Andrew	James
James	John	James	John
John	Andrew	John	Andrew
Philip	Philip	Philip	Philip
Bartholomew	Bartholomew	Bartholomew	Thomas
Thomas	Matthew	Matthew	Bartholomew
Matthew	Thomas	Thomas	Matthew
James, son of Alphaeus	James, son of Alphaeus	James, son of Alphaeus	James, son of Alphaeus
Thaddaeus	Thaddaeus	Simon Zealot	Simon Zealot
Simon Zealot	Simon Zealot	Judas son James	Judas son James
Judas Iscariot	Judas Iscariot	Judas Iscariot	Matthias (*elected to replace Judas)

c. The First Set of Miracles (1:21-2:12). According to the Gospel of Mark, Jesus' ministry began in Capernaum. Why in Capernaum and not in his hometown Nazareth? We do not know. It could be that his first two disciples, Peter and Andrew, lived there. Or perhaps, since Capernaum was a populous city and an important port on the Sea of Galilee, a cross-road city, it made a better "audience." It is in the synagogue and in the midst of this busy pulsing life that Jesus performed his first healing miracle—the exorcism of the demoniac (1:21-28). Then he healed the mother-in-law of Peter (1:29-31). Apparently, the news of these healings spread all over the city, and great crowds gathered with their sick around the house where Jesus was lodged. And Jesus healed them.

After spending an evening in a solitary place, Jesus continued his healing ministry in other towns, performing miracles such as the healing of a leper and the healing of a paralytic (1:38-2:12). This had an amazing effect on the ordinary people but irritated "the teachers of the Law," who exclaimed, "He is blaspheming! Who can forgive sins but God alone?" (2:6).

d. <u>The Conflict With the Religious Custodians of Judaism</u> (2:13-3:6). After this first "offensive" episode, Jesus further offended the custodians of the law. First he called to apostleship a publican by the name of Levi (2:13-17). A publican was a tax collector for Rome, despised by the Jews from whom he extorted money (Matt. 9:10-13; 13-17; 21:23). Next Jesus broke the Sabbath with his disciples by picking some heads of grain (2:23-27), and healing a man on the Sabbath (3:1-6). Sabbath was the seventh day of the Jewish week, sacred to Yahweh and dedicated to rest and worship. It was a memorial of Yahweh's repose after six days of creation, and was strictly observed by Jews. When admonished for Sabbath breaking, Jesus replied, "The Sabbath was made for man, not man for the Sabbath" (2:27).

e. <u>Jesus' True Family</u> (3:31-35). According to the Gospel, Jesus had, in addition to his mother Mary, four brothers (James, Jude, Joses, and Simon), and at least two sisters (who are not named). Roman Catholic and Ancient Orthodox Churches regard these as "relatives" of Jesus, not brothers and sisters. They hold to the notion of the "perpetual virginity" of Mary.[53] Most Protestants believe that they were really blood brothers and sisters of Jesus—and that one of them, James, was the first bishop of the church in Jerusalem.

Jesus was told, "Your mother and brothers are outside waiting for you." He asked, "Who are my brothers and sisters?" This is one of the most shocking of Jesus' questions! Were these words meant to repudiate family ties? No, because in verse 35 Jesus stated "Whoever does God's will is my brother and sister and mother." By these words Jesus was, in fact, extending the circle of God's family.

f. <u>Parables of the Kingdom</u> (4:1-32). Jesus was a teacher, a rabbi. In spite of the fact that Mark is a Gospel of action, and presents Jesus as the Great Doer of Deeds, it nevertheless includes eight parables of Jesus. After telling his followers that his new concepts cannot be fitted in the old traditions, just as "new wine" should not be put in the "old wineskins" (2:22), Jesus told the Parable of the Sower, in which his message is likened to planting seed. Just as some seeds die, some grow sparsely, and some flourish according to the kind of soil on which they fall, so does Jesus' word find varying degrees of success according to the receptivity and good will of his hearers (4:3-20).

The next two parables, the Growing Seed (4:26-29) and the Parable of the Mustard Seed (4:30-34), both stress the fact that the kingdom of God grows with a small beginning, quietly, imperceptibly, and irresistably moving on to the day of harvest.

    g. The Second Set of Miracles (4:35-5:43). In this section, there are these miracles recorded: the storm stilled, the Gerasene demoniac, the daughter of Jairus, and the woman with the issue of blood.

In a tossing boat, during a storm on the Sea of Galilee, the disciples were frightened while Jesus was calmly sleeping. Jesus stilled the raging waters and rebuked the disciples for their lack of faith (5:35-41).

Mark 5:1-20 reflects the demonology of the day and relates the story of a dangerous Gerasene demoniac, dwelling naked in the tombs. In the Gospel of Matthew, there are two demoniacs (Matt. 8:28-34). The demoniac(s) recognized the authority of Jesus. The demons were driven out of the lunatic(s) and entered the two thousand swine who jumped into the sea, following which the natives wanted Jesus to get out of their town. They thought more of their swine than they did of their people.

After the healing of the demoniac, Jairus, one of the rulers of the synagogue, fell at the feet of Jesus pleading him to heal his dying daughter, at which time a woman who had been subject to bleeding touched Jesus' clothes to be cured. The woman was restored to complete health of body, and the girl, who had in the meantime died, was raised from the dead. (5:21-43).

B. *Jesus' Ministry Beyond the Sea of Galilee* (6:1-9:58). Heretofore Jesus' ministry is centered around the Sea of Galilee and primarily around Capernaum. Beginning with chapter 6 a new division begins, recounting his visit to Nazareth, another circuit of Galilee, a journey to Bethsaida, a visit to the region of Tyre and Sidon, a return via Decapolis, a visit to Dalmanutha, a stop at the village of Caesarea Philippi, another trip to Bethsaida and a return to Capernaum through Galilee. In chapters 6-9, following the rejection at Nazareth and the commissioning of the disciples, Jesus is mostly outside Galilee proper, or rather outside the jurisdiction of Herod Antipas.

a. <u>Jesus' Visit to Nazareth</u> (6:1-6). The first stop of these wider journeyings is Jesus' visit to Nazareth (6:1-6). This seems to have been his second visit to "his own country" after he began his public ministry, about a year after the visit recorded in Luke 4:16-30. The presence of "his disciples" indicated that the purpose of his journey was evangelization, not a family visit. His preaching and his "mighty works" astonished Jesus' townfolks. They took offense at him and rejected him by saying, "Isn't this the carpenter? Isn't this Mary's son and the brother of James, Joses, Judas, and Simon? Aren't his sisters here with us?" (6:3). Jesus' reaction to this attitude is realistic, not one of cynicism or self-pity. Quoting a familiar proverb, he said, "A prophet is not without honor, except in his own country" (6:4).

b. <u>The Mission of the Disciples</u> (6:7-13). Jesus commissioned the Twelve disciples and began to send them out two by two. He charged them to take nothing for their journey (v.8) and if any place would not receive them "to shake the dust off their feet and leave" (v.11)—a symbolic act denoting a complete break in relations.

c. <u>The Death of John the Baptist</u> (6:17-29). John the Baptist had criticized the tetrarch of Galilee and Perea, Herod Antipas, for divorcing his wife and marrying his brother's wife, Herodias. The latter, reacting violently to this moral reproof, used her daughter (Salome) to trick Herod into decapitating the Baptist.

d. <u>Another Series of Mighty Deeds</u> (6:45-8:26). Mark again records a series of Jesus' mighty works:

— the feeding of the five thousand (6:30-44), where Jesus multiplied five loaves of bread and two fish to feed five thousand people;

— Jesus' walk on the sea (6:45-52), a sign of his command over nature;

— the healing of the Syrophoenician woman's daughter (7:24-30), one of the few cases of ministry to Gentiles; Jesus refers to her in a derogatory way (calling her a "dog"). This story has received various interpretations: a) Jesus' reluctance to minister to those outside Israel; b) testing the faith of this woman; c) a lesson that persistence in prayer is essential; d) a demonstration that trust in him was not confined to Israel; e) a humorous reference echoing what was in the minds of the Jewish people toward non-Jewish people. Undoubtedly, the Syrophoenician woman's persistence, humility, and faith won her request;

— the healing of a deaf and dumb man (7:31-37); Jesus not only restored his hearing but also cured an impediment in his speech, cautioning the man to keep quiet in order to avoid publicity;

— the feeding of the four thousand (8:1-10) could be, according to some scholars, a second version of the same story of the feeding of the multitudes. Both accounts illustrate the "messianic banquet" theme, "that of the chosen people enjoying feasts of abundance in the coming kingdom,"[55] as well as Jesus' compassion for the hungry;

— the healing of the blind man of Bethsaida (8:22-26), whose healing was gradual, requiring two treatments, (two "touches").

e. <u>Peter's Confession</u> (8:27-30). "Who do people say I am?" asked by Jesus of his disciple, is a timeless question, which represents the starting point for an understanding of Jesus—what others have thought of him. Jesus wanted his followers to answer the same question, "But who do you say that I am?" Peter's answer, "You are the Christ," was a great act of faith.

f. <u>The First Passion Announcement</u> (8:31-33). After charging the Twelve not to reveal his messiahship to anyone, Jesus made his first passion announcement; he was going to be rejected by the Jewish leadership, killed, and after three days raised from the dead. In Mark the same prediction is made two more times: while passing through Galilee (9:31), and near Jerusalem (10:32-34). Parenthetically, in the Synoptic Gospels the Passion is foretold five times between Peter's confession and the arrival of Jesus and his disciples in Jerusalem: First, after Peter's confession (Matt. 16:21, Mark 8:31, Luke 9:22). Second, after the Transfiguration (Matt. 17:9, 12; Mark 9:9-12). Third, after the healing of the epileptic (Luke 9:44). Fourth, while passing through Galilee (Matt. 17:22-23; Mark 9:31). Fifth, near Jerusalem (Matt. 20:17-19; Mark 10:32-34; Luke 18:31-34).

g. Transfiguration (9:2-8). The vision of the Transfiguration immediately follows the unveiling of the idea of the Suffering Messiah. Jesus is seen in a glorified state, involved in a three-way conversation with Moses and Elijah, two of the greatest personalities of his people. Moses represents the lawgiver, and Elijah, the Prophets. This demonstrates that Jesus is the final culmination of the Law and the Prophets.

3. Jesus' Perean Ministry (10:1-52). In this section, Jesus departed from Galilee and went to Perea, or in modern topography, Trans-Jordan. The activities covered in this chapter include:

a. *Marriage and Divorce* (10:1-12). What Jesus had to say about this issue was uttered against the background of an ongoing rabbinical debate about divorce originating in Deuteronomy 24:1-2. Jewish law at the time made divorce almost impossible for a woman. It was a man who could put away his wife if he found "some indecency" in her. The implication of Jesus' words are that women as persons are equal with men in the sight of God. In marriage husband and wife "become one;" they still retain their individual identity, but each adds to himself/herself the identity of the other. Jesus seems to permit divorce on the grounds of adultery.

b. *Blessing of the Little Children* (10:13-16). In childhood Jesus found the perfect analogy for membership in the kingdom of God. The unquestioning faith and the sense of dependence characterizing children are qualities that Jesus commended.

c. *The Meaning of Discipleship* (10:17-31). In this section there are three items that deal with discipleship: the rich young man, the danger of riches, and the reward of renunciation. Jesus did not frown upon wealth and riches. The rich young man's problem was not the fact that he had great possessions, but that the possessions had *him*—they had come between himself and God. Jesus impressed the fact that no one can become a disciple until he rearranges his priorities and gives his first loyalty to God.

d. *The Request of James and John* (10:35-45). The request

of the two brothers, James and John, was to be honored as the greatest among the followers of Jesus. Jesus turned upside down the disciples' (and the world's) concept of greatness. The world says: The greatest people are those who have the most servants. But for Jesus, "Whoever wants to become great among you must be your servant"(v. 43).

4. Jesus' Last Week In and Around Jerusalem (Mark 11:1-15:47). This division of the Gospel narrates Jesus' activity during the final week. The crowded events covered in these five chapters quite possibly belonged to a larger period and perhaps to more than one visit to Jerusalem. The chronology of events related in the Gospel According to John allows for several visits of Jesus to Jerusalem.[56] These five chapters are divided into two parts: A. Controversies and Apocalyptic Discourse; B. The Passion Narrative.

A. Controversies and Apocalyptic Discourse Include:

a. The Triumphal Entry (11:1-11). Here Jesus who had walked on foot all the way from Galilee in the north, down along the east bank of the Jordan through Perea, stopped within sight of the Holy City to borrow a donkey for the remaining two mile journey. Why? Because riding into Jerusalem on a donkey was a Messianic statement. "Tell the daughter of Zion, behold, your king is coming to you, humble, and mounted on an ass" (Zech. 9:9). Why is this event called "The Triumphal Entry" when there was nothing triumphant about it? It was a triumph over a precarious situation. Jesus was coming to Jerusalem where he knew that both civic and religious leadership was against him. He knew that Jerusalem was a danger zone where he would be treated violently. Yet, in spite of all these, "He set his face to Jerusalem." On donkeyback, Jesus entered Jerusalem. As a sign of honor, "garments and leafy branches" were spread before him on the road. And the crowd cried out "Hosanna" (*Hashiahna*, meaning, "save now!" or "God in heaven save him!") "Blessed be he who comes in the name of the Lord! Blessed be the kingdom of our father David that is coming! Hosanna in the highest!" (11:10).

b. Cursing of the Fig Tree and Cleansing of the Temple (11:12-19). Entering Jerusalem, Jesus went into the Temple. As it was already late, he went out to Bethany with the Twelve. On the following day, when they came from Bethany, on the way to Jerusalem, he cursed a fig tree, which looked good from the outside, but bore no figs. Probably this was an "enacted parable," intending a reference to the Temple and the religious folk of Jesus' day who were "infertile" and made religion into a sham.

With the barren fig tree and the barren temple religion as a backdrop, Jesus went to the Temple and cleansed it from the traders and money-changers, telling them that they had made "my house ... of prayer " (Isa. 56:6-8) a den of robbers (v. 17).

c. Questions Asked of and by Jesus (11:27-12:34). Following the cleansing of the Temple, the opposition of the Jewish secular and religious leadership against Jesus intensified. The chief priests, scribes, and elders questioned Jesus' authority asking, "*By what authority are you doing these things?*" (11-27). In good rabbinical style Jesus answered with a counterquestion "Was the baptism of John from heaven or from men?" (11:30). Afraid of the people's reaction, they refused to answer, and Jesus in turn refused to answer them.

After telling the Parable of the Tenants, an allegory which predicts the rejection of the Messiah by the leaders of the Jews (12:1-12), Jesus was asked another question, "*Is it right to pay taxes to Caesar or not?*" (12:14). This was a trap set for Jesus. Jesus did not give an absolute answer as to what they ought to do, but gave them the basis for making their own decision. "Give to Caesar what is Caesar's and to God what is God's" (12:17). There have been various interpretations of this statement. Some have interpreted it as an appeal to religious liberty and the separation of church and state, and have asserted that the two powers to which men give their loyalty should be kept completely and permanently distinct.[57] Others have understood that to mean Christians are called to be citizens of two worlds: the Kingdom of God and the Kingdom of this world. Most of the time there is no conflict between the two. But should conflict ever come Christians know their first loyalty is to God.[58] Both interpretations are logical and meaningful.

The third question came from the Sadducees *concerning resurrection*. The Sadducees, who did not believe in the resurrection of the dead, probably had used this question against the Pharisees, who believed in resurrection. But now the two factions joined hands in conspiracy against Jesus. They wanted Jesus to answer *"In the resurrection, will there be marriage or not?"* (12:18-27). Jesus once again turned the table upon his opponents by quoting from the Torah, which both groups recognized as their final authority. Jesus affirmed that there is resurrection, and explained that the risen people are "like angels in heaven" (v. 25) and thus there is no marriage in the resurrection.

The fourth question was that of the *greatest commandment*: *"Of all the commandments, which is the most important?"* (12:28-34). Jesus combined the two "great commandments" of Deuteronomy 6:4 and Leviticus 19:17 into a summary of the law: "Love the Lord your God with all your heart and with all your soul and with all your mind and with all your strength ... and love your neighbor as yourself" (12:30-32).

The last question is one asked by Jesus himself: *"Whose Son is the Christ?"* (12:35-37). The point in the question is how could a man call his own son "Lord?" Simple as the answer seems, it silenced his opponents.

d. The Widow's Mite (12:41-44). After Jesus' denunciation of the Scribes and Pharisees, the event that Mark describes in graphic detail is the widow's mite. A dear old widow gave all she had to God. Jesus paid tribute to the widow because out of her poverty and without reservation she gave her whole living to God. Her gift foreshadowed the one Jesus was about to make: His very life. In Mark "this poor widow becomes a type of Him who 'though he was rich, yet for (our) sake became poor, so that by his poverty (we) might become rich' " (II Cor. 8:9).[59]

e. The Apocalyptic Discourse (13:1-37). This section deals with apocalyptic eschatology. *Apocalyptic* means a revealing, unveiling, uncovering. *Eschatology* is the study of the "last things." Jesus prophesied the impending fall of the temple (13:1-2), the signs of the end of the age (13:3-8), the persecution of the disciples (13:9-13), persecution in Judea (13:14-23), and the Parousia of the Son of Man (13:24-37). One of the most interesting things stated in Mark 13 about the end times is that even Jesus did not know when the end would occur. In his words, "No one knows about that day or hour, not even the angels in heaven, not the Son, but only the Father" (v. 32). This declaration "countered everything the first-century Jews would have expected of the Messiah."[60]

B. *The Passion Narrative* (14:1-15:47). Mark 14 and 15 record 16 events from the last days of the life of Jesus: the plot against Jesus (14:1-2), the anointing in Bethany (14:3-9), Judas' treachery (14:10-11), preparation for the Passover (14:12-16), prediction of the betrayal (14:17-21), the Last Supper (14:22-26), prediction of Peter's denial (14:27-31), Jesus in Gethsemane (14:32-42), Jesus' arrest (14:43-50), the flight of a naked young man (14:51-52), Jesus before Pilate (15:1-5), Jesus condemned to death (15:6-15), the mocking (15:16-20), the Crucifixion (15:21-32), Jesus' death on the Cross (15:33-41) and Jesus' burial by Joseph of Arimathea (15:42-47).

The highlights of the last couple of days of Jesus' earthly life include:

a. <u>Jesus' Betrayal and the Last Supper</u> (14:1-11). Following Jesus' prophecy of judgment, Mark records an incident where Jesus is prepared for death: a woman anointing Jesus with expensive perfume at the home of Simon the Leper; Jesus interprets her action, saying, "She has anointed my body beforehand for burying" (14:8).

In contrast to this magnanimous gesture was Judas Iscariot's decision to betray Jesus and make arrangements to hand him over to the authorities (14:10-11).

On the evening before his crucifixion, Jesus observed the Passover feast of the unleavened bread with his twelve disciples in a guest chamber of an unnamed friend. The Paschal feast is a celebration that solemnly recalls the Jews' last night in Egypt when the Angel of Death "passed over" their homes to slay the Egyptian first born (Exodus 11:1-13, 16). That night Jesus built upon the symbolism of the historic feast and gave it new meaning. The bread is to represent his body, and the wine "the blood of the covenant shed for many" (14:32-42). Following this *Last Supper*, Jesus and the Eleven (Judas had separated himself from Jesus and his other disciples) retired to a grove or vineyard called Gethsemane. Mark describes the loneliness and agony of Jesus while his disciples slept. Jesus demonstrated submission in the face of dread, praying "Abba, Father, ... take this cup from me, yet not what I will, but what you will" (14:36).

    b. Jesus' Arrest (14: 43-51) . While they were still in the Garden of Gethsemane, an armed mob "sent from the chief priests, the teachers of the law, and the leaders" (v. 43) appeared to arrest Jesus. Judas led them to him after the city had gone to sleep. Identified to the crowd by Judas' kiss, Jesus was arrested. The cowardly disciples deserted him and fled. Mark even includes an interesting story of the flight of a "young man" who in panic "fled naked, leaving his garment behind" (v. 52). Because this curious episode is reported in Mark alone, some scholars suggest that "young man" was the author himself.[61]

    Biblical scholars also have dealt with the question of Judas' betrayal of Jesus. Why did he do it? Various motives have been suggested, such as love of money, jealousy, fear, revenge, or an attempt to force Jesus' hand to declare himself the Messiah. [62]

    c. Jesus Before the Sanhedrin (14:53-65) . Jesus was conveyed to the Sanhedrin and accused of claiming to be the Messiah. The high priest asked him if indeed Jesus thought he was the Messiah (14:62). This is the only time recorded in the book of Mark that Jesus spoke openly to confirm that he was the Messiah. The self-revelation cost him his life: the Sanhedrin judged him deserving of death (14:63-64).

    d. Jesus Before Pilate (15:1-15). At daybreak Friday the chief priests, with the elders, the teachers of the Law, and the whole Sanhedrin held a meeting, perhaps implying that the Thursday night meeting had been illegal (or as John 18:31 states), the Jewish Council did not have legal authority to inflict capital punishment. The Council sent Jesus to Pontius Pilate, the Roman procurator who was in Jerusalem to maintain order during Passover week. Cognizant that their accusation of Jesus was purely religious and unlikely to carry much weight with a Gentile procurator, the Jewish leadership fabricated a charge of treason saying Jesus had claimed to be a king (a threat to Roman occupation). Pilate asked Jesus: "Are you the king of the Jews?" (15:2).

Mark's presentation of the two trials emphasizes the important distinction drawn between the religious and political accusations made against Jesus. Whereas the high priest had asked if Jesus were the Messiah (Christ), Pilate demanded to know if he claimed to be the "King of the Jews."[63]

Mark then introduces Barabbas (whose name means "Son of the Father"), a rebel (probably a terrorist) who had committed murder in the uprising (15:7). It was the custom at the Feast of Passover to release a prisoner. Pilate asked of the people, "Which shall it be, Jesus or Barabbas?" There is a dramatic fitness in the choice. Barabbas and Jesus represented two irreconcilable reactions to the Roman occupation—violent and non-violent resistance. It is not surprising that the people, faced with such a choice, preferred Barabbas; what is surprising is that Pilate should have found himself in a position where he had to release a declared enemy of Rome.[64]

e. The Crucifixion (Mark 15:21-32). Mark reports that Jesus, exhausted from the emotional and physical torture, was too weak to carry his cross to Golgotha, the hill of execution outside Jerusalem. The Roman soldiers impressed a passerby, Simon of Cyrene, to carry it for him (15:16-21). Taken to Golgotha ("Place of the Skull"), Jesus was crucified between two thieves. He was crucified at 9:00 in the morning (15:25) and died about three in the afternoon (15:16-21).

f. The Death of Jesus (Mark 15:21-32). Mark's Passion narrative includes the following details: the casting of lots for Jesus' clothes, darkness enveloping the earth, Jesus' recital of Psalm 22 (which opens with the lament "my God, my God, why have you forsaken me"), someone offering wine vinegar to Jesus on the cross and speculating whether "Elijah would come to take him down", Jesus' loud cry and death. Highlighting the spiritual blindness of the Jewish tormentors, Mark records the Gentile Roman centurion's exclamation, "Surely this man was the son of God" (15:39).

g. The Burial of Jesus (Mark 15:42-47). Mark's narrative then relates the story of Joseph of Arimathea who obtained permission to remove Jesus' body from the cross and provided a rock-hewn tomb that he sealed by rolling a stone across the entrance. (15:47).

h. <u>Jesus' Empty Tomb</u> (Mark 16). Because the Jewish Sabbath had begun by the time Jesus' body was removed from the cross, the women followers of Jesus were unable to prepare the body properly for its permanent entombment. Early on Sunday morning they went to the tomb "to anoint Jesus' body" (16:1). They found the entrance stone already rolled back and the tomb empty, except for "a young man dressed in a white robe sitting on the right side" (16:5). Trembling and bewildered, the women fled from the tomb (16:8).

The oldest and most reliable manuscripts of the Gospel of Mark abruptly end in mid-sentence with the Greek word "gar" which means "for." Later manuscripts contain a short two-sentence ending which appears as a footnote in some English versions of the New Testament or as a long ending designated as Mark 16:9-20. [65]

What happened to the original end of Mark? Did the author die as a martyr before he had time to finish it? Did the ending get torn off of the most ancient manuscript? Or, did Mark expect the *Parousia*, Jesus' sudden return, in the near future and consequently omit Jesus' resurrection?[66] Nobody knows. One thing is clear; the women did not keep quiet. They told their experience to others. That testimony was reinforced as Jesus "appeared to the Eleven" (16:14). Jesus' reappearance and commissioning of his disciples to "go into all the world and preach the good news to all creation" (16:15) becomes the climax of Mark's Gospel.

3. The Gospel of Luke

In some ways Luke is the most attractive of the four Gospels, containing a variety of detail and vividness of expression and being pervaded with a sense of joy. It is commonly agreed among people trained both in New Testament scholarship and in literature, that Luke is the best life of Christ ever written.

Scholars are also generally agreed that Luke is the most valuable of the Gospels from a historical point of view. Although

Mark is the earliest Gospel, it is Luke who ties the story of Christ into historic personages and events of the secular world of the time and gives its readers firm historical moorings.

Luke is the longest of the Gospels, almost twice as long as John and about three times as long as Mark.

The Gospel According to Luke is the first volume of Luke-Acts, a work that deals with the origin of Christianity and its early expansion in Palestine and other parts of the Roman Empire.

The author of this two-volume work was Luke, who was a physician (Col. 4:14; Philem 24; II Tim. 4:11). He was Greek, making him the only Gentile writer in the New Testament. This sole non-Jewish author is responsible for about 27% of the total contents of the New Testament.

According to most scholars, Luke-Acts was written after 70 A.D., when Jerusalem was destroyed by the Roman armies under Titus.[67] Luke uses a large percentage of Mark's Gospel and certain passages reveal detailed knowledge of the Roman siege (Luke 19:41-44; 21:20-24). These factors suggest that Luke may have been written around 85-90 A.D.

Besides drawing on Mark, Luke includes many sayings and teachings of Jesus that appear in Matthew but are absent from Mark. Scholars believe that this shared material was taken from the *Q* document. In addition to these, Luke acquired some material unique to his Gospel, including the birth stories, prayers, anecdotes about women, and parables, from private sources which scholars call the *L* source.

We know a good deal about Luke the author from evidence within the New Testament. In the Book of Acts (Luke's companion volume) there are sections known as "we" sections—portions written in the first person plural. Scholars generally agree that Luke must have traveled with Paul at times and that these "we" sections in Acts are a travel diary.

From biblical references, from his association with Paul, from the things he wrote, together with some educated guesses, scholars have inferred a number of things about Luke. It is certain that Luke was a cultured, educated Greek. He was a beloved physician of great ability, of warm and gentle disposition, having great interest in the world and in people. His vocation is indicated by medical terms unique to Luke on a number of pages of both the Gospel and Acts. It is no wonder that Luke presents Jesus as the Great Physician and Healer.

There are some scholars who claim Luke was probably trained at the University of Tarsus and there might have met Paul who was being trained in law. Upon completing his medical training, Luke returned to Antioch where he came into contact with the Christians and was converted. He later moved to Troas and practiced medicine there.[69]

Other scholars are not so sure about Luke's authorship. They believe that Luke-Acts is an anonymous two-volume work; that the author's identity is not conclusively settled. The most they concede is that because of his interest in a Gentile audience and his ease in handling Greek, he may have been a Gentile.[70]

The purpose of Luke's Gospel is found in its first four verses. These verses, which constitute the prologue to the Gospel, are highly stylistic. In comparison with the other Gospels, Luke provides a completely different frame of reference. By including such a prologue he follows the prevailing literary fashion of his day—a device not found in the other three Gospels.

Luke begins his Gospel with what is the best Greek in the New Testament on the model of the best Greek writers. His preface tells us that Luke was not completely satisfied with the stories of the life of Christ which had thus far appeared. He seeks to awaken a feeling of historical reliability in the things he reports. That he would offer information on his sources, their worth, and his own procedure, is quite unique.

The preface tells us that this Gospel is addressed and dedicated to Theophilus, the same person to whom he dedicated the Book of Acts. Theophilus was possibly a government official. The title "most excellent" was used for Felix, a Roman governor (Acts 2:43). The name Theophilus means "lover of God," and marks Theophilus as a representative of the Gentiles who were interested in a historical account of the origins of Christianity. Theophilus also may have been a well-to-do patron who had underwritten the expenses of publishing and distributing Luke's composition. A third theory is that "Theophilus" refers to the type of person Luke intended for his audience—"lovers of God."

Luke's purpose was to write a clear, accurate, orderly account of the life and teachings of Jesus Christ. This purpose grew out of several factors operating when Luke wrote.

First, about six decades had passed since the crucifixion and resurrection of Jesus Christ and there was confusion among some Christians regarding certain aspects of Christian faith. Luke's intention was to guard his Christian readers from error or heresy and to render the full Christian story.

Second, Luke's purpose was to support the claim that Christianity is a world religion and not a Jewish sect. The Gospel therefore prepares the way for the story in the Book of Acts of the spread of Christianity from Palestine to the rest of the Roman Empire. [71]

Third, Luke wrote to clarify the misunderstanding that Christianity was a subversive movement. During the first few decades of its history Christianity was regarded as a Jewish sect by the Roman officials. Jews made every effort to repudiate Christianity. They regarded Christians as apostates. So Luke points out that on four occasions Jesus was acquitted by Roman officers (Luke 23:4, 23:11; 23:14; 23:20), that it was not the Romans but the followers of Herod who mocked Jesus, that Roman Governor Pontius Pilate wanted to release Jesus, that it was a Roman soldier at the cross who said, "Surely this was a righteous man" (Luke 23:47).

A variety of religious ideas and themes characterizes the narrative of Luke:

A. *First, Luke presents a distinctive portrait of Jesus as a Savior-Friend for all people.* It is a *people-centered* and *people-concerned Gospel*. So Luke presents Jesus in such a way that the reader learns not only of Jesus' unique nature and message but also becomes aware of Jesus as the universal man, ideal and perfect, and as the Son of Man, our friend, redeemer, and guide.

This picture of Jesus as the *Superlative Friend* is presented in several ways by Luke:

a. He presents Jesus as the friend of the poor, the downtrodden, the disinherited. Luke is the Gospel of the Poor, the Gospel of Compassion, the Gospel of the Underdog.

In the birth stories, Jesus is born in the poorest surroundings, so none are excluded because of their low estate. When Mary offers her sacrifice of purification, she offers two doves, the offering of the poor. Jesus sends word to John the Baptist that "the good news is preached to the poor" (7:22). The words from Isaiah Jesus reads at the synagogue in Nazareth state his commission to the poor, the broken-hearted, the captives, the bruised. In Matthew, the beatitude reads, "Blessed are the poor in spirit" (5:3); while in Luke it is, "Blessed are you who are poor" (6:20). In the *Magnificat*, Mary sings "He has filled the hungry with good things"(1:53).

Only Luke tells of the Good Samaritan, an example of unparalleled friendliness to the unfortunate; of Dives and Lazarus; of the Rich Young Fool; and of the Great Banquet to which the poor, the maimed, the blind, and the lame are invited. In Luke, Jesus is the dependable friend of the poor and disinherited.

b. Luke presents Jesus as the compassionate and understanding friend of the sinners and outcasts of society. In Jesus' day, to be seen socializing with a tax-gatherer, or to associate with a "sinner," or to eat with such, was to forfeit all respect of so-called decent people. Yet, in spite of this attitude, Jesus accepts an invitation to the home of Zacchaeus, a dishonest tax-collector (19:1-10).

It is Luke who tells the story of the Pharisee and the Publican at prayer in the Temple, when the confessed sinner is justified and the proud self-righteous one is condemned (18:9-14). It is Luke who gives the story of the Prodigal Son and his father's redeeming compassion (15:11-32).

c. Luke presents Jesus as the Superlative Friend of Women. Women are present in all the Gospels, but they are usually relatively passive. In Luke they are dynamic actors in the story. There are more stories about women in Luke than in any other Gospel[72]. Women are numbered among the larger group of disciples who followed Jesus about (8:2-3). They are apparently included among the company of disciples who witness the Ascension at the end of the Gospel; therefore, they would seem to be included in the commission to be witnesses (24:50-53). A woman, Anna, is the first person to preach about Jesus (2:36-38).

Luke alone records the parables of the persistent widow and of the woman's lost coin (18:1-8; 15:8-10), as well as the conversation between Jesus' mother Mary and her cousin Elizabeth (1:29:56). It is only Luke who records the story of the widow whose child Jesus resurrects (7:11-17). In Luke we learn of the various women of Galilee with whom Jesus associates. Luke alone records the words of Jesus to the women of Jerusalem as he himself goes to the cross. Luke states that some of Jesus' most faithful disciples were women, "several wealthy enough to support his ministry" (8:1-3). Mary Magdalene, from whom Jesus drove seven devils, and Joanna, whose husband was a steward to Herod Antipas, were present at the crucifixion and were also among the women who found Jesus' tomb empty (23:55 - 24:12).

That Luke's presentation of Jesus as a befriender of women is remarkable may best seen against the status of women of that day. In the Jewish morning prayer, the orthodox man thanked God that God had not made him, "a Gentile, a slave, or a woman." Considering this background, Jesus goes out of his way to befriend women.

Luke is the Gospel of the Elevation of Women as persons in their own right .

d. Luke presents Jesus as the Superlative Friend of the sick; Jesus is the Great Physician, the Healing Friend. Luke emphasizes Jesus' miraculous healing powers . There are more instances in his Gospel of Jesus' ministry to the ills of people than in any other, and many are unique to Luke. Of the twenty miracles related by Luke, four appear in this Gospel alone: cleansing ten lepers (17:11-19), healing a man with a dropsy (14:1-6), curing a crippled woman (13:10-17), and raising a widow's dead son (7:11-17).

B. *A second theme in Luke is the presentation of Christianity as a universal faith.* Luke presents Christianity as a religion intended for "all nations" from the outset. As Simeon prophesied over the infant Jesus, the child was destined to become "a revelation to the Gentiles" (2: 32) . Luke is the universal gospel, presenting Jesus as Lord of all people. While Matthew traces

Jesus' lineage back to Abraham, the "Father of the Hebrew Race," Luke shows Jesus' line all the way back to Adam, the "Father of the Human Race." In Luke's birth narrative the angel announces that the birth of Jesus is "good news of great joy that will be for all people" (2:10). Only Luke tells the story of the Good Samaritan (10:29-37), a non-Jewish hero, the last person of whom the Jews of the day would think anything good. Jesus' last teaching, in the Emmaus experience, declares that "repentance and forgiveness of sins will be preached in his name to all nations" (24:27).

C. Third, *Luke is the Gospel of Prayer*. It emphasizes the prayer life of Jesus. Luke lists more occasions when Jesus prayed than do the other Gospels. Every milestone in Jesus' life is preceded by prayer. In his account of Jesus' baptism, Luke states that the Spirit descended upon Jesus while he was praying (3:21). According to Luke, Jesus chose his disciples after prayer (6:12). He prayed before he revealed his identity to them (9:18). He prayed before and at the time of his transfiguration (9:28-36). Jesus taught his disciples the model prayer, what we call "The Lord's Prayer" (11:4). He had been praying before his arrest (22:47-54). His last words on the Cross were a prayer: "Father, into your hands I commit my spirit" (23:46).

D. Fourth, *Luke is the Gospel of Praise*. It is often called the father of Christian hymnody. Nowhere else in the New Testament is there such interest in the sung praise of God. Luke reports four hymns of praise in the opening section: Mary's Song, the *Magnificat* (1:46-55); Zechariah's Song, the *Benedictus* (1:67-79); the Angel's Song, the *Gloria in Excelsis* (2:13-14); and Simeon's Song, the *Nunc Dimittis* (2:29-32).

In Luke's writings, the phrase "praising God," appears more often than in any of the other gospels. Many oratorios and anthems have borrowed much from Luke and hymnals are full of hymns taking their inspiration both from the spirit and content of Luke's Gospel.[73]

E. Fifth, *Luke emphasizes the work of the Holy Spirit*. Mark has six references to the Holy Spirit, Matthew has twelve, but

Luke has seventeen. If we include the Book of Acts (the second volume of Luke), there are fifty-seven references. It was by the Spirit that Jesus was conceived (1:26-38), and was baptized (3:21-22). The Holy Spirit led him into the wilderness (4:1) and empowered his ministry in Galilee (4:14). The Spirit was conferred through prayer (11:13). In the inaugural sermon of his ministry at Nazareth, Jesus quoted the passage from Isaiah 61:1-2 that begins "The Spirit of God is upon me ..." It is the essence of the Christian faith that God is in His world and involved with it.

F. Sixth, *Luke is the Gospel of Stewardship and Philanthropy.* He records the parables of the rich fool (12:16-21), the dishonest steward (16:1-10), the rich man and Lazarus (16:19-31). After his first contact with Jesus, Zacchaeus promised to give half of his goods to feed the poor. Jesus epitomized the generosity of the widow. Wealth is presented as a trust to be used for ministry to people; the possessor of material goods is but a steward of what has been given to him.

The Gospel of Luke is divided into the following major parts:
1. Preface (1:1-4)
2. Birth Narratives of John the Baptist and Jesus (1:5-2:22)
3. Introduction to Jesus' Public Ministry (3:1-4:13)
4. Jesus' Ministry in Galilee (4:14-9:50)
5. Jesus' Ministry on His Way to Jerusalem (9:51-19:27)
6. Jesus' Ministry in Jerusalem (19:28-24:12)
7. The Risen Christ and Post Resurrection Appearances (24:13-53)

1. Preface (1:1-14). Luke is the only Gospel writer to introduce his work with a formal statement of purpose. It follows carefully the pattern of introduction used by the great Greek historians.[74] Luke adopts this practice here and in Acts 1:1. Luke dedicates this Gospel as well as his second volume, the Book of Acts, to Theophilus, a Gentile patron.

The author states that although there have been other compilers, as well as eyewitnesses and servants of the word, he proposed to write a more "orderly account" than anything yet presented (1:3). Luke implies that there are stages of the Gospel tradition. There are "eyewitnesses"—those who had been with Jesus, such as the Twelve Apostles. There are "servants of the word," — those who passed on the eyewitness tradition by preaching. Finally, there are compilers of the tradition, such as Luke himself. By writing "an orderly account," Luke did not mean to arrange his account differently, for Luke generally follows Mark's order of events. Probably Luke refers to his intentions of arranging his presentation in a proper literary form acceptable to educated Gentile readers. [75]

2. Birth Narratives Concerning John the Baptist and Jesus (1:5-2:52). The first two chapters of the Gospel of Luke are concerned primarily with the birth and infancy stories of John the Baptist and Jesus. These stories are unique to Luke's Gospel. Both Matthew and Luke record that Jesus was born in Bethlehem to Mary and Joseph, but Luke also introduces John the Baptist, the forerunner of Jesus in the story (1:5-25; 39-45; 57-80). He begins his account of Jesus by devoting long passages to Zechariah, a priest, and Elizabeth, his wife, thus linking the birth of Jesus with the birth of John. Both Mary, the mother of Jesus, and Zechariah, the father of John, experience miraculous revelations concerning their coming children. John is the "prophet of the Most High" (1:76); Jesus is the "son of the Most High" (1:32). John the Baptist serves as a witness and a prophet to Jesus (1:80; 2:40, 52).

Luke carefully sets the story within the context of world history: "In the days of Herod" (1:5); "In the sixth month" (1:26); "In those days Caesar Augustus issued a decree" (2:1).

Luke chooses to include different details than Matthew. He records the angel's announcement to the shepherds and their worship of the baby Jesus while omitting the visit of the wise men and the threat of murder by Herod.

Luke's depiction of Jesus' childhood differs from Matthew's account in two other respects: Jesus' circumcision and presentation (2:21-40) and his visit to the temple when Jesus was twelve (2:41-52). Upon seeing Jesus, Simeon, an old pious man who was patiently "waiting for the consolation of Israel," exclaimed, "Lord, dismiss your servant in peace, for my eyes have seen your salvation" (2:29-30). He prophesied that Jesus would be "a light for revelation to the Gentiles" (the *Nunc Dimittis* hymn, Luke 2:29-32). In the final part of the Simeon episode an old prophetess, Anna, appeared (2:36-38), who also anticipated "the redemption of Jerusalem."

Luke recounts the only incident of Jesus' boyhood. Twelve-year-old Jesus visited the temple and impressed some learned scribes (2:41-52). When his parents questioned him, "Son, why have you treated us like this?" Jesus replied, "Why were you searching for me ... didn't you know I had to be in my Father's house?"(2:48-49). The final statement of this section of Luke, "Jesus grew in wisdom and stature, and in favor with God and men" (2:52), paves the way for Jesus' future ministry.

3. Introduction to Jesus' Public Ministry (3:1 - 4:13). Chapters three and four in Luke emphasize that Jesus is the universal savior. Among the Gospel writers, Luke alone extends John the Baptist's citation from Isaiah 40 to include the prophecy: "And all mankind will see God's salvation" (3:4). The ancestry of Jesus is then traced to beyond Abraham, the father of the Jews, back to Adam, the progenitor of all humans (3:28-38). Luke goes on to declare that the Son of God was like Adam, tempted by Satan, but he did not yield to temptation (4:1-13).

Luke's tradition also gives prominence to the work of the Holy Spirit; everyone who participated in the miracle of Jesus' birth was "filled with the Holy Spirit." Luke states that after Jesus had received baptism with water, "the Holy Spirit descended on him in bodily form like a dove" (3:22). "Full of the Holy Spirit," Jesus returned from the Jordan and "was led by the Spirit in the desert, where for forty days he was tempted by the devil" (4:1-2).[76] While praying, both Jesus and his disciples receive the direction of the Holy Spirit (Luke 4:19; 10:21; 21:36; 22:40-46).

4. Jesus' Ministry in Galilee (4:14-9:50). The section includes the following:

a. *Jesus' Rejection in Nazareth*. Luke chooses to show the beginning of Jesus' public ministry with an example of him preaching in Nazareth, a different starting point than shown in either Matthew or Mark. In Mark, Jesus' first public act is to exorcise a demon (Mark 1:21-28); in Matthew, it is to deliver the Sermon on the Mount (Matt. 5-7); in Luke it is to preach in his home synagogue at Nazareth (4:14-30). Luke places this episode almost at the outset of Jesus' career. He also adds an incident (not found in Mark and Matthew) in which Jesus' former neighbors tried to kill him (4:16-30). Luke probably included these events to illustrate that from the beginning Jesus was destined to be rejected and killed.[77] In Luke, Jesus is rejected not because he claims authority (as Mark points out in 6:1-6), but because he extends salvation to the wrong people—the poor, the imprisoned, and the physically afflicted (4:18). When asked to perform miracles as he had in Capernaum (v. 23), Jesus rejected their request and declared that a prophet is not acceptable in his own country. He then spoke of the miracles of Elijah and Elisha which were performed not for the people of Israel, but for foreigners. The audience's anger was further aroused.

b. *The Call of the First Disciples.* A comparison between the calling of disciples in Luke (5:1-11) and in Mark (1:16-20) shows that the stories are quite different. Luke includes the miracle of the great catch of fish. Upon witnessing the miracle, Simon Peter made a confession of sin and repentance, and he and those with him became "fishers of men."

Luke emphasizes the importance of repentance in this section, beginning with Simon Peter's confession, which is followed by the Pharisees' and scribes' criticism of the disciples for "eating with tax collectors and sinners" (5:30). Jesus once again reiterated his mission: "I have not come to call the righteous, but sinners to repentance" (5:32).

c. *Luke's Sermon on the Plain* (6:20-49). Luke's "beatitudes" are four in number and are written in the second person. He follows the beatitudes with a list of "woes" in which the "rich" are cursed with future loss and hunger. Luke highlights Jesus' condemnation of this rich and complacent people whom the society considers fortunate. Jesus repeatedly attacked the wealthy and predicted their present affluence would be exchanged for misery.[78]

d. *Jesus' Special Interest in Women* (7:11-50). In Luke, Jesus is presented as a special friend to the dispossessed and the poor. The raising from the dead of the young man of Nain (7:11-17) is an illustration of Jesus' special love for the poor and unfortunate (especially women). Luke alone includes this episode in his Gospel. Luke's sympathy for women is manifest in the attention he devotes to them. Luke tells us that after providing comfort to the sorrowing widow at Nain, Jesus showed similar compassion for a prostitute who in a penitent spirit falls before the feet of Jesus and anoints him with costly ointment (7:36-50).

e. *Jesus Widens the Scope of his Ministry* (8:4-9:50). In the introduction of this passage, a number of witnesses are recorded to have gathered around Jesus: the Twelve and the women who not only follow Jesus but also support him from their own financial resources (8:1-3). There is an emphasis upon the movements of Jesus indicating the acceleration and widening of his activity, as well as that of the Twelve. Here Luke introduces another segment of Mark's parable of the Sower (8:4-5) and depicts the importance of hearing and holding the word of God.

Luke's wider application of the parable of the lamp (8:16-18) which is also found in the Gospel of Matthew (Matt. 5:15) is noteworthy: in Matthew the light is to give illumination to those in the house; in Luke, the light enables those outside to find the door. The widening scope of Jesus' ministry is best illustrated when Jesus' mother and brothers came to see him, and were told, "My mother and brothers are those who hear God's word and put it into practice" (8:21).

The next episodes in Luke—calming a storm at sea (8:22-25), healing a raging demoniac (8:26-39), raising the daughter of Jairus and healing a hemorrhaging woman (8:40-56)—follow the Markan sequence of events. This series culminates "when Jesus called the Twelve together, and gave them power and authority to drive out all demons and cure diseases, and he sent them out to preach the kingdom of God and to heal the sick" (9:12).

At the close of this section instead of Mark's "whoever is not against *us* is for *us*" (Mark 8:40), Luke's version of Jesus' words are "whoever is not against *you* is for *you*" (9:50).

5. Jesus' Ministry on His Way to Jerusalem (Luke 9:51-19:27). Luke begins this section with Jesus "setting his face toward Jerusalem." The journey seems to take much longer than the actual distance (about sixty miles) would have warranted. There is an extensive account about a trip which could have been traveled in about three days. Luke tells us Jesus said he had to go to Jerusalem because "surely no prophet can die outside Jerusalem" (13:3). Luke undoubtedly viewed Jesus as Messiah in the prophetic role (see 1:76; 4:24; 24:19), and, as prophet, appropriately going to die at the capital city of Jerusalem. [79]

a. *Hostile Samaritans; Half-Hearted Disciples* (9:51-56). On his way from Galilee to Jerusalem, Jesus passed through Samaria, carrying his message to several villages. The Samaritans, who hated Jews because Jews held them in contempt over their rival interpretation of the Mosaic laws, did not welcome Jesus. Disciples James and John wished to invoke a punitive miracle—"fire from heaven"—upon the villagers (v. 54). It is interesting to note the differences of Luke's and Matthew's account. In Matthew (10:5-6), Jesus forbids a mission to the Samaritans; in Luke, however, Jesus forbids the disciples to punish an inhospitable Samaritan village.

b. *Seventy Missionaries* (9:57-10:29). After explaining the demanding nature of discipleship (9:57-62), Jesus sent seventy other disciples "two by two" to preach the Gospel (10:1-6). In Jewish terminology, the number seventy or seventy-two represented the sum total of non-Jewish nations, as the Twelve sent to evangelize Israel symbolized the traditional twelve Israelite tribes.[80] Upon the successful return of the missionaries, Jesus praised the Father for His methods, assured the disciples of God's power and blessing, and answered a question about who should receive ministry.

c. *The Parable of the Good Samaritan* (10:17-37). The parable of the Good Samaritan was told by Jesus in response to the question asked by a lawyer (a scribe), "What shall I do to inherit eternal life?" When Jesus, in his typical rabbinic fashion asked him "What do you read in the Law?" the Torah expert defined the essence of the Mosaic Law in the two commands to love God (Deut. 6:5) and neighbor (Lev. 19:18). The lawyer then asked Jesus to explain what the Torah means by "neighbor."

Instead of answering directly, Jesus once again responded in rabbinic fashion and told the story of the Good Samaritan. A Jew was traveling from Jerusalem down to Jericho. On the way he was mugged and needed help. In succession three different people came along: a Levite, a priest, and a Samaritan. The Levite and the priest just passed him by. The Samaritan was the only one to show compassion. Then Jesus made the lawyer answer his own question: "Which of these three do you think was a neighbor to the man who fell into the hands of robbers?"(v. 37). The lawyer apparently could not bring himself to utter the hated term "Samaritan." Instead, he vaguely identified the hero as "the one who had mercy on him" (v. 37).

By telling this illustrative narrative, Jesus forced the Jewish audience to recognize that a "neighbor" does not necessarily belong to one's racial or religious group but can be any person who demonstrates or who needs human kindness, compassion, and love.

d. *Martha and Mary* (10:38-42). Following the Samaritan parable, Luke relates Jesus' visit to two sisters, Martha and Mary. The village is not named, but the author of the Gospel of John tells us that it was Bethany (John 11:1; 12:1-3). Jesus again draws a distinction between strict adherence to duty and a sensitivity to spiritual values. Martha, the mistress of the house, "was distracted" by household chores, while Mary "sat at the Lord's feet listening to what he said" (v. 39). Jesus commended Mary for recognizing "what is better," i.e. the learning experience that will remain with her forever.

e. *Instructions on Prayer* (11:1-13). Luke's emphasis on prayer is evident in this section. Luke's version of the Lord's Prayer is shorter than Matthew's. While Matthew locates his version in the Sermon on the Mount, Luke ties the Lord's Prayer with the parable of the importunate friend to emphasize the importance of persistence in prayer; like Jacob's wrestling with the angel, insistent prayer is not to persuade God but to overcome our own wills and egos. The grounds for Jesus' confidence in the efficacy of prayer is that if we can trust our human fathers, how much more should we trust our heavenly Father.[81]

f. *Concerning the Exorcism of Demons* (11:14-28). Jesus'

healing of the dumb demoniac created controversy. Some who were present said, "He casts out demons by Beelzebub, the prince of demons"...while others "tested him by asking for a sign from heaven" (11:15-16). In other words, some went so far as to ascribe Jesus' actions to the power of evil. Others were incapable of seeing heaven near at hand.

    g. *Concerning Signs* (11:29-36). In response to the demand for a messianic sign, Jesus said, "No sign shall be given to this generation except the sign of Jonah" (11:29). "The sign of Jonah" could be a reference to the burial and resurrection of Jesus. It also could mean the message of repentance. *Jonah* proclaimed the judgment of God to *the men of Nineveh* in ancient time, so the *Son of Man* proclaimed to *this generation* (v. 36).

    h. *Denunciation of Pharisees and Lawyers* (11:37-54). Here we find six "woes" against the Pharisees and the scribes (lawyers). The first three are for the Pharisees and deal with ceremonial rituals—ritual ablutions before meals and ceremonial purity of dishes, ostentatious practices, and hypocrisy (11:37-42). Jesus criticized the Pharisees for their emphasis on and preoccupation with their externalism and legalism at the expense of the inner religion of the heart.

With his triple denunciation of the lawyers, Jesus criticized them for burdening the common folk with a lot of laws and evading the responsibility they imposed on others (11:45-46). Jesus had in mind the interpretations and applications of individual precepts of the law that had accumulated from the time of Ezra (5th century B.C.) and that ultimately were committed to writing in the Mishnah (second century A.D.).[82] Jesus also accused the scribes of sharing in the guilt of their ancestors, who murdered the prophets (11:47).

    i. *On the Responsibilities and Privileges of Discipleship* (12:1-13:9). Luke stresses the spiritual riches of the Kingdom of God. The Lukan Jesus assures his followers that if God provides for nature's birds and flowers He will care for His children (12:22-31).

Luke also emphasizes stewardship through a series of Jesus' parables. For example, the *rich fool* (12:16-21) forgot that everything he had belonged to God; everything he was, he owed to God. He forgot also his dependence upon his fellow men. What he had was a trust from God. This man's barns were full, but his soul was empty; his bankbook was fat, but his heart was starving, because he forgot *who* he was and *whose* he was.

Following the Parable of the Rich Fool, Jesus told the Allegory of the Waiting Servants (12:35-38). This allegory has certain features in common with the parables of the doorkeeper (Mark 13:33-37) and of the wise and the foolish virgins (Matt. 25:1-13). The waiting servants appear to represent the early church; the absent master, the risen Christ; and the master's return, the Second Coming of Christ.[83] This allegory is a metaphorical summons to preparedness for Christ's return, even though it may be long delayed. Christians are *servants* of Christ, left for a while with certain duties, and do not know when the Master will return to demand an accounting (12:40).

Similar is the Parable of the Faithful and Unfaithful Servants (12:41-46). The faithful and wise servant will be rewarded by promotion (12:43-44), but the drunken and cruel servant will be punished (12:45-46).

To conclude the discourse begun with 12:2, Luke records Jesus' Parable of the Fig Tree (13:6-9), a reiteration of the theme of impending judgment and a call to repentance. The owner of the orchard had given the fig tree ample opportunity to demonstrate its fruitfulness. It had not done so and must now be felled. But the gardener urged the owner to give the tree another chance (v. 9).

j. *Various Teachings* (14:1-35) The first six verses of Luke 14 deal with a Sabbath healing. Jesus had healed a woman in the synagogue and this involved a breach of Sabbath legislation. Jesus maintained that every person is dear in God's sight and that healing on the Sabbath is consonant with Sabbath praise (14:5).

— Advice to Guests (14:7-11). Jesus insisted that self-seeking assertiveness defeats its own aim. It is better to be humble, for the humble shall receive final exaltation (v.11).

— Kindness to the Unfortunate (14:12-14). There is no virtue in entertaining those whom you expect to return the favor. Rather, spend the effort on those who cannot reciprocate your favor, for the only generosity that God will recompense is that which is extended to those who cannot repay (14:13-14).

— Excuses (14:15-24). This is the Parable of the Great Banquet, a variant of Matthew 22:2-10. The man giving the dinner represents God offering His salvation, first to the Jews, as invited guests, then to the rest of the world. Some invited guests did not want to attend and made excuses. Jesus knew that many of the Jewish leadership would flout him and his offer of eternal redemption, giving the most trivial excuses.

— Cost of Discipleship (14:25-35). Jesus demanded undivided allegiance from his followers. They were to follow Him unconditionally. They were to bear their own cross and follow him (v. 27). Disciples who do not sacrifice everything in Christ's service are as useless as salt that has lost its taste (14:34-35).

k. *On God's Love for the Lost* (15:1-32). In this section Jesus is presented as a Friend of the Lost. This is illustrated by three parables: *The Lost Sheep, The Lost Coin,* and *The Prodigal Son.* The first two parables pose an interesting problem of interpretation, for the general conclusions of each speak of a sinner's repenting (15:7,10), yet such repentance is hardly exemplified in the parables themselves. A lost sheep or a lost coin does not repent. The first two parables emphasize the initiative of the one who seeks out the lost.[84] Both the shepherd and woman exhibit intense concentration on a single action—searching for lost property—showing Jesus' demand to seek God's rule first, to the exclusion of all else (6:22, Matt. 6:33).

— The Parable of the Prodigal Son (15:11-32) might be called the Parable of the Good and Forgiving Father, for the climax of the narrative focuses on the latter's attitude to his two very different sons.[85] The Parable falls into two parts. The first (11-24) illustrates the joy with which God welcomes the repentant sinner. When the spendthrift prodigal returned home, his father rushed to embrace him, forgive him, and throw a lavish celebration in his honor. There is joy for one who was lost and is now found (v. 24). The second part of the parable (vss 25-32) deals with a self-righteous older brother, full of jealousy, self-pity and pride, who criticized his father's joyful reception of the one who "squandered his wealth in wild living" (v. 13). He could not understand this reception, much as Pharisees and scribes could not understand Jesus' actions. He was prodigal at heart in spite of the fact that he had not left home and squandered his father's wealth. He needed to repent and accept the good news of God's forgiveness. The father's behavior is a lesson that God, like a loving father, loves unconditionally and makes no distinction between the deserving and the undeserving children.

1. *Teaching on the Use and Abuse of Riches* (16:1-31). Chapter 16 gives us two parables on stewardship: the *Dishonest Steward* (16:1-13), and *Lazarus and the Rich Man* (16:19-31).

— In the Parable of the Dishonest Steward we read about a conniving and dishonest businessman who cheated his employer. Jesus commended his foresight, not his dishonesty. He invited his followers to emulate the cleverness of this steward for better ends. One of the important lessons of the parable is the wise use of money. As the dishonest steward used money to make sure that people would receive him into their houses after he had been dismissed of his stewardship (v. 4), so followers of Christ are to use it to assure "eternal dwellings" for themselves (vs. 9). In a real sense, this parable is the *Parable of the Shrewd Manager*. After Jesus told this parable the Pharisees ridiculed Jesus' teachings about money, because they were "lovers of money" (16:14-15). The Pharisees claimed their wealth was proof that they were righteous, but Jesus repudiated that claim, stating "God knows your hearts" (v. 15).

— The Parable of Lazarus and the Rich Man is the story of a poor man, Lazarus, who suffered from hunger and sickness and a rich man, Dives, who lived in luxury. Both men died. Lazarus went to heaven. The rich man went to hell. The rich man requested two things of Father Abraham: that Lazarus would be sent "to dip the tip of his finger in water and cool my tongue" (v. 24), and that Lazarus might go to his father's house and warn his five brothers, so that they will repent "and not also come to this place of torment" (v. 28). Both requests were denied; the first on grounds that it was impossible, and the second on grounds that it would be ineffective.

Two distinct themes are discussed in this parable. Verses 19-26 demonstrated a reversal of values in the life to come. The poor beggar enjoyed all the rewards Jesus promised, and the rich and indifferent man went to hell. Verses 27-31 assert that the inpenitent rich man had ample warning to repent and would not repent even if someone were to return from the dead to reiterate that warning.[86]

Luke implies in this parable that in life people need people. Lazarus needed the rich man; he needed food, medical attention, and friendship. Dives also needed Lazarus; he needed to share his concern, love, time, and substance with Lazarus.

m. *On Forgiveness, God's Grace, and Man's Ingratitude* (17:1-19).

— Offenses and Forgiveness (17:1-6). Luke has joined three sayings in the first six verses of chapter 17 which were perhaps distinct at first and spoken at different times. They are linked as follows: *offenses* come in part by the failure to forgive, and forgiveness is so hard that it requires a new access of faith. The offender who shows the spirit of contrition is to be forgiven, no matter how often the offense is repeated.[87]

— Parable of the Farmer and the Slave (17:7-10). The next parable in Luke 17 talks about our responsibility to obey God. The slave who only carries out his master's orders has not earned any right to his gratitude. By the same token, men who carry out God's work entrusted to them should not expect any rewards (vs. 10). They are doing as they should.

— The Grateful Samaritan (17:11-19). This is another story of healing lepers (Luke 5:12-14, Mark 1:40-45). But in this passage the number of lepers who were healed by Jesus is *ten* and the miracle is effected at a *distance* (vs. 12). Luke's emphasis in this story is that only *one* man said thank you for the cure; the other *nine* quickly forgot. In addition, that grateful man was a *Samaritan* rather than a Jew. (In other words, true faith is not the monopoly of the so-called religious people.)

n. *On the Kingdom of God and the Son of Man* (17:20-37). In the days of Jesus, religious leaders debated by what "signs" God would foreshadow the Kingdom of God and the coming of the Messiah. Jesus told them that the Kingdom will come suddenly, like lightning (v. 24) and as the deluge in the days of Noah (v. 27).

o. *Parables on the Practice of Prayer* (18:1-14). Over again, we see Luke's emphasis on prayer. In this section he records two parables of Jesus on Prayer: the *Parable of the Widow and the Judge* and *The Parable of the Pharisee and the Tax Collector*.

— The Parable of the Widow and the Judge (18:1-8) extols the value of persistence in prayer. The parable resembles that of the importunate friend in 11:5-8. They have the same theme: Persistence in prayer brings results. The widow who sought justice from a cynical and corrupt judge succeeded only through persistent petitioning. The judge "who neither feared God nor cared about men" (vs. 3) granted the widow's petition because she refused to give him any peace until he acted. If an unscrupulous judge finally gave what the widow asked of him, how much more is God going to respond to those who call on him, plead with him, and wait for him (18:7-8).

— The Parable of the Pharisee and the Tax Collector (18:9-14). In this parable, Luke contrasts two kinds of prayers: self-righteous and penitent. Each man described himself in his prayer. The *Pharisee* was *righteous* by common tests: he gave a tenth of his income to religion and observed the Judaic laws. Conversely, the *tax collector* was a crook, extorting money and goods from his Jewish countrymen. His confession was true. The Pharisee was congratulating himself; the tax collector kept smiting his breast and confessing his shortcomings. It is "the honest outcast who wins God's approval and not the conventionally good man."[88] The fundamental basis of our approach to God should be a realization of our sinfulness and our need of his mercy.

p. *Conditions of Entrance to the Kingdom* (18:15-34). Luke had temporarily abandoned the Markan narrative at 9:45 (Mark 9:40) in order to include material he had gathered from other sources. Here he resumes following his major source, Mark. In this section, he includes two incidents: *The Little Children* and *The Rich Young Ruler*.

— The Little Children (18:15-17). Matthew as well as Mark also records this incident (Matt. 19:13-15, Mark 10:13-15). Jesus called the little children to him and told his audience "the kingdom of God belongs to such as these" (v. 16). The childlike qualities of candor, openness, trustfulness, and dependence are required of all believers.

— The Rich Young Ruler (18:18-27). This incident also is recorded in the other Synoptic Gospels (Matt. 19:16-22; Mark 10:17-31). The rich ruler asked Jesus what he must do to inherit eternal life (vs. 18). Jesus invited his questioner to become a disciple, asking him to sell all his possessions and distribute the proceeds to charity. The rich man, too in love with his riches, found discipleship too costly. He departed sadly. Jesus' response was that the salvation of a rich man is very hard, sometimes as hard as "a camel going through the eye of a needle" (vs. 25), but with God's power everything is possible.

q. *Jesus in Jericho* (18:35 - 19:27). In this section, Jesus had arrived in Jericho en route to Jerusalem. Three imporant incidents distinguished his ministry in this small Judean town on the Jordan River: *Healing of a Blind Beggar, Jesus and Zacchaeus*, and *The Parable of the Ten Minas.*

— The Healing of the Blind Beggar (18:35-43) is told also in Matthew 20:29-34 and Mark 10:46-52. Matthew says there were two blind men. Mark and Luke mentioned only one. Mark called him Bartimaeus. The blind beggar asked Jesus to heal him. Jesus healed him and told him, "Your faith has healed you" (vs. 42).

— Jesus and Zacchaeus (19:1-10). Zacchaeus was a chief publican, head of a large office of tax collectors. Publicans were considered hirelings, collaborators with the occupying Romans; they were despised by the Jews from whom they typically extorted money and were classed with harlots (Matt. 21:31-32). Jericho was a city of priests. Jesus chose a publican rather than a priest to visit. Zacchaeus was converted immediately. As a result of his new relationship to Jesus he vowed to give half of his "possessions to the poor" (vs. 8), and Jesus pronounced him an heir of salvation (vs. 10).

— The Parable of the Ten Minas or The Parable of the Pounds (19:11-27). This parable in some ways is similar to *The Parable of the Talents* in Matt. 25:14-30, but in some points the two parables are different. In the Lukan version of the parable, the nobleman went into a *far country* to receive kingly power, a hint that in Luke's eschatology the king will return again only after a long journey. Before leaving he gives ten *minas* to ten citizens with explicit instructions to invest the money. Some citizens did not want him to be king; they resisted him. The surprise of the parable is that when he returned, he condemned the one who in fear of him as a severe judge had simply hidden the gift away. [89] The Gospel story teaches that the Parousia—the Second Coming of Christ—will be delayed; that followers of Christ have specific duties in the interim; and that there will be a last judgment with rewards and punishments.[90] Just as the servants of the nobleman were given *minas* to invest, so, teaches the Gospel, followers of Christ are given opportunities; some are given more, some less, but all are accountable to the Lord for the way they use their means and time.

Of special interest is the behavior of the one-mina servant who did not invest his money because he wanted to play it safe. His master took away his trust, called him "wicked," and punished him. "Wicked" is a strong word of denunciation that the New Testament writers used sparingly. The Lord called him wicked because he did nothing. Luke wanted to point out that in the sight of the Lord idleness is wickedness. The parable also points out the costliness of doing nothing. Furthermore, it teaches that if we do not use our God-given talents and opportunities we may lose them.

6. Jesus' Ministry in Jerusalem (19:28 - 24:12). This segment of Luke's narrative focuses on Jesus' ministry in Jerusalem. It includes Jesus' Triumphal Entry into Jerusalem, attempts to incriminate Jesus, views on the end of time, the final conflict, and the passion story.

A. *Jesus' Triumphal Entry into Jerusalem* (19:28-46). Luke's account of the Triumphal Entry is very similar to those of Matthew and Mark. This passage is primarily based on Mark 11:1-10, but Luke also employs another source. He stresses the site of Jesus' proclamation of his messiahship, perhaps under the influence of the prediction of Zechariah 14:1-4. He omits Mark's comment that "others spread branches they had cut in the field" (Mark 11:8). The disciples' joyful praise was directed to *God*, who had been responsible "for all the miracles they had seen" (v. 37).

The Hebrew "Hosanna" is omitted from the disciples' cry of jubilation (v. 38). Mark's "Hosanna in the highest!" is replaced by "Peace in heaven and glory in the highest!" This last clause is reminiscent of the angelic chorus in 2:14.[91]

Following the Triumphal Entry, Jesus cleansed the Temple (19:45-46). Luke's account again is modeled on Mark's. It shows Jesus' indignation at the secular traffic which had made the temple courts resemble a market place.

B. *Attempts to Incriminate Jesus* (19:47-21:4). The chief priests, the teachers of the Law, and the leaders wished to kill Jesus, yet they could not find any way to do it, because "all the people hung on his words" (19:47-48). The Sanhedrin, the supreme judicial council of the Jews, had heard of Jesus' activities in Galilee and had been watching him with suspicion. The Sadducees who controlled the Sanhedrin, the priesthood, and the Temple and who cooperated with Roman rule of Palestine, were concerned that Jesus' ministry might cause a political disturbance or lead to a messianic uprising. They wanted to trap Jesus into an admission that could be framed as a charge warranting the death penalty. So they asked him, "Who gave you this authority?" (20:2) hoping that Jesus might make some explicit messianic claim. Jesus answered with a counterquestion: "Was John's baptism from heaven or from men?" (v. 3). The questioners hesitated to answer. Then Jesus told them *The Parable of the Vineyard and its Wicked Tenants* (20:9-18). This parable likened God to the owner of the vineyard, the vineyard to Israel, the tenants to the hierarchs of Judaism, the servants to the prophets of the Old Testament times, the beloved son to Jesus Christ, the murder of the heir to the crucifixion of the Son of God, and the new tenants to the apostles. In Luke's account of the parable, when Jesus completes the story, the people respond, "May it never be," showing they are on his side, not on the side of those who were rejecting him.

C. *Luke's Views On the End of Time* (21:5-38). According to many scholars, Luke did not anticipate a very imminent *parousia*. His emphasis on the church's long-range commission to witness about Christ "to the ends of the earth" (Acts 1:8) expresses his belief that "Christians have much unfinished business to accomplish before the End arrives."[92] Luke does not deny the imminence of Christ's Second Coming, but he maintains that the readers are told not to believe premature reports of Jesus' arrival. Cataclysmic events such as Jerusalem's siege and fall may not be the prelude for the cosmic events that signal Jesus' return (21:9, 20-23).

In Luke's modified apocalypse, there are two stages of the End: the fall of Jerusalem and the Parousia. Luke claims that between the fall of Jerusalem and the Parousia there will be an age of foreign domination. He also borrows terms from Jewish apocalyptic writers. Only after the climactic events, Christians are assured that their freedom is near (21:25-28).

D. *The Final Conflict and Passion Story* (22:1-23:56). Although Luke's account of the last days of Jesus in Jerusalem parallels that of Mark (14:1 16:8), it differs in enough details to suggest that Luke may have used another source as well.[93] In this section, for example, Luke stresses that Jesus' death was a conspiracy premeditated and executed by the Jewish leadership. In Jesus' trial the charges brought against him were unfounded. Luke points out that Herod does not find Jesus guilty of anything treasonous. Pilate is reluctant to condemn Jesus (23:14-15). Only when he is pressured by the mob does Pilate consent to Jesus' crucifixion. Luke notes the Roman centurion's protest, "Certainly this man was *innocent*" (23:47).

a. The Last Supper (22:14-23). Luke's version of The Last Supper has a few minor differences from Mark's. In Luke Jesus passed the wine cup first and then the unleavened bread. According to some scholars Luke may have presented this order because he wanted to avoid giving Jesus' statement about drinking wine again in the kingdom the apocalyptic meaning that Mark gave it.[94]

b. The Agony in Gethsemane (22:39-46). Luke's version of Jesus' ordeal in Gethsemane is shorter than those of Matthew and Mark, but it includes two striking additions which demonstrated the agony under which Jesus labored to decide to accept the cross. Luke tells us that after Jesus asked God to spare him, God sent an angel from heaven who strengthened him (vs. 43). Luke underscores the anguish of Jesus by describing a physical response: Jesus' sweat drops of blood (vs. 44).

    c. Hearing Before the Sanhedrin (22:66-71). In describing Jesus' hearing before the Sanhedrin, Luke makes several changes in the Markan sequence of events. In Mark the High Priest questions Jesus, Jesus is then physically abused, and Peter denies knowing him (Mark 14:55-72). Luke describes Peter's denial first, the physical mistreatment second, and the priests' interrogation third (22:63-71). In Mark the High Priest asked Jesus, "Are you the Christ, the Son of the Blessed One?" (Mark 14:61), to which Jesus responded "I am" (Mark 14:62). In the Lukan version, the chief priests and the teachers of the law say, "If you are the Christ tell us;" and Jesus says, "If I tell you, you will not believe me" (22:67).

    d. Jesus' Examination by Herod Antipas (23:6-16). When governor Pontius Pilate learned that Jesus was a Galilean and therefore under the jurisdiction of Herod Antipas, he sent Jesus to be tried by Herod, who was in Jerusalem for the Passover (23:6-12). This episode, which is found only in Luke, reinforces Luke's picture of an innocent Jesus.

    e. Jesus Surrendered to the Jews by Pilate (23:17-25). Luke's account presents Pilate as a man anxious to acquit Jesus. Twice Pilate declared Jesus' innocence: "He has done nothing to deserve death" (vs. 15), and "I have found in him no grounds of death penalty" (vs. 22). It is interesting to note that Pilate, whom other contemporary historians depict as a ruthless tyrant, is here "only a weak pawn manipulated by a fanatical group of his Jewish subjects."[95]

    f. The Crucifixion (23:26-43). Crucifixion, first employed by the Carthaginians and then adopted by the Romans, was a cruel method of execution. It was a most agonizing method used for slaves, foreigners, and criminals who were not Roman citizens. The condemned, after a brutal scourging, was obliged to carry his own cross to the place of execution. The outstretched arms of the victim were nailed or tied to a cross beam which was then nailed to a vertical pole. The victim was left hanging in agony, starvation, thirst, convulsions of pain and eventual suffocation. Sometimes the victims lingered in anguish for hours or even days. In Jesus' case, death on the cross came in six hours.

Crucifixion was also infamy. To Jews who remembered the biblical statement, "Anyone who is hung on a tree is under God's curse" (Deut. 21:34), the thought of a crucified Messiah was a "stumbling block," and to Greeks a crucified Savior appeared "foolishness" (I Cor. 1:23).[96]

In his crucifixion account, Luke provides a couple of "last words" that illustrate important Lukan themes. For instance, only in Luke do we find Jesus' prayer to forgive his executioners because "they do not know what they are doing" (vs. 34). This statement harmonizes with Jesus' known position on forgiving one's enemies (6:27-28). According to Mark 15:32, both robbers who were crucified with Jesus joined the bystanders in mocking him. In Luke, one of the thieves crucified next to Jesus recognized Jesus' innocence and repented. The penitent criminal was promised paradise with Jesus (vs. 43).

g. The Discovery of the Empty Tomb (24:1-12). Luke's story of the Empty Tomb is primarily based on the Markan narrative (Mark 16:1-6). But Luke slightly revised Mark's story and supplemented it with additional data. In Mark's version the women see "a young man dressed in a white robe" (Mark 16:5) as soon as they enter the tomb. In Luke, "two men in clothes that gleamed like lightning" (vs. 4) appear after the discovery of the Empty Tomb. Instead of fleeing in terror from the tomb and saying nothing to anyone, as in Mark 16:8, the women remembered Jesus' prophecy of his resurrection and returned to report what they had seen and heard "to the Eleven and to all the others" (vs. 9).

7. The Risen Christ and Post-Resurrection Appearances (24:13-53). In writing of the resurrection, Luke departs from both Mark and Matthew. The first post-resurrection appearance Luke records occurred on the road to Emmaus, a village about seven miles northwest of Jerusalem. Jesus appeared to Cleopas and an unnamed companion. These two disciples did not recognize that the stranger walking along with them was Jesus. Probably they failed to recognize him because of their preoccupation with the tragic events of the preceding days (vss. 19-21).

The crucial moment of recognition came only during the meal: "Then their eyes were opened and they recognized him" (vs. 31).

Following that incident, Luke reports another post resurrection appearance taking place in Jerusalem: *Jesus Appearing to the Disciples* (24:36-49). Even though Jesus appeared directly to the disciples and told them to look at his hands and feet, they still "did not believe it because of joy and amazement" (vs. 41). Only after he ate was he recognized by them. Again, eating seemed to be crucial for full recognition. Only in breaking bread—symbolic of the Christian communion ritual—was Jesus' living presence discerned. The closest previous reference to "breaking bread" was during the Last Supper with the apostles (22:14-19) at which Jesus said, "I have eagerly desired to eat this Passover with you before I suffer. For I tell you, I will not eat it again until it finds fulfillment in the kingdom of God" (22:16). Evidently, Jesus would not eat until suffering was accomplished. That he now ate with the disciples indicated that his suffering had been completed and he was risen. Now they could recognize him. [97]

Linking the Emmaus and Jerusalem events, Luke also emphasizes that the risen Jesus offered post-resurrection teaching that connected his ministry and life with the Hebrew Bible. By choosing to include the fact that the risen Christ interpreted biblical texts, Luke shows that "Jesus continues to guide the Christian church, inspiring fresh insights into the meaning of the Hebrew Scriptures."[98]

The last words of Jesus reported in Luke anticipate the gift of the Holy Spirit after his forty days of post resurrection ministry (24:44-53). A Christian mission "to all the nations" was Jesus' declared goal, and the followers of Jesus would return to the temple with great joy (24:52-53).

In summary, Luke is a skilled writer, a careful historian, and a competent theologian. His careful use of his sources and his preservation of some of the most beautiful parables in the synoptic tradition are great contributions to the portrait of Jesus. For him Jesus is the Savior and Friend of mankind, who opens a new era in God's plan for human salvation. Without Luke's work the New Testament would be lacking a great deal.

4. The Gospel of John

The Gospel of John is not a narrative of the life and teachings of Jesus in the sense that Matthew, Mark, and Luke are. Rather, it is an interpretation of the meaning of the Person of Jesus in terms of certain concepts of Greek philosophy. Out of this fact, and the difference in nature between this Gospel and others, certain descriptive statements or characterizations of this Gospel are often made.

A. *Characterizations*
1. John is called "*the spiritual Gospel.*" John is not so much interested in the mere facts about the life of Jesus as he is in the truth and spiritual meaning of the Person Jesus.[99] For John, events in the life of Jesus are not just events in time, they are "windows" revealing eternal truth and spiritual reality.
2. John is called "*the didactic Gospel* "—the Gospel which uses events to reveal and teach meaning beyond the actual events.[100] It is like a series of homilies, or inspirational material, based on historical events and pointing out the deeper and higher implications of those events.
3. John is called "*the theological and philosophical Gospel.*" Various theological and philosophical themes pervade the Gospel: Jesus as Logos ("Word of God") preexistent and made incarnate; Jesus as sacrificial lamb, humbled and exalted; the judgment of the world; the resurrection of the dead.[101]
4. John is called "the dramatic Gospel." It is the dramatic presentation of the coming of God into the world to bring light, truth, and life.
5. John is called "*the Gospel of symbolism.*" The events of this Gospel are there not primarily as historical events, but are there as symbols of truth which is eternal. The events are not told for themselves but as symbols of something beyond the mere facts of history.[102]

6. John is called "*the Gospel of dialogue.*" Compared to the Synoptics, John shows little action. Rather, there is much more emphasis on dialogue, conversation. John is essentially in the form of most Greek philosophical literature of the period.

7. John is called "*the devotional Gospel.*" Of the four Gospels, it is the most useful in the nurturing of one's inner devotional life. Chapters 14 through 17, particularly, are classic devotional material.

8. John is called "*the Charter of Christian Experience.*" It sets before its readers the eternally living and present Christ. Unlike the Synoptic Gospels, which anticipate the Second Coming, expecting that Jesus will soon return to complete his work, John views that work as already complete; he portrays Christ as a constantly present, an eternally living, vibrant spirit available to his followers. The Jesus John brings before us is at once a historical Person and the invisible Lord who is ever present with his people.[103]

9. John is called "*the Greek Gospel.*" It is a simple yet profound Gospel written for the Greeks, in Greek literary form, using Greek philosophical concepts. [104]

B. *Authorship, Place, and Date*

Biblical scholars are divided over the issues of authorship, place, and date of the Gospel of John. According to the ancient tradition of the church, the Gospel of John (commonly labeled the Fourth Gospel to distinguish it from the Synoptics), as well as the Johannine Epistles and the book of Revelation, are the work of the apostle John, who lived to an advanced age in the city of Ephesus.[105] Conservative biblical scholars still believe that the author of the Fourth Gospel is John the son of Zebedee, one of the twelve apostles.[106] According to this view John, "the disciple whom Jesus loved" (13:23, 19:26), had presumably escaped the early martyrdom of his brother James (executed by Herod Agrippa I between 41-44 A.D.) and attained a ripe old age in Ephesus, where he wrote the Gospel.

Most contemporary scholars doubt that the Apostle John wrote the Gospel bearing his name. The Gospel itself does not mention the author's identity. Only in chapter 21 is the author identified as "the disciple whom Jesus loved" (21:20-24; cf. 19:35), and the reference, according to some scholars, may have been inserted by a later editor of the Gospel or may refer to another disciple.

Many biblical scholars believe that Apostle John suffered the same fate as his brother at about the same time, as Jesus had foretold he would (Mark 10:39; Acts 12:1-2). If so, he could not have written the Fourth Gospel, which, biblical critics insist, was written at least two generations later. There were some scholars in the nineteenth century who argued that John was written in the latter half of the second century. The discovery of papyrus fragments in Egypt containing parts of the text of the Gospel and dating from 140-150 A.D. excludes this possibility. These oldest New Testament fragments indicate that the Gospel of John circulated in the first half of the second century. It was probably written by a church leader identified by scholars as the Presbyter John, who included the memoirs of John the disciple, as well as drew upon the other Gospels.

The place of the Gospel's origin is likewise uncertain. Three cities have been suggested: Ephesus, Antioch, and Alexandria. To most scholars, Ephesus remains the most likely place.[108]

C. *Relation to the Synoptic Gospels*

The Gospel According to John differs from the Synoptic Gospels in a number of ways:

1. In John there is no genealogy of Jesus or reference to Jesus' virginal conception. Jesus from the very beginning of the Gospel is described as the Incarnate God—the eternal Word (Logos) who "became flesh" (1:14).

2. John does not contain Jesus' baptism by John, perhaps emphasizing Jesus' independence of and superiority to the Baptist.

3. John has no account of the temptation of Jesus by Satan. John's Jesus is portrayed as one who could not be tempted; He is one with God.

4. In John, Jesus speaks not in parables (as he does in the Synoptics), but in lengthy meditative discourses. He uses philosophical discourses frequently, rather than crisp, pithy sayings, as in the Synoptics.

5. Unlike the Synoptics, John does not record communion as a new covenant between Jesus and his followers at the Last Supper. Stating that the meal took place a day before Passover, John chooses to recall the washing of the disciples' feet—Jesus' act of humble service—rather than the Eucharist (13:1-16).

6. In John there are no references to Messianic expectation, the Parousia. There is only one brief reference to the Kingdom of God (3:3-5). John's Jesus is the "Eternal Contemporary." John also speaks of the Holy Spirit that would be the ever-present Comforter of Christians.

7. John does not record Jesus' agony before his arrest in the Garden of Gethsemane.

8. In John there is no mention of the fall of Jerusalem, a topic that dominated the Synoptic Gospels (Mark 13; Matt. 24-25; Luke 21).

9. In the Synoptics, the miracles of Jesus are seen as acts of compassion. In John, they are signs of his divine power.

10. Conversely there are some things which are found only in the Gospel of John and not in the Synoptics:

   a. The miracle of changing water into wine at the wedding at Cana

   b. The healing of the cripple at the pool of Bethesda

   c. The restoration of the sight of the man born blind

   d. The raising of Lazarus

   e. The woman of Samaria at the well

   f. The washing of the disciples' feet

   g. The extended farewell discourse and prayer with the disciples

D. *Differences in the Chronology of Events*

Even more striking than the omissions and additions in John are the apparent differences in the timing and ordering of events between the Fourth Gospel and the Synoptics.

1. In the Synoptics, Jesus did not emerge as a preacher until after John the Baptist was imprisoned. In John, there is considerable time in which the two ministries overlap (3:23-4:3).

2. In the Synoptics, the main locale of Jesus' ministry is Galilee. With the exception of his visit to the temple at age 12,

Jesus is not seen to go to Jerusalem until the last week of his life. John presents much of Jesus' ministry in and around Jerusalem. In the Fourth Gospel, Jesus is described as traveling back and forth between Galilee and Jerusalem.

3. In the Synoptics, the ministry of Jesus seems to cover only one year. In John, there is reference to three Passovers (2 :13, 6:4; 11:55) in Jerusalem at which Jesus was present, thus giving the ministry of Jesus a duration of at least three years.

4. In the Synoptics, the *Last Supper* is presented as a Passover Meal; John states that it occurred the evening before Passover and the Crucifixion took place on Nisan 14, the day of the preparation, when the paschal lambs were being sacrificed (13:1, 29; 18:28; 19:14). Many historians believe that John's chronology is more accurate, for it is improbable that Jesus' arrest, trial, and crucifixion took place on Nisan 15, the most sacred time of the Passover observance.[109]

5. In the Synoptics, the cleansing of the temple is mentioned near the end of Jesus' ministry; in John, Jesus' assault on the temple is presented at the beginning of his career (2:13-21).

E. *The Purpose of John's Gospel*

The Gospel of John was written for three major reasons:

1. *It was written to the Graeco-Roman world.* By the time the Gospel of John was written, Christianity had been exported from Palestine to the rest of the Roman empire, and there needed to be a Gospel that could reach that world. If the message of Christianity was to be presented to that world, then it had to be presented in the thought forms which the people understood. It was not that the message, the Gospel, the Person Jesus Christ, had changed. It was that the categories of thought had changed! If the unchanging truth of Christ was to be understood and accepted, it had to be restated in the new categories. John was trying to present Jesus as Incarnate God—the *Logos* (Creative Reason, the Word) Who became man—through whom people might know truth, themselves, God, light, and life.

2. *It was written to refute Gnosticism.* Gnosticism, a widespread and extremely diverse movement in early Christianity, was a form of mystical dualistic philosophy that divided the

cosmos into light and darkness, good and evil. The Gnostics believed that matter was evil and that spirit was good, and God was so spiritual and the earth so material that God could not touch the earth or create it. They believed that God put forth a series of emanations from Himself—each emanation a bit further removed from Him, until at last, there was an emanation so far removed from God that it was evil, and this evil emanation created the world and was in hostile opposition to God. In sharp opposition to this heresy, John begins his Gospel with the ringing word, "In the beginning was the Word, and the Word was with God, and the Word was God ... through him all things were made; without him nothing was made that has been made" (1:1-3). Further, this is why, in John 3:16 in what is often called "the Gospel in a single verse," the author affirms the love of God for the world: "For God so loved the world that He gave His one and only Son, that whoever believes in him shall not perish but have eternal life." This is a direct attack on Gnosticism.

The Gnostics also denied both the full divinity and the humanity of Jesus. Gnosticism declared that Jesus was one of many emanations which had proceeded from God, that he was a kind of demi-god. On the other hand, it also denied his humanity; Jesus had no real body; he was a kind of phantom without a body, since a body was material and therefore evil.

In answer to these heresies, John affirms that Jesus was truly God. So the Gospel of John speaks of Jesus' preexistence—the Word was with God from the beginning. It stresses the omniscience of Jesus—he knew the past of the Samaritan woman at the well. He knew how long the cripple beside the pool had been ill. He knew Judas would betray him. He knew the death of Lazarus before anyone told him.

John also affirms the real humanity of Jesus, that the Logos really became flesh. The incarnation of the Logos is the keystone of the Gospel. So Jesus physically expressed his anger with those who defiled the temple. He got physically tired. He was thirsty and needed water. He needed food like anyone else. He knew grief and wept. He was human!

3. *It was written to address polemical considerations.* There were two facets of polemics:

a. *A rebuttal of Judaism's criticism of the early Church.* There are some rather pointed remarks regarding the Jews in this Gospel. At the time of John's writing, the Jewish community was engaged in maligning the story of Jesus and ridiculing his claims. Against the statement that Jesus was just an obscure teacher, John asserts that Jesus taught at the very headquarters of the national religion (7:4; 18:20). Against the statement that Jesus could not hold the loyalty of his own disciples, and one betrayed him, John asserts that Jesus knew what Judas would do and permitted it for his own ends (6:64; 13:11). Against the statement that Jesus died a malefactor, John states that Pilate could find no fault in him (19:4).

b. *An affirmation of the subordinate position of John the Baptist.* There had arisen among the Jewish people a group of followers of John the Baptist declaring that John the Baptist, not Jesus, was the Messiah, the Christ. The "John the Baptists" were a recognized sect within the Jewish community. The Mandaean, a sect surviving to this day in Iraq, revere John the Baptist.[110]

The Gospel of John holds John the Baptist in high regard, but every time he is mentioned there is great care to point out the subordinate position of the Baptist to Jesus. The Baptizer himself declares repeatedly and specifically that he is not the Christ, but the forerunner of Christ, whom he identifies as Jesus.

F. *Organization of the Gospel of John*

The Gospel of John is framed by a prologue and an epilogue. The main narrative (2-20) is divided into three sections. The Gospel may be outlined as follows:
1. The Prologue (1:1-51)
2. The Book of Signs (2:1-12:50)
3. The Book of Service (13:1-17:26)
4. The Book of Sacrifice (18:1-20:31)
5. The Epilogue (21:1-25)

1. The Prologue (1:1-51) is very likely taken from an early Christian hymn. Scholars suggest that the hymn was originally developed within the community of John the Baptist. The prologue deals with the incarnation and identification of the Son of God. The key term in this section is the *Logos*, translated "the

Word." *Logos* is a Greek philosophical term which means creative reason. It denotes a rational principle that created and informed the universe. It represents the mediator between God and material creation. John blends it with a parallel Jewish tradition about divine Wisdom that existed before the world began. According to the book of Proverbs (8:22-31), Wisdom was Yahweh's companion when he created the universe, transforming the original dark chaos into a design of order and light.[111]

The Jews were familiar with the concept of God's *word*. God spoke and creation occurred. The creative reason of God put the order and majesty into creation. God said, "Let there be light," and there was light. John's emphasis on light recalls the position of light in the Genesis account of creation.

The Greeks believed that *logos*, creative reason, is, in some measure, in man, making it possible for man to think, to know, to sense the order in nature. They spoke of the spark of the divine in man.

John's Gospel is simply stating that *logos* and God are equivalents. And this *logos* has visibly come to earth in Jesus: "In the beginning was the Word (the Logos), and the Word was with God, and the Word was God ... through him all things were made ... in him was life, and that life was the light of men ... the Word became flesh and lived for a while among us. We have seen his glory, the glory of the one and only Son, who came from the Father, full of grace and truth" (1:1-3, 16). The Greeks could understand that. It talked to them in their own language.

John's statement that the Word became flesh is the summation of the New Testament view of Christ.

The prologue continues to introduce Jesus' ministry by referring to the witness of John the Baptist. The Baptist was a man sent from God and a witness sent beforehand that all people may believe. He was not the light (1:8), but he proclaimed that Jesus is the light (1:5). This and subsequent statements of the Baptist in which he denies he is the Christ and clearly subordinates himself to Jesus may represent a subtle polemic against John.[112] Pointing out the Baptist's inferiority, the author has him bear witness against himself: he is neither a prophet nor the Elijah figure, but "a voice" whose sole function is to announce Jesus

(1:21-23). Thus, the Baptist witnesses the Holy Spirit descend upon Jesus (1:32) a phenomenon that Mark reports as Jesus' private experience of his calling (Mark 1:10-11).[113]

In the remainder of chapter 1 the author deals with the call of the first disciples: John, Andrew, Simon, Philip, and Nathanael. They had been prepared by the preaching of John the Baptist, and all five later became Apostles. This was another great contribution of the Baptist's ministry to the work of Christ.

2. The Book of Signs (2:1-12:50). Chapters 2 through 12 are designated by several interpreters as "The Book of Signs."[114] This cycle of miracle stories forms the basis for the first major section of the Gospel.

A. *Seven Signs.* John organizes his interpretation of the meaning of Jesus' mission around seven miracles, or signs, among which he inserts long discourses and dialogues. Each sign manifests Jesus' glory. One scholar has rightly observed that John's concern is "everywhere apparent that Christ himself may not be overshadowed by anything ... Jesus alone is the true divine gift to which all other gifts can and should only point."[115]

The seven signs are:

a. *Changing of Water into Wine at Cana* (2:1-11). This miracle, found only in John, is not performed to impress gullible onlookers, but is a deeply symbolic act. First, Jesus' producing wine of high quality is a symbolic suggestion of the superiority of his new religion of the spirit (1:26, 33) to the old "watery" religion with its external and ceremonial rites. Moreover, wine, the sacramental element of the Christian communion, symbolizes the blood of Jesus shed on the cross. Above all, however, the purpose of this "sign" was to manifest Jesus' glory, now first revealed to his disciples.

b *Healing the Nobleman's Son* (4:46-54). This miracle also took place at Cana, a Galilean town, four miles northeast of Nazareth. Called "the second sign" (vs. 54), this was the second miracle performed in the region of Galilee. Jesus had done miracles in the meantime in Jerusalem (2:23). The nobleman was one of Herod's officials in Capernaum, 15 miles northeast of Cana. Thus this "long distance" miracle was spoken in one town and healed a person in a town 15 miles distant. This story has much in common with the episodes recorded in Matthew 8:5-13 and Luke 7:1-10. In all accounts what is commended by Jesus is the faith of the nobleman.

    c. *Curing the Lame Man at Bethesda* (5:1-15). Jesus' healing of this chronic invalid on the Sabbath created an uproar and resulted in the Sanhedrin's determination to kill him (vs. 18). This miracle was one of the seven healings of Jesus on the Sabbath recorded in the Gospels. The others were a demoniac in Capernaum (Mk. 1:21-27); Peter's mother-in-law in Capernaum (Mk. 1:29-31); a man with a withered hand (Mk. 3:1-6); a woman doubled over (Lk. 13:10-17); a man with dropsy (Lk. 14:1-6); and a man born blind (Jn. 9:1-14).

    d. *Feeding the Five Thousand* (6:16-21). The miraculous feeding of the five thousand people (the fourth sign) is the only miracle that appears in all four Gospels (Matt. 14:13-21; Mark 6:30-44; Luke 9:10-17). John uses this event to symbolize Jesus' providing the world with spiritual nourishment. As usual in John, some of Jesus' followers misunderstood his intent. This time they wanted to enthrone him as king (vs. 15), not realizing that his kingdom "does not belong to this world" (18:36). In spite of the fact that Jesus regarded himself a king only in a spiritual sense, his assertions of kingship were used as the main accusations against him in the trial leading to his death.

    e. *Walking on Water* (6:16-21). This fifth sign demonstrated Jesus' power over nature. The spiritual lesson of this episode seems to be that without the serenity that faith in Christ gives to human minds and hearts, man is doomed to sink in the dark and tempestuous "seas" of life.

    f. *Restoring Sight to a Blind Man* (9:1-41). This sixth "sign," performed by Jesus at Jerusalem during the Feast of Tabernacles, symbolizes the giving of spiritual insight to those who believe in him. It illustrates John's theme that Christ is the "light of the world" (8:12). His gift of light dispels the darkness. Those, like the Pharisees, who deny his messiahship remain spiritually blind.

    g. *Raising Lazarus from the Dead* (11:1-44). This the seventh and most potent sign was performed by Jesus at Bethany, probably a month before his own death. This episode also precipitates the Jewish leadership's conspiracy to kill Jesus (11:45-53). The Gospels tell of two other times Jesus raised someone from the dead: Jairus' daughter in Mark 5:21-43 and the son of the widow of Nain in Luke 7:11-17. Fearing that Jesus might accept the people's desire to "make him king of the Jews," which could incite the Romans to destroy Israel, High Priest Caiaphas told the people, "It is better for you that one man die ... than that the whole nation perish" (11:50). It is ironic that the High Priest unwittingly expressed the truth that Jesus' death would redeem the world.[116]

B. *Seven Discourses.* John inserts seven long discourses and dialogues among the seven "signs" around which he organizes his interpretation of the meaning of Jesus' mission.

a. *Dialogue with Nicodemus* (3:1-21). Jesus' conversation with Nicodemus, a Pharisee and member of the Jewish Religious Council (Sanhedrin) is unique to John. The discussion on spiritual rebirth starts with a dialogue and ends as a monologue. When Jesus remarks that unless one is "born again" he cannot "see the kingdom of God," Nicodemus mistakenly thinks he refers to reemerging from the womb. Jesus then explains that he means rebirth "from water and spirit," referring to the spiritual renewal that accompanies Christian baptism. In perhaps the most familiar passage of the New Testament, Jesus states his purpose in coming to earth. "God so loved the world that He gave his one and only Son, that whoever believes in him shall not perish but have eternal life" (3:16). This verse is often called the miniature Bible, the Bible within the Bible.

b. *Conversation with the Samaritan Woman* (4:1-26). As does Luke, John shows "Jesus ignoring the rigid social conventions that segregate the sexes."[117] Astonishing the disciples by his violation of the social code (4:27), Jesus publicly discussed fine points of theology with a Samaritan woman who gave him water to drink at Jacob's well. Recalling the deep hostility then existing between Jews and Samaritans, the Samaritan woman was surprised at Jesus' willingness to talk with her. Jesus' proclamation that neither the Jerusalem Temple nor the Samaritans' rival shrine on

Mount Gerizim were the only places to worship was not only a rebuke to those who localized and monopolized God, but also a proclamation of God's universal Fatherhood and the brotherhood of all people.

c. *Life Through the Son* (5:16-47). Criticism directed at Jesus' breaking of the Sabbath in healing a nobleman's dying son in Cana provided the opportunity for this extended discourse on Jesus' special relation to the Father.

Jesus was accused of claiming equality with God. He explained that he derived all his authority from the Father, whose example he followed and whose purpose he carried out (5:19-23). He had the authority to pronounce sentence upon men and to withhold doom by preserving and conferring life. Thus, those who dishonored the Son by disputing his saving power were dishonoring the Father.

d. *Jesus the Bread of Life* (6:25-59). This fourth discourse took place in the synagogue at Capernaum. A remnant of the five thousand who had been fed had followed Jesus. The Lord criticized their failure to discern the "sign" in the miraculous meal. He told them that he would give them not merely perishable food, but food that nourishes the life which is life indeed (vs. 27). Like the Samaritan woman who said, "Sir, give me this water so that I won't get thirsty and have to keep coming here to draw water" (4;15), these Galileans exclaimed, "Sir, from now on give us this bread" (6:34).

Jesus identified himself with "the bread from heaven" (v. 32), "the bread of God" (v. 3), by saying "I am the bread of life" (v. 35), "I am the living bread" (v. 51), "I am the bread that came down from heaven" (v. 41). In this passage, John alludes to the Eucharist; he asserts that by truly partaking in the communion ("eating his flesh" and "drinking his blood") one can gain eternal life.

e. *Jesus the Living Water* (7:37-52). This discourse was given on the last day of the Feast of Tabernacles. The Feast of Tabernacles was a reminder of the water given to the Jewish people from the rock in the desert in their time of need. On each of the seven days of the festival a full golden pitcher was carried in procession to the temple. But on the last day that rite was dispensed with, for now they were celebrating the entrance into the Promised Land with its springs and water courses. "It was in such a setting that Christ promised, not symbolism, but reality, a living water, abundant, satisfying, overflowing." [118]

f. *Jesus the Light of the World* (8:12-20). This is an eloquent example of one of the famous "I am" sayings so characteristic of the Gospel of John where Jesus announces, "I am the light of the world. Whoever follows me will never walk in darkness, but will have the light of life." He is himself the life, the life-giving power, which is "the light of men" (1:4). Those who claim to be his followers pass the test for eternal life through their attraction to Jesus, while others judge themselves by preferring the world's darkness (3:17-21).

g. *The Shepherd and his Flock* (10:1-18). In these verses we have a description of a sheepfold, with door and gatekeeper, intruders climbing the wall to steal, and the shepherd who is recognized by the gatekeeper and whose voice is known to the sheep as he calls them by name. In metaphoric language the author is speaking "of the Christian church and of the difference between fold and flock, between Judaism and Christianity, between Pharisees and Jesus, and of the relation between Christian pastors and the Good Shepherd."[119] Jesus is the door in relation to the fold (vss. 7-10); he is also the shepherd in relation to the flock (vss. 11-18). He is a good shepherd, mindful of his own, ready to risk his life for the sheep.

Noteworthy in the Book of Signs are Jesus' "I am" pronouncements, which express an important aspect of John's Christology. They echo Yahweh's declaration of being to Moses at the burning bush (Exodus 3:14), in which God revealed His sacred personal name: *I am who I am*. Jesus uses the "I am" expression in a number of instances, such as "I am ... the bread of life" (6:35); "I am the good shepherd" (10:11); "I am the resurrection and the life" (11:25); "I am the way, the truth, and the life" (14:6). In all these expressions, John points out Christ's unity with God, the eternal "I am."[120]

3. The Book of Service (13:-17:26). Chapters 13-17 contain a number of discourses. After demonstrating the extent of his love by washing his disciples' feet, Jesus instructed his disciples regarding three crucial relationships: to one another, to himself, and to the world.

    a. *The Last Supper* (13:1-30). This part of the Gospel opens with an account of the Last Supper that differs considerably from that related in the Synoptics. John's account contains no reference to the new covenant and to Jesus' distributing the ceremonial elements of bread and wine. Instead, John dramatizes the concept of Jesus' "servanthood"—washing his disciples' feet.

    Scholars do not agree on John's silence about the Eucharist. Some interpret the inclusion and or the substitution of the story of the feet washing as a symbolic representation of the Eucharist. It combines "the obvious lesson of humility shown in self-forgetful service with a sacramental allusion."[121] The feet washing incident expresses the self-humiliation of Jesus who "emptied himself" of all but love, and "was obedient unto death, even the death of the cross."

    b. *Jesus Predicts His Betrayal* (13:21-20). The disciples are plainly told, "one of you is going to betray me" (v. 21). So shrewdly had Judas kept his secret that none of them suspected him. Judas knew that Jesus knew his secret. In fact, Jesus identified him, when asked "Lord, who is it?" He answered, "It is the one to whom I give this piece of bread, when I have dipped it in the dish" (v. 26). After receiving the piece of bread, Judas immediately went out to betray his Master.

    c. *Jesus' Farewell Discourses* (13:31-17:26). This section includes a number of farewell discourses and dialogues, *Paraclete* sayings (*Paraclete* is a Greek term meaning an "advocate" or "intercessor summoned to aid" used to denote the Holy Spirit; it is variously translated as "Comforter," "Helper," or "Spirit of truth"—John 7: 39; 14 :12; 15: 26), and Christ's prayer for the unity of the church.

    — The New Commandment (13:31-35). Jesus stated the nature of what is involved in following him: "A new command I give you: Love one another. As I have loved you, so you must love one another" (v. 34). From this we get the name "Maundy Thursday." "Maundy" comes from the Latin word "*mandatum*," which means "commandment" or "law." It was on Thursday night Jesus gave this new commandment, the new "*mandatum*."

— Dialogue on Christ's Departure and Return (13:31-14:31). Facing his imminent crucifixion, Jesus thought of those he loved. To comfort them and give them strength to face life, he told them of new life in God and he shared his own hope and faith with them, speaking of life and truth and love. He admonished his disciples, "Do not let your hearts be troubled." The grounds of this admonition were threefold:

First, their hearts need not be troubled if they believed in God the Father who had empowered Jesus and who will answer their prayers.

Second, their hearts need not be troubled if they believed in Christ, who will show them the Father and provide for their immediate comfort through the Holy Spirit as well as for their eternal welfare through his sacrifice and resurrection.

Third, their hearts need not be troubled if they believed in heaven, for heaven is a mansion with many rooms and a home where their loving Heavenly Father awaits them.

— The Paraclete Sayings (14:15-16:15). In chapters 14-16, there are five separate sayings about the promised presence of the Holy Spirit (14:15-17; 14:25-26; 15:26-27; 16:5-11; and 16:12-15).

Unlike the Synoptics, which emphasize the Second Coming of Christ, John teaches the perennial presence of Christ. Brief allusions to Christ's reappearance after death (14:3) are fulfilled when he sends the *Paraclete*. The *Paraclete*, translated as "Advocate," "Helper," "Counselor," or "Comforter" is synonymous with the Holy Spirit. It is the Holy Spirit who enables the disciples to understand the true significance of Jesus' teaching (16:1-15).

John maintains that Jesus imparted the Paraclete at his resurrection by breathing on the disciples and saying, "Receive the Holy Spirit" (20:21-23).

The Holy Spirit is God's presence active in human life. The *Paraclete* is a witness and spokesman for Jesus. He is to be a consoler of the disciples in Jesus' absence. Moreover, he is to be their teacher and guide. Jesus' promised return is therefore partially fulfilled in the sending of the *Paraclete*. By such means, Jesus "abides" with his own who are in the world, while yet present with the Father. The presence of Jesus with his disciples is not a substitute for or in opposition to the final coming of Jesus,[122] but a greater emphasis is placed upon the former in the Gospel According to John.

— <u>Jesus' Intercessory Prayer</u> (17:1-26). This prayer is like a summary of the Fourth Gospel. The prayer has three divisions.

First, Jesus consecrates himself before offering his life as a sacrifice for the world. He signals that the hour has come (vs. 1) and prays that his crucifixion might be the means of God's glorification, of bringing eternal life to his own, and of reuniting the Son with the Father (17:1-5).

Second, the delegated work having been accomplished, Jesus then consecrates his disciples that they might reach out through their testimony (17:6-19).

Third, Jesus prays for the church of the future and its unity in God—the final union of believers with himself in the presence of the divine glory (17:20-26). The union of God with Christ and believers and the union of believers with one another achieves tangible form and visible expression in the love of Christians for one another. Not until the Church becomes one can the world know God's purpose of love in sending Jesus Christ. Thus, the unity of the church is a unity of love in and through Jesus Christ.

4. The Book of Sacrifice (18:1-20; 31). This section records Jesus' arrest, his trial before the high priest and before Pilate, his crucifixion and burial, and his resurrection appearances. The central aspect in these episodes is the kingship of Christ. Jesus went to the cross as a king ascends to his throne. His kingship transcended national lines. The allegiance he claimed was that of obedience to truth (18:33 ff).

John emphasizes that the death of Christ was a voluntary act. When the soldiers came, he gave himself up; when death approached, the initiative again was taken by Jesus (18:4-9; 19:17; 19:28-30).

In this section although John follows the tradition preserved in the Synoptic narrative, he also draws upon an independent source.

a. *Jesus' Arrest* (18:1-2). The story of the arrest is also recorded in Matthew 26:47-56, Mark 14:43-50, and Luke 22:47-53. John's account differs slightly from the synoptic record. For example, in the case of those who arrested Jesus, Mark tells us Judas was accompanied by "a crowd with swords and clubs, from the chief priests and the scribes and the elders." Matthew agrees, but omits "and the scribes." Luke simply mentions a crowd under the leadership of Judas. John tells that "Judas came to the grove, guiding a detachment of soldiers, and some officials from the chief priests and Pharisees ... carrying torches, lanterns, and weapons" (18:3).

John again emphasizes that Jesus was in control and voluntarily laid down his life: While the Synoptics speak of Judas' kiss as the sign given to the temple police, in John, Jesus stepped forward to meet those who would arrest him and asked them "Who is it you want?" (18:4).

b. *Jesus' Trial* (18:12-19:16). Although John agrees with the Synoptics that Jesus' arrest was followed by a trial, he presents a slightly different version of the episode. Whereas the Synoptics tell us about Jesus being accused of blasphemy before the whole Sanhedrin, John shows Jesus being examined at the residence of Annas, father-in-law of the High Priest Joseph Caiaphas who, in turn, handed him to Pontius Pilate. John does not tell us of questions asked of Jesus about his teachings and his disciples, nor of his messianic claim or his alleged threat to destroy the temple. John does not record a charge or a judgment. [123]

Unlike the Synoptics, which present an extended narrative of Jesus' trial before the Jewish authorities, John concentrates on Pilate's hearing of the case. The evangelist relates Jesus' trial in six stages: 1. Pilate was dissatisfied with the validity of Jewish accusations against Jesus (18:28-32); 2. Pilate interrogated Jesus and asked if Jesus indeed claimed to be the King of the Jews (18:33-38); 3. Pilate tried to evade judgment by appealing to the custom of releasing a prisoner at the Passover (18:38-40); 4. Foiled in that attempt, Pilate then tried to work on the pity of the Jews.[124] The Jews had no pity and their leaders shouted the more "crucify him" (19:1-7); 5. Pilate requestioned Jesus (19:8-12); 6. Pilate made a last attempt to release Jesus but the Jews threatened him with the charge of indulgence to Caesar's rivals (19:13-16).

c. *Jesus' Crucifixion and Burial* (19:17-42). John follows the Synoptic tradition in describing Jesus' crucifixion as fulfillment of the prophecies of the Hebrew Bible. He includes the soldiers' casting lots for Jesus' garment (19:24) and Jesus' thirst (19:28). John emphasizes Jesus' "carrying his own cross" and is silent about Simon of Cyrene, who helped bear the cross because it was heavy for Jesus (Mark 15:21). This emphasis of "Jesus bearing his own cross" (19:17) was important for the evangelist to counteract the claim of the Gnostic heretics that "Simon and Jesus changed places, so that Jesus did not actually suffer death."[125]

Like the Synoptic authors, John records Jesus' crucifixion between two others. He also includes the superscription on the cross, but adds that the inscription specifically mentioned the name of Jesus of Nazareth and that it was written in Hebrew, in Latin, and in Greek. A trilingual inscription would have been necessary in Jerusalem, for Latin was the official language of the administration, Greek the international language, and Hebrew, the language of the Jews.

Unique also to John's Gospel is the incident of the Roman soldier's piercing Jesus' side with a spear, "bringing a sudden flow of blood and water" (emblems of redemption and truth). This and other grisly details are recorded to counteract Gnostic and Docetic claims that the death of Jesus was a mere semblance. The evangelist makes an emphatic declaration that Jesus' death was a historical fact.

Joseph of Arimathea, who sought release of Jesus' body from Pontius Pilate, is named in all four Gospels. John adds that Joseph "was a disciple of Jesus, but secretly because he feared the Jews" (19:38). Helped by Nicodemus he buried the body of Jesus in a new tomb.

John omits mention of the natural phenomena—earthquakes, thunder, and midday darkness—that, according to the Synoptics, accompanied Jesus' death.

d. *Appearances of the Risen Lord* (20:1-29). John, like Luke, mentions Jesus' resurrection appearances in and around Jerusalem (instead of Galilee as Mark and Matthew do). John only mentions Mary Magdalene as the first witness of the empty tomb of Jesus

(20:1). In the Synoptics Mary Magdalene is accompanied by two other women, Mary, the mother of James the Little, and Salome (Mark 15:40; Matt. 27:56), or Mary, the mother of James, and Joanna (Luke 24:10). Luke also adds "the others with them who told this to the Apostles" (Luke 24:10).

Unique in John's Gospel is the story of Thomas. On the first Easter evening, Christ appeared to his disciples, infusing them with the Holy Spirit. Thomas was absent. When the other disciples told him of what had happened, Thomas did not believe this alleged appearance to the ten. He demanded a tangible test: "Unless I see the nail marks in his hands and put my finger where the nails were, and put my hand into his side, I will not believe it" (20:25). A week later Thomas was present in the house with the rest when Jesus appeared and challenged the "Doubting Thomas" to carry out his test. The sight of the wounded hands and side of the risen Lord vanquished Thomas' skepticism.

5. The Epilogue (21:1-25). Many scholars believe that this section is an appendix added by another editor who may have prepared the Gospel manuscript for publication. It emphasizes the complimentary roles of Peter, leader of the Twelve, and the unidentified "Beloved Disciple"[126] and reminds the church that Peter, who had denied his Lord, was forgiven and reinstated. It was also to affirm that the testimony of the "disciple whom Jesus loved" lies behind this Gospel; thus, this was sufficient guarantee that it was worthy of acceptance.

a. *The Appearance Beside Lake Tiberias* (21:1-14). The disciples returned to Galilee, which Jesus had told them to do (Matt. 28:7,10; Mark 16:7). Jesus, standing on the beach of Lake Tiberias (Sea of Galilee), was at first unrecognized. It may have been at, or near, the spot where he called them to become "fishers of men." This time, as at first, he gave them a miraculous haul of fish. He may have intended it as a "symbolic hint of the great success of the redemptive movement among men which they were about to initiate."[127]

b. T*he Reinstatement of Peter* (21:15-23). Jesus questioned Peter about the depth of his love. There was a threefold question and a triple commission, corresponding to the triple denial. Jesus emphasized that love for him means feeding his "lambs," providing spiritual and other care for the future believers.

c. *Conclusion* (21:25). The Gospel concludes with an interesting hyperbole: "Jesus did many other things as well. If every one of them were written down, I suppose that even the whole world would not have room for the books that would be written."

References

1. Maurice Goguel, *Jesus and the Origins of Christianity*, 2 Vols., trans. Olive Wyon (New York: Harper and Brothers, Torchbooks, 1960), Vol. 1, "Prolegomena to the Life of Jesus," pp. 91-94.
2. *Ibid.*, pp. 95-97.
3. *Ibid.*, pp. 98-104 .
4. Josephus, *Antiquities of the Jews*, Loeb edition, Vol. 9, trans. L.H. Feldmann (Cambridge, Mass.: Harvard University Press, 1965), pp. 43-44.
5. *Ibid.*, p. 20.
6. Joseph Klasner, *Jesus of Nazareth: His Life, Times, and Teaching,* trans. Herbert Danby (Boston: Beacon Press, 1964), p. 46.
7. Dennis C. Daling, *Jesus Christ Through History* (New York: Harcourt Brace Jovanovich, Inc . 1979), pp. 7-8 .
8. John B. Gabel and Charles B. Wheeler, *The Bible as Literature* (New York, Oxford: Oxford University Press, 1986), p. 183.
9. *Ibid.*, pp. 183-184.
10. W.O. Walker, Jr., Ed. *The Relationship Among the Gospels* (San Antonio: Trinity University Press, 1978), pp. 2-3.
11. Stephen L. Harris, *UnderstandingThe Bible* (Palo Alto; Mayfield Publishing Company), pp . 266-267.
12. Martin Dibelius, *From Tradition to Gospel*, Trans. by G.L. Woolf (Philadelphia: Westminister Press, 1935), p . 4 .
13. Chamberlin and Feldman (Ed.), *The Dartmouth Bible* (Boston: Houghton Mifflin Co., 1961), p. 858.
14. Walker, pp . 60-65 .
15. B.H. Streeter, *The Four Gospels: A Study of Origins* (London: Macmillan & Co ., 1930), pp . 15-22 .
16. Henry J. Cadbury, "The New Testament and Early Christian Literature," *The Interpreter ' s Bible*, Vol. VII (New York: Abingdon Press, 1962) pp. 37-38.
17. W.F. Howard, "Introduction and Exegesis to the Gospel of John," *Interpreter's Bible*, Vol. VIII (New York: Abingdon Press, 1962) pp. 485-490.
18. Dwight Moody Smith, "Gospel of John," I*nterpreter's Dictionary of the Bible: Supplementary Volume* (Nashville: Abingdon Press, 1976) pp. 482-86 .
19. William H. Marty, *Surveying the New Testament* (Dubuque, Iowa: Kendall/ Hunt Publishing Co., 1987), p. 28.

20 George A. Buttrick, "The Gospel According to St. Matthew," *The Interpreter's Bible,* Vol. VII (New York: Abingdon Press, 1962), p. 231.
21 Streeter, pp. 505-23.
22 Harris, p. 272.
23 Streeter, p. 562 .
24 Harris, p. 273.
25 Marty, p. 31.
26 Gabel and Wheeler, p. 198.
27 Streeter, pp. 518-20.
28 Harris, p. 274.
29 Nelson Beecher Keyes, *The Story of the Bible* (Pleasantville: The Reader's Digest Association, 1962) p. 131; also, Chamberlin and Feldman, p.963.
30 James S. Stewart, *The Life and Teaching of Jesus Christ* (New York: Abingdon Press, n.d.), p. 37.
31 Harris, p. 279.
32 Chamberlin and Feldman, p. 967.
33 *Ibid.*, pp. 971-72; also, Steward, pp. 106-114.
34 B.W. Bacon, *Studies in Matthew* (New York: Holt, 1930), pp. 53-62.
35 Harris, p. 283.
36 Buttrick, p . 582 .
37 Chamberlin and Feldman, pp. 978-79.
38 Henry H. Halley, *Bible Handbook: An Abbreviated Bible Commentary* (Grand Rapids: Zondervan Publishing House, 1960), p. 414.
39 William Barclay, *Daily Study Bible* (Philadelphia: The Westminster Press, 1956), p. xiii.
40 Edgar J. Goodspeed, *Introduction to the New Testament* (Chicago: University of Chicago Press, 1938), p. 145.
41 Gabel and Wheeler, p. 191.
42 Frederick C. Grant and Halford E. Luccock, "The Gospel According to Mark," *Interpreter's Bible*, Vol. VII (New York: Abingdon Press, 1962) p. 630; Harris, p.185.
43 Frederick C. Grant, *The Growth of the Gospels* (New York: Abingdon Press, 1933), pp. 136-137.
44 Frederick Buechner, *Peculiar Treasures* (New York: Harper & Row, 1979), p. 97.
45 *Ibid.*, pp. 98-99.
46 Marty, p. 41.
47 Gabel and Wheeler, pp. 192-193; Harris, pp. 287-288.
48 Harris, p. 287.
49 *Ibid.*
50 Stewart, pp. 50-51.
51 Harris Franklin Rall, *New Testament History* (New York-Nashville: Abingdon-Cokesbury Press, 1929), pp. 69-77.
52 Harris, p. 288 .
53 Donald Strobe, *Secretary to St. Peter* (Knoxville: Seven Worlds Publishing, 1989), p. 41.
54 Grant and Luccock, p. 726.
55 Harris, p. 290.
56 Grant and Luccock, p. 823.
57 Chamberlin and Feldman, p. 976.

58 Strobe, p. 196.
59 Lamar Williamson, Mark, "Interpretations" (Atlanta: John Knox Press, 1983), p. 234.
60 Robert Jewett, *Jesus Against the Rapture* (Philadelphia: The Westminister Press, 1979), p. 14.
61 Chamberlin and Feldman, p. 978.
62 Stewart, pp. 151-154.
63 Stephen L. Harris, *The New Testament: A Student's Introduction* (Mountain View, California: Mayfield Publishing Co., 1988), p. 81.
64 F.F. Bruce, *The New Testament* (Garden City, New York: Doubleday & ompany, Inc., 1969), p. 204.
65 Strobe, p. 261.
66 Harris, *The New Testament*, p. 84.
67 *Ibid*., p. 116.
68 Howard Clark Kee, *Understanding the New Testament*, 3rd. Ed. (Englewood Cliffs: Prentice Hall, 1973), pp. 369-385.
69 Vernon A. Loescher, *The Gospel of Luke* (New York: F.C.C. Press, 1975), p. 2.
70 Robert A. Spivey and D. Moody Smith, *Anatomy of the New Testament*, 4th Ed. (New York: Macmillan Publis ~ ., 1989), p. 126; Harris, The New Testament, p. 116.
71 S.M. Gilmour, "The Gospel According to St. Luke, Introduction and Exegesis," *The Interpreter's Bible*, Vol. 8 (New York and and Nashville: Abingdon Press, 1951), pp. 6-7.
72 Pheme Perkins, *Reading the New Testament* (New York: Paulist Press, 1977), p. 231.
73 Loescher, p. 4.
74 Loescher, p. 3.
75 Harris, *The New Testament*, p. 116.
76 James L. Price, *The New Testament: Its History and Theology* (New York: Macmillan Publishing Co., 1987), p. 134.
77 Harris, *The New Testament*, p. 123.
78 *Ibid* p. 124.
79 Spivey and Smith, p. 142.
80 Harris, *The New Testament*, p. 127.
81 John Knox, "The Gospel According to St. Luke," *The Interpreter's Bible* (New York: Abingdon Press, 1952), p. 204.
82 *Ibid*., p. 217-
83 *Ibid*, p. 231.
84 A.T. Cadoux, *The Parables of Jesus* (New York: The Macmillan Co., 1931), p. 180.
85 Hugh Martin, *The Parables of the Gospels* (New York: The Abingdon Press, 1937), p. 167.
86 John Knox, p. 289.
87 *Ibid*., pp. 294-295.
88 Harris, *The New Testament*, p. 128.
89 Spivey and Smith, p. 146.
90 Knox, p. 328.
91 *Ibid* pp. 337-38.
92 Harris, *The New Testament*, p. 132.
93 *Ibid*., p. 134.

94 *Ibid.*; Knox, pp. 377-380.
95 Harris, *The New Testament*, p. 135.
96 Chamberlin and Feldman, p. 979.
97 Spivey and Smith, p. 151.
98 Harris, *The New Testament*, p. 136.
99 Raymond E. Brown, *The Gospel According to John* Vol. 1 (Garden City, NY: Doubleday, 1966, 1970), p. 18.
100 C.H. Dodd, *The Interpretation of the Fourth Gospel* (New York: Cambridge University Press, 1953), pp. 118-122.
101 R. Kysar, *The Fourth Evangelist and His Gospel* (Minneapolis: Augsburg, 1975), pp. 101-103.
102 Brown, pp. CXVI-CXXI.
103 E.F. Scott, *The Fourth Gospel* 2nd. Ed. (Edinburgh: T. & T. Clark, 1908), p. 359.
104 R.C. Briggs, *Interpreting the New Testament Today* (Nashville: Abingdon, 1973), pp. 85-96.
105 C.K. Barrett, *The Gospel According to St. John: An Introduction With Commentary and Notes on the Greek Text*, 2nd Ed. (Philadelphia: Westminister, 1978), pp. 100-134.
106 Halley, p. 484; Marty, p. 52.
107 Brown, Vol. 29, pp. cii-f; Barett, p. 149-152.
108 *Ibid.*
109 W.F. Howard, "Introduction and Exegesis to the Gospel of John," *The Interpreter's Bible*, Vol. VIII, (New York and Nashville: Abingdon Press, 1954), pp. 775-779; Harris, 146.
110 Rudolf Bultmann, *The Gospel of John* (Philadelphia: Westminister, 1971), pp. 17-18.
E.L. Drower, *The Mandeans of Iraq and Iran* (Leiden: Brill, 1962), pp. 17-18.
111 Harris, p. 149.
112 Spivey and Smith, pp. 165-166.
113 Harris, p. 152 .
114 C.H.Dodd, pp. 497 ff; Brown, Vol. 29, pp. cxxxvii; Harris, pp. 152-155.
115 Ernst Kasemann, *The New Testament: A Study of the Gospel of John in Light of Chapter 17* Translated by G. Krodel. (Philadelphia, Fortress Press, 1968), p. 19.
116 Harris, p. 155.
117 Harris, p. 153.
118 Howard, p. 588 .
119 Howard, pp. 622-623.
120 Harris, pp. 152-153.
121 Howard, pp. 678-679.
122 Price, p. 445.
123 Howard, p. 759.
124 Howard, p. 771.
125 Howard, p. 779 .
126 Harris, p. 159; Howard, pp. 446, 802, 811.
127 Halley, p. 510.

PART 3

THE ACTS OF THE APOSTLES

The Acts of the Apostles is the second major part of the New Testament. People casually call it *Acts*. The full title of the book is *The Book of the Acts of the Apostles*. It is not "The Book of the Thoughts or Speculations of the Apostles." It is the book of their *acts*. It is a book filled with action, thrilling stories, suspense, accomplishments, hazards, defeats, and victories.

The value of the Book of Acts is impossible to overestimate. It is a very important historical document. It traces the birth and the growth of the Church from Jerusalem to Rome. If it had been lost or never written, we would have little clear knowledge of the church from the crucifixion and resurrection to the death of St. Paul—some thirty-five crucial years. It is "the only bridge we have across the seemingly impassable gulf that separates Jesus from Paul, Christ from Christianity, the gospel *of* Jesus from the gospel about Jesus."[1]

The first verse of the Book of Acts connects it with the Gospel of Luke. Written to Theophilus, Acts is the second volume in Luke's account of Christ and the Church. In fact, the Third Gospel and the Book of Acts are two parts of a single whole from the pen of Dr. Luke. The first part, the Gospel of Luke, tells the story of Jesus; the second part, Acts, tells the story of the influence of Jesus, the founding, development, and early expansion of the Christian Church.

The Book of Acts, like the Gospel of Luke, is dedicated to Luke's dear friend, Theophilus, a representative of the Greek and Gentile world. It presents Christianity as both the natural fulfillment of Judaism and as a universal faith intended for all nations. The author emphasizes that the apostles and the early followers of Christ continued essentially the same ministry that Jesus had begun; they maintained the same ethical and spiritual quality that distinguished Jesus' ministry.[2]

Scholars hold various opinions about the date and place of origin of the Book of Acts. Dates spanning ninety years, from 60 to 150 A.D., have been suggested. The majority of scholars, however, believe Acts was written about 85 A.D. The place of origin of the book is quite uncertain. Here again, there is diversity of opinion. The majority believe Rome is the most probable place of origin.

A reading of the Book of Acts evokes several questions, such as, *Where did Luke get the materials he incorporated in Acts? What were his sources of information?*

The first fifteen chapters contain material of which he had little, if any, direct personal knowledge. These materials, according to biblical scholars, came from two kinds of sources. There were, first, the records of certain churches—some records written and some transmitted orally. So there were the records of the Jerusalem church (chs. 1-5;15-16). There were the records of the church at Caesarea (chs. 8:26-40; 9:31-10:48). There were the records of the church at Antioch (chs. 11:19-30; 12:25-14:28). The second source for materials in these chapters was the stories which clustered around some of the great figures of the church, like Peter, John, Philip, and Stephen.

In chapters 16-28, the so-called "we" sections, there is evidence of a third source of material. Luke was with Paul during this period and what he writes in these chapters is, in effect, Luke's travel diary. These chapters grow out of the experiences Luke had with Paul and information he learned from Paul.[3]

Another question is: *Why did Luke write this second volume of his story?*

a. *The first and most obvious reason was to bring his friend, Theophilus, up to date on what had happened.*

b. *The second purpose was to commend Christianity to the Roman authorities.* Luke was writing during a period when Christians were disliked and were under the threat and actuality of persecution. The author goes out of his way to repeatedly show how courteous and fair various Roman officials had been in dealing with Paul and that Christians were good citizens of the Roman Empire and had always been regarded as such by the authorities. It has even been suggested by some that the Book of

Acts is essentially the brief prepared for Paul's defense as he stood trial before the Roman Emperor.[4]

c. *Luke's third purpose for writing the Book of Acts was to show that Christianity is a universal religion for all people of all countries.* Christianity had broken the shackles of the "chosen people" concept. So Luke shows Philip preaching to Samaritans; Stephen making Christianity a universal thing and getting killed for it; Peter taking Cornelius (a Gentile) into the Church; Christians preaching to the Gentiles at Antioch; Paul traveling far and wide winning people of all kinds and nations to Christ; and finally, the Church making the great decision to accept Gentiles into the Church on equal terms with the Jews.[5]

d. *The fourth purpose was to describe the expansion of Christianity in widening circles from Jerusalem to Rome.* The expansion occurred in the following stages: the first was the expansion from the little church in Jerusalem to encompass the whole city; the second was from Jerusalem throughout Palestine; the third, from Palestine to Antioch and all of Syria; the fourth, from Syria to Asia Minor; the fifth wave carried Christianity to Europe and occupied Greece and Macedonia; the last stage witnessed the expansion of the new faith to Rome, the capital of the world.

e. *The fifth and most important purpose of Luke in the Book of Acts was to demonstrate the work of the Holy Spirit in the lives of the Apostles and to show how they realized the prophetic words of Jesus, "You will be my witnesses in Jerusalem, and in all Judea and Samaria, and to the ends of the earth"* (1:8).

The title *"Acts"* (the Greek word *praxeis*) was used to summarize the accomplishments of the Apostles. Through Acts, Luke continues his account of Jesus Christ by describing what the resurrected Lord accomplished through his chosen witnesses. Luke relates how Christianity, which began as a small movement, had in three decades spread across the then civilized world and reached the capital of the Roman Empire.

The Book of Acts provides valuable information concerning the founding of the church at Jerusalem, its early extension and expansion. But it does not attempt to provide comprehensive record of its subject. The author lists the names of the original eleven Apostles (1:13) but tells us almost nothing about the majority of them. He tells us nothing about other geographical expansion except in the one direct line from Jerusalem to Rome. There is no mention of the church planting in Crete (Titus 1:5), Illyricum (Rom. 15:19), or Pontus, Cappadocia, and Bythynia (I Peter 1:1), not to mention the Church's expansion eastward toward Mesopotamia, northward toward Armenia, or southward toward Egypt.

There have been various ways of dividing the book. It has been frequently divided on the basis of Luke's interest in Peter (1-12) and Paul (13-28), or in the geographic expansion of the Gospel from Jerusalem to Antioch (1:1-12:25) and from Antioch to Rome (13:1-28:31), or in terms of the fulfillment of Jesus' promise: "You shall be my witnesses ... in Jerusalem, in all Judea and Samaria, and to the ends of the earth" (1:8).

In a broad way, the Book of Acts may be outlined as follows:

1. The Establishment of the Church: Jerusalem (1:1-6:7)
2. The Extension of the Church: Judea and Samaria (6:8-9:31)
3. The Expansion of the Church: To the Ends of the Earth (9:32-28:31)

1. The Establishment of the Church: Jerusalem (1:1-6:7). In the period of establishment, the focus is on the birth and growth of the church in Jerusalem. After commissioning his followers and promising to send them the Holy Spirit, Jesus Christ ascended into heaven. On the day of Pentecost, the resurrected and ascended Christ fulfilled his promise by sending the Holy Spirit.

a. *The Birth of the Church: A New Beginning* (1:1-2:47). In chapter 1, Luke explains two things: First, he shows the meaning of Jesus' departure and the indefinite period before his return. Second, through his treatment of the reconstitution of the twelve apostles, he shows the continuity between Jesus and his disciples. It is interesting to note that Luke is the only New Testament writer to describe the ascension of Jesus (1:9-12), and the selection of the twelfth Apostle, Matthias, as a replacement for

Jesus' betrayer, Judas Iscariot (1:12-26). The original appointment of the twelve must have had a symbolic reference to the twelve tribes, and the disciples wished to preserve this national symbolism by keeping the number intact.[7] It is also interesting to note that after Matthias' selection, Luke says nothing more about him. He is also silent about most of the Apostles. He describes only those whose activities were conducive to the direct expansion of the Church from Jerusalem to Judea, Samaria, Asia Minor, and Europe.[8]

Chapter 2 falls into two parts, verses 1-13, the descent of the Holy Spirit upon the disciples and the reaction of the bystanders, and verses 14-47, an account of the earliest evangelistic preaching by Peter.

The Holy Spirit descended upon the Apostles during the celebration of Pentecost, ten days after the Ascension and fifty days after the Passover. (Pentecost, also called the Feast of the First-Fruits, was an ancient Jewish harvest festival).

Jesus had spoken of the coming of the era of the Holy Spirit (John 16:7-14). It was now inaugurated in a mighty manifestation of the Holy Spirit with sound "as of a roaring wind" and with split tongues "as of fire" upon each of the followers of Jesus. This was the opening proclamation to the world of the resurrection of Jesus. The Jews and Jewish proselytes assembled at Jerusalem for Pentecost from all the countries of the then known world (15 nations are named in 2:9-11) were on hand to receive this announcement; the Galilean Apostles spoke to them in their own languages.

Peter delivered a Spirit-inspired sermon, the first Christian missionary sermon. Peter's sermon is a model representative of apostolic preaching. It is an apostolic "proclamation," *kerygma*, (a word borrowed from the Greek word *kerysein*, meaning "to proclaim;" *kerygma* connotes "the active sense of proclaiming Jesus Christ").[9]

Peter's proclamation included four points: 1. The day of fulfillment has dawned with the coming of the Messiah; 2. the Messiah is Jesus who was unjustly crucified, but was raised from death, in accordance with the Scriptures; 3. through his resurrection, God has made Jesus "Lord" as well as "Messiah;"

4. the time of God's hoped-for-salvation of his people is here, "whoever calls upon the name of Jesus Christ will be saved ... repent, and be baptized in the name of Jesus Christ."[10]

The result of Peter's kerygmatic message was spectacular: three thousand souls repented and were baptized, giving rise to the new-born Church. This was also the beginning of communal life among the earliest Christians in Jerusalem. The earliest Christian community was characterized by the fellowship of all believers sharing together, "devoting themselves to the apostles' teaching and fellowship, to the breaking of bread and prayers" (2:41-42). Luke also reports that the believers sold their possessions so that money and goods could be distributed according to individual members' needs (2:43-45).

b. *The Growth of the Church: Work of Peter and the Apostles* (3:1-42). The early followers of Christ wrought miracles of healing evidencing the power of the risen Lord. Peter's healing a lame man by invoking Jesus' authority (3:1-10) demonstrated that the disciples continued their Master's work. The healing of the crippled man at the gate of the Temple, his attribution of this miracle to the power of the risen Christ, and his second sermon to the crowd (3:11-26), led to Peter's first serious clash with Jewish authorities. The priests and the captain of the temple and the Sadducees arrested Peter and John, held them overnight, and at a hearing the next morning, forbade them "to speak or teach at all in the name of Jesus" (4:17). The Apostles were released and resumed their teaching and healing in Solomon's Colonnade (5:12). Once again, they were arrested and put in jail. But during the night an angel of the Lord opened the door of the jail, and at daybreak they entered the temple courts and began preaching (5:17-41). Peter and his friends were brought before the Sanhedrin. The High Priest told them, "We gave you strict orders not to teach in the name of Jesus." To which Peter replied, "We must obey God rather than men!" The members of the Sanhedrin were so enraged they wanted to kill Peter and his friends. Protection came from an expected source: Gamaliel, a rabbinical scholar. He told his fellow Council members, "Leave these men alone. If their purpose or activity is of human origin, it will fail. But if it is from God, you will not be able to stop these men; you will only find yourselves fighting against God" (5:38).

c. *Persecution of the Hellenist Jewish Christians: Appointment of the Seven* (6:1-6). Accompanying the growth of the church in Jerusalem, tensions developed within the community itself, a tension based on traditional lines between Jerusalem (or Aramaic-speaking) Jews and the diaspora (Greek-speaking Jews). The Hellenists were Jews from the diaspora who were now living in Jerusalem. Many such Hellenists returned to Jerusalem in their later years to die and be buried by Mount Zion. Since they were not native in Jerusalem, when they died their widows had no regular means of sustenance. These widows were cared for by daily subsidies; this care caused a considerable economic strain in Jerusalem. Apparently there was a cleavage within the membership of the church. When the collections were taken, the widows of the Palestinian Jews were given help, but the widows of Hellenist Jews were discriminated against. That kind of discrimination created tensions, hostilities, and complaints.

The twelve disciples called the people together and told them to elect seven members to organize and supervise the collection and fair distribution of funds to the needy. Thus they elected seven men headed by Stephen.

In this action, two things were important: first, this was the first organizational committee set up in the Christian church, virtually the first Board of Deacons, to translate the love of Christ into practical ministry to meet human need. Second, implicit in this action there was the first step in breaking the bondage of the Church to exclusiveness of the Palestinian Jews in the Church; Hellenistic Jews of the Church were to be treated with the same concern as Palestinian Jews in the Church. It is interesting to note that all seven members of the Board of Deacons had Greek names, and one of them, Nicolaus, the proselyte of Antioch, was a Gentile. Christianity was beginning to reach out to the whole world.

2. The Extension of the Church: Judea and Samaria (6:8-9:31). This section depicts the gradual extension of the Church beyond the confines of Jerusalem. Luke focuses on three men: Stephen, Philip, and Paul. Each one is a preacher to a different group of people: Jews, Samaritans, and Gentiles.

    a. *The Martyrdom of Stephen* (6:8-8:1). Stephen was the first head deacon of the Church. He first appears not as an administrator or a supervisor of the Church's collections, but as a wonder worker and especially as a debator, incurring the hostility of the Jews (6:8-15). The Jews could not refute this intelligent and enthusiastic spokesman of the new faith. They got some men who would say that they had heard Stephen speak blasphemy against Moses and the Temple. They brought Stephen before the Sanhedrin and accused him of attacking the two things that were most sacred to the Jews: the Temple as the only place where sacrifices could be made and the only place where Yahweh could be truly worshipped, and the unchangeable law of Moses.

    The High Priest asked Stephen if the charges against him were true. In his response, which was mainly a recital of Old Testament history, Stephen delivered a stinging rebuke for the murder of Jesus (7:51-53). His accusers were enraged; "they were furious and gnashed their teeth at him" (7:54). They rushed upon him like wild beasts. They dragged him out of the city and hurled stones at him to kill him. It was a lynching. The Sanhedrin, before which Stephen had spoken, had no power to issue the death penalty. It was the surge of blind rage that killed Stephen.

    One of the persons watching the stoning was the most fanatical, cold-blooded persecutor of the Christians in the land, "a young man named Saul" (7:58), who guarded the garments of those stoning Stephen. This is the first reference to Saul in Acts. Here he appears as a silent witness to the death of Stephen, to which he gave his full consent: "Saul was there, giving approval to his death" (8:1). Saul was not necessarily a member of the Sanhedrin that condemned Stephen. But as a member of the Cilician synagogue (his hometown, Tarsus, was the capital of the Asia Minor province of Cilicia), he may have taken part in the original dispute, and Luke suggests that the moral consent he gave to the execution carried with it as much responsibility as the actual execution. The last words of Stephen, "Lord, do not hold this sin against them" (7:60), which echoed the last words of

Jesus on the cross, were planted in the mind of Saul, there quietly working to make him receptive to the great Vision on the road to Damascus (26:14). Stephen put the first crack in Saul's Pharasaic armor of self-righteousness and started the process by which Saul was transformed into Paul.

Stephen became the first martyr of the Christian Church. There were to be many others who would follow. It was, as church father Tertullian put it later, "the blood of the martyrs that became the seed of the church."

b. *Dispersion of the Church* (8:1-4). Luke notes that on the day of Stephen's death "a great persecution broke out against the church at Jerusalem" (8:2). Saul of Tarsus, who dragged men and women into prison (8:3), was a leader in the persecution.

This persecution resulted in the dispersion of the Church. Christians were driven out of Jerusalem; they were scattered abroad. That very disaster, however, was to be the dispersal of the seed. Once they were scattered they went about preaching the Word (8:5).

c. *The Story of Philip: Mission to Samaria and Judea* (8:4-40). The first Christian missionary seems to have been Philip, not the Philip who was among the original followers of Jesus, but a new convert, one of Stephen's Hellenist associates. He had been chosen as a deacon to look after the welfare of the church members in Jerusalem, but when they scattered following the stoning of Stephen, he also left the city (11:19).

Philip traveled up into Samaria, where he preached and performed many miracles. Among his converts was Simon Magus, a notorious purveyor of black magic (8:9-13). When the Jerusalem church heard of this phenomenon, they sent Peter and John, and only then did the Samaritans receive the Holy Spirit (8:14-17). Simon later tried to buy Peter's gift of imparting the Holy Spirit, but he was rebuked by the Apostle.

The mission to Samaria was the first geographical expansion of the Gospel carried by the Hellenists.

On another trip south of Jerusalem to Gaza, Philip baptized a "God-fearing" Ethiopian eunuch, who was on his way home from a pilgrimage to Jerusalem. Philip met him and "told him the good news of Jesus" on the basis of the Suffering Servant passage from Isaiah 53, which the eunuch had been reading when Philip encountered him (8:26 ff). Throughout this section of Acts, Luke repeatedly refers to Jesus as a "servant" (3:12, 26; 4:27, 30), the only New Testament writer to do so (compare Luke 22:26-27).[11]

From Gaza Philip made his way north along the Palestinian seaboard, evangelizing the cities on the way until he reached Caesarea. There he appears to have settled, making Caesarea a base for further evangelistic activity. It is there that we meet him twenty years later, known to his fellow Christians as "Philip the Evangelist," as well as the father of four daughters with the gift of prophecy (21:8).

d. *The Conversion of Saul* (9:1-31). Saul, who is also called Paul (Acts 13:9), was born in Tarsus, the capital city of Cilicia. His year of birth is unknown. Philemon 9 may refer to him as an "old man," but that is rather vague. According to Acts 7:58 he was a "young man" present at the stoning of Stephen.

That Tarsus in Cilicia was Paul's birthplace is mentioned only in Acts, which also mentions a popular characterization of it as "no mean city" (21:39). At that time it was also a famous center of learning.

Paul himself reports that his family belonged to the tribe of Benjamin (Phil. 3:5) and that he belonged to the party of the Pharisees. His occupation, according to Acts 18:3, was that of a "tent-maker" (the word can also mean a leather or textile worker in the broader sense), a trade common in and around Tarsus.

Luke mentions in Acts that Paul held Roman citizenship. How the Roman citizenship came into Paul's family we have no means of knowing.

According to Acts 22:3 and 26:4, Paul received his education in Jerusalem from the famous rabbi, Gamaliel. Paul describes himself as a "Pharisee of Pharisees," and a "Hebrew of Hebrews" (Phil. 3:5), and his radicalism sent him out to persecute the Christians. He himself tells us that before his conversion he was an active persecutor of the Church. In Galatians 1:13, he describes that activity as "violent," with the intent to destroy the Church.

His reputation was well known among the Christians who regarded him as a real plague upon them.

It was with this spirit and this purpose that Saul set out for Damascus to persecute the Christians there.

On the road to Damascus Saul had a dramatic encounter with the spirit of Christ which turned around his whole life and orientation. It was on the road to Damascus that he was enveloped in a brilliant light, fell to the ground, and heard the voice of Jesus. Not only was this conversion experience important as a turning point in the life of Saul of Tarsus, it was important as a turning point in history, for out of it grew the beginning of the spread of Christianity. Indeed this climactic experience confirmed the Christian Gospel for Paul, transformed him from an active persecutor of the Church to the outspoken proclaimer of its message, and made of him an unparalleled missionary.

Luke regards Paul's conversion experience as crucial and gives three lengthy accounts of it in the Book of Acts (9:1-19; 22:1-21; 26:1-23). Paul also refers to it in his own letters (I Cor. 9:1, 15:8); Gal. 1:15ff, Eph. 3:3; Phil. 3:12). In Galatians 1 Paul takes great pains to state that his status as both apostle and missionary could never depend on official commissioning by the twelve Apostles. He sees his conversion and his missionary call as inseparable. He does not seek other people's approval. He claims that the Gospel he received and now came to preach, he received through his "revelation," his encounter with Jesus (Gal. 1:12).

Upon his conversion, Paul immediately began to preach his new found faith in Damascus, where he lived on a street called Straight. He preached with conviction and energy, but the Jews of Damascus plotted to kill him. He was finally forced to escape in a basket which his friends lowered over the city wall (9:20-25).

e. *Barnabas: Paul's Sponsor* (9:26-31). Barnabas, whose original name was Joses or Joseph, was a relative of John Mark (author of the Second Gospel). He had come from Cyprus. An early convert, he had turned his wealth over to the Apostles, who had given him the surname Barnabas, which means encourager (4:36-37). It was he who "took Paul and brought him to the

Apostles" (9:27), and helped overcome the suspicion of the disciples in Jerusalem toward the new convert, Saul of Tarsus, who had been the most violent persecutor of Christians; and it was he who enlisted the Christian Paul years later and brought him to Antioch (11:25-26).

An observation should be made concerning the gaps in Luke's record relative to Paul's ministry. We tend to think that almost immediately after his conversion Paul began his missionary journeys. Actually, there is a gap of 13 years between his conversion experience and his first missionary journey. We know from his writings that he spent three years "into Arabia" (Gal. 1:17-18). There is no mention of this sojourn in the Acts. We do not know how he spent the remaining ten years. Presumably, he spent those ten years in missionary activity in Syria and Cilicia as his words suggest, "Later I went to Syria and Cilicia" (Gal. 1:21), before he was brought to Antioch by Barnabas (11:25-26).

3. The Expansion of the Church: To the Ends of the Earth (9:32-28:31). During the Period of Expansion, the Church experienced unprecedented growth. The Gospel was carried to the ends of the earth. Luke skillfully prepared the reader for the "historic transformation of Christianity from a movement within Judaism to an independent world religion."[12]

Peter is portrayed by Luke as the founder of the mission to the Gentiles, and as an advocate of the position that the Gospel can be preached to those outside the bounds of organized Judaism.

a. *Peter's Preliminary Mission* (9:32-43). After Pentecost, Peter spent some time in Jerusalem, preaching and teaching as well as providing leadership to the Apostles. His first missionary work beyond the city and its environs took him north into Samaria, accompanied by the Apostle John.

It was probably the following year that Peter, presumably alone this time, set out down the road toward Joppa, stopping in all villages along the way. In Lydda, a town between Jerusalem and Joppa, a center for rabbinical learning, he healed Aeneas who had palsy. At Joppa, he raised Tabitha, or Dorcas, from the dead, and performed other miracles that led many to believe (9:35,42).

b. *The Conversion of Cornelius* (10:1-11:18). Acts gives a lengthy account of the conversion of Cornelius and the subsequent discussion of its meaning. In chapters 10 and 11, Luke narrates the conversion of the first Gentile Christian, the Roman military officer, Cornelius.

Cornelius had a vision at Caesarea in which he was instructed to summon Peter from Joppa (10:1-8). Even while his emissaries were on the way, Peter in turn had a vision (10:9-16). After stating the purpose of their mission, Cornelius' men took Peter to Caesarea (10:17-19). Peter gave an evangelistic sermon, the result of which was spectacular: the centurion, his family, and others received Christ and were baptized (10:34-48).

When Peter returned to Jerusalem he was criticized by the Circumcision Party (Jewish Christians who strictly observed the Mosaic Law) for eating and associating with the uncircumcised men. So Peter, to justify his actions, recounted the entire course of events. Once again, he related his vision to them implying that all foods, as well as all non-Jewish people who eat them, are "clean" and acceptable to God. In Peter's words, "I now realize how true it is that God does not show favoritism but accepts men from every nation who fear him and do what is right" (10:34-35).

Using the Cornelius incident, once again Luke skillfully emphasizes the landmark significance of the mission of the Church to the Gentiles. This bold step was to be a support for the position of Peter and Paul in receiving the Gentile converts into the Church without any prerequisites and restrictions.

c. *The Church at Antioch* (11:19-26). Antioch was the third largest city of the Roman Empire with a population of five-hundred thousand. Surpassed only by Rome and Alexandria, it was the Mediterranean doorway to the great eastern highways. "Embellished with everything that Roman wealth, Greek aestheticisim, and Oriental luxury could produce, it was called 'Antioch the Beautiful—Queen of the East'." [14]

The Church at Antioch was founded after the death of Stephen by those who were scattered abroad in the persecution that followed. It consisted at first only of Jewish Christians (11:19).

Some years later, certain Christians of Cyprus and Cyrene,

possibly having heard of the reception of Cornelius into the Church, came to Antioch and began to preach to the Gentiles that they could be Christians without becoming Jewish proselytes (11:21).

The Jerusalem Church had heard of this. The Apostles dispatched Barnabas to report on the situation. Impressed by the converts' zeal, Barnabas went to Tarsus and found Paul, and brought him to Antioch to help instruct them. Paul now became an active leader in this new-born center of Gentile Christianity. It was in Antioch that "the disciples were first called Christians" (11:26); it was also the Church at Antioch that organized the first Christian relief fund for a sister church. When the Christians in Antioch heard of the famine of Jerusalem, they commissioned Barnabas and Paul to deliver their relief fund to the mother church in Jerusalem (11:27-30).

d. *Persecution Under Herod Agrippa I* (12:1-24). Herod Agrippa I, son of Aristobulus and grandson of Herod the Great, who ingratiated himself at the imperial court in Rome under Emperor Claudius, was made king over most of Palestine (41-44 A.D.). He was known for his hostile policy toward Christians in order to please the Jews (12:3). He executed one of the Twelve Apostles, James the son of Zebedee, and imprisoned another, Peter. Peter escaped from prison the night before Herod was to bring him to trial, delivered by an angel (12:1-19).

Because Herod assumed divine honors, Luke claims that "God struck him down, and he was eaten by worms and died" (12:23).

e. *First Missionary Journey of Barnabas and Paul to the Gentiles* (13:1-14:28). In Acts 13 and 14 we find the first description of missionary activity beyond Palestine and Syria. This trip, occuring in 41-48 A.D., is called Paul's First Missionary Journey; in fact, it was under the leadership of Barnabas with Saul as the second member and John Mark as an assistant. They were commissioned by the Church at Antioch (13:1-3). Antioch was the starting point of their missionary tour. Their destination was central Asia Minor. The route would have been more direct by land, going through Tarsus, but Paul had already been in Tarsus for a number of years. So they went through the island of

Cyprus; then from the west end of Cyprus north into central Asia Minor. They may have chosen Cyprus as their first destination because it was Barnabas' homeland. They preached from the east end of the island to the west end of it. One episode in the island is singled out for attention. The proconsul of Cyprus, Sergius Paulus, became a convert. Some think that Saul's admiration of this convert led him, from this point on, to use his own Roman name, Paul.

The second leg of the journey took them to Asia Minor; from Paphos of Cyprus they sailed to Perga. At Perga, John Mark deserted the team (13:13) for reasons unknown to us. There seems to have been an estrangement, between John Mark and Paul. After Perga, Paul and Barnabas traveled to Pisidia.

In Antioch of Pisidia, Paul, as was his custom, started his work in the synagogue. Many Jews and Gentiles believed, but some unbelieving Jews stirred up a persecution, and drove Paul and Barnabas out of the city (13:17-41).

They then spent considerable time in Iconium (modern Konya), about 100 miles east of Pisidian Antioch, but again they were forced to leave (14:17) and head for Lystra.

In Lystra, they were mistaken for gods in human form. The citizens of Lystra called Barnabas Jupiter (Zeus), and Paul Mercury (Hermes), but later they stoned Paul, and dragged him outside the city, thinking that he was dead (14:8-19). It was in Lystra that Timothy, son of a Jewish mother and a Greek father, was converted. He later became Paul's secretary and companion.

In Derbe, about thirty miles southeast of Lystra, they made many disciples. Then they returned through Lystra and Iconium back to Antioch.

f. *The First Church Conference in Jerusalem* (15:1-35). The First Missionary Journey of Paul was followed in 49 A.D. by the first Church Council, held in Jerusalem. The problem which here came to focus plagued the Church for some time: Should uncircumcised Gentiles be received into the Christian fellowship? The question was first raised in Caesarea when Peter converted the Roman centurion Cornelius and other Gentiles. The Apostles and elders were convinced circumcision was unnecessary (11:18), yet a small minority, the Judaizing Party, persisted in teaching that Gentile converts be circumcised and observe Jewish dietary regulations. The great success of Barnabas' and Paul's missionary work in converting large numbers of Gentiles not only revived the issue but also brought the Church to its first major crisis.

The Judaizers of Antioch and Jerusalem were basing their argument on the Hebrew Bible. According to Genesis 17:9-14, circumcision is required of all Israelite males if they are to be a part of the covenant community. They insisted that a Gentile believer must first become a Jew in order to become a Christian. Barnabas and Paul strongly opposed this view (15:1-2).

The first church conference at Jerusalem was to decide the issue. Initiating the conference, Antioch sent delegates, including Paul and Barnabas, to Jerusalem, and the Apostles and Elders investigated the problem, allowing the two sides to debate the issue.

Representing Palestinian apostolic authority, Peter vehemently opposed the Judaizer's position citing his own key role in bringing Gentiles into the Church (15:7-11). Similarly, Barnabas and Paul effectively pleaded their case for the Gentiles (15:12).

Finally, it was James (Jesus' brother) who decided the issue and persuaded the conference to adopt his resolution that no restrictions be imposed upon Gentile converts except the commands "to abstain from food polluted by idols, from sexual immorality, from the meat of strangled animals and from blood" (15:20).

Following the Jerusalem Conference, the Apostles and Elders, with the whole church, sent Judas Barsabbas and Silas to accompany Paul and Barnabas back to Antioch to deliver the Council's verdict (15:22-29).

Apparently, this important Apostolic Decree did not relieve all contention. Paul's report in his Letter to Galatians reveals he was unwilling to make any compromise to the Judaizers (Gal. 2:1-10); he states, "we did not give in to them for a moment, so that the truth of the Gospel might remain with you" (Gal. 2:5). It seems that there is a discrepancy between Galatians 2 and Acts 15. According to Galatians 2, Paul accepted no restrictions, whereas according to Acts 15, he willingly complied to the resolutions (i.e., legal prohibitions) of the Jerusalem Conference. Some scholars find these differing accounts irreconcilable; but since "Paul's is a contemporary witness and Acts was written many years after the event," [15] they prefer Paul's version. The differences between these two accounts is simply a matter of perspective. The author of Acts did not write to preserve an accurate record of the doctrinal disputes that divided the early Church but to idealize the Church's unity and cooperation in spite of differences. As a historian writing to the Graeco-Roman world, Luke does not involve himself in the theological intricacies of the Jewish Torah, and minimizes the existing pluralism and at times dissension of the early Church.

g. *Paul's Quarrel With Barnabas Over John Mark* (15:31-41). After their return from the Jerusalem Conference, Paul and Barnabas remained in Antioch for some time doing evangelistic work (15:35). Then Paul proposed to embark on a second journey to "visit the brethren in every city where we proclaimed the word of the Lord" (15:36). Barnabas wanted to take John Mark. Paul refused because Mark had deserted his friends during their First Missionary Journey (Acts 13:3). Paul's rejection of John Mark led to a "sharp disagreement" causing a break between Paul and Barnabas.

h. *Paul's Second Missionary Journey: Mission to Greece* (16:1-18:17).   Upon his estrangement from Barnabas, Paul launched on what is generally known as his "Second Missionary Journey." This journey was three years in length—49-52 A.D. Paul was in command. He was accompanied by Silas, and later by Timothy and Luke.

Little is known of Silas. He first appears as one of the leaders of the Judean Church (15:22, 27, 32). Like Paul, he was a Jew and a Roman citizen (16:21, 37). He was also called Sylvanus.

At Lystra Paul found Timothy, son of a Greek father and a Christian Jewish mother (16:1; II Tim. 1:5). To please the Jews, Paul circumcised Timothy before taking him on his Second Missionary Journey (16:3).

On his way to Ephesus, somewhere on the high plateau of Asia Minor, Paul faced a crucial question as to which way was he to go next. He turned northward into Bithynia, "where the

Spirit of Jesus would not allow them" to go (16:7). Then he turned northwest, and came to Troas, where a divine vision revealed to him that they should go to Macedonia "to preach the Gospel to them" (16:10). This was a most fateful decision whose dramatic significance cannot be underestimated. For the first time the Gospel was being exported westward into regions destined to become part of modern Europe.

At Troas (ancient Troy), Luke joined Paul's missionary team. Beginning with verse 10, notice in the book the usage of the so-called "we" passages—a change from the third person to eyewitness narrative in the more intimate first person.

In Philippi, a city of eastern Macedonia, Paul established the first Christian Church in Europe (16:11-15), and the Philippian Church became his favorite church (20:6; Philipp. 4:16; II Cor. 11:9). In Philippi, Paul and Silas were accused of illegally converting Romans to Judaism. They were wrongfully flogged and imprisoned. At night Paul and Silas were praying and singing hymns to God, and the prisoners were listening to them (16:25). Freakish earthquakes were common in this region, and, when we consider wooden-beam dungeons of the period, there is no reason to question the facts of the dramatic story of how the earthquake opened the doors of the prison and how the chains and stocks were detached from the wall.[16] Filled with a shuddering fear that the prisoners had escaped, the jailer was ready to commit suicide. The responsible action of his prisoners had a great impact on his life. When the jailer asked, "What shall I do to be saved?" the reply was: "Believe in the Lord Jesus, and you will be saved" (16:30-31).

Philippi's legal authorities released Paul and Silas, finding that not only did they have no case against them but that they had violated the civil rights of these Roman citizens. The authorities apologized for this flagrant violation (16:35-40).

Luke remained behind while Paul, Silas, and Timothy went to Thessalonica, which was the capital of the province and, like modern Salonika, a flourishing commercial city with a good port.[17] Paul labored valiantly there, preaching three days in the synagogue and winning many converts, including Greeks. However, persecution forced his missionary team on. They traveled southwest another fifty miles to Berea. There he met with considerable success (17:10-15).

Leaving Silas and Timothy in Berea, Paul continued to Athens, the cultural center of philosophy, literature, science, and art, seat of the greatest university of the ancient world.[18]

Paul's efforts in Athens seem to have borne little fruit. The most noteworthy event of his visit in this pagan city was his famous speech at Areopagus (in English, "Mars Hill"), a bare rock on the slope just below the Parthenon, which held in full view "the superb statues and temples which symbolized the older glory of Helenic culture and the old religion."[19] In the open-air court in front of the rock, where speakers came and expressed their views, Paul spoke to the Greek thinkers. He identified the "unknown god" of Athenians as the Judeo-Christian Creator. Only a few among Paul's audience were converted and baptized; others, however "sneered" and did not appreciate his message (18:32-34). Considering the less than enthusiastic reception of Paul's speech, and the fact that there is no reference to a Christian church at Athens in the New Testament time, it would seem that the results of Paul's missionary endeavors were not very successful ln the Greek capital.

From Athens Paul moved on to Corinth, the great commercial port through which passed the traffic between the two major sections of Greece. Corinth was the capital of the province of Achaia and notorious for its wealth, gaudy vice, and houses of prostitution.

In Corinth, Paul found two Jewish compatriots, Aquila and his wife, Priscilla, recently forced to leave Rome by Claudius' edict of 49 A.D. He was glad to join these fellow craftsmen and pay his way as a "tent maker." After a short time, however, Silas and Timothy returned from Macedonia bringing gifts from the converts there. This enabled Paul to devote himself entirely to his ministry. This ministry was carried on for some weeks in the synagogue, until trouble began when the Corinthian Jews "opposed Paul and became abusive" (18:6). One of his converts, a Gentile Christian named Titius Justus, placed his home at Paul's disposal. Thus the number of believers continually increased.

The Jews in Corinth intensified their attacks on Paul "and brought him into court" (18:12). At that time the governor (proconsul) of Achaia was the newly appointed Gallio. Historians tell us that he was the elder brother of the philosopher Seneca, prime minister to the infamous Nero. An inscription in Delphi places the term of Gallio between 51-53 A.D.[20] The practical value of the mention of his name is that it gives us one of the few precise dates in Paul's ministry. Gallio dismissed the case, and ejected the accusers of Paul from the court (18:17).

Legally exonerated, Paul and his companions spent several more months in Corinth, establishing the Christian community which they had planted in that unpromising city.

i. *Paul's Third Missionary Journey: Revisiting Asia Minor* (18:19-20:38). Realizing at length that there was much territory yet to be covered, Paul embarked on another missionary journey. Taking Aquila and Priscilla as traveling companions, Paul sailed to Ephesus, some two hundred fifty miles directly east. Ephesus was at this time the greatest commercial city of Asia Minor (the western part of modern Turkey). Standing on one of the main routes from Rome to the eastern provinces, it enjoyed political as well as economic importance. It had an ethnically mixed population and a great variety of religious cults. It also housed the famous Temple of Artemis (Diana), a fertility goddess not related to the Diana, chaste huntress, of Greek and Roman mythology. Ephesus also had a sizable Jewish community maintaining a large synagogue.[21]

The existence in Ephesus of a dozen disciples of John the Baptist is regarded by some scholars as evidence that the movement founded by him had not died.[22] Luke points out that baptism in the name of Jesus is superior to that of "John's baptism."

Furthermore, Luke illustrates the superiority of Christianity by contrasting Paul's ability to heal with the inability of some Jewish "competitors" (19:13-14).

In Ephesus, Paul's success in converting Ephesians brought him into conflict with the worshippers of Artemis. The Greek silversmiths of Ephesus, who fashioned images of the goddess of Diana for sale to the tourists, tried to force Paul to stop his anti-idolatry campaign which was hurting their business. Once again, the local authorities (this time a city clerk) argued that the Ephesian protesters had no legal ground to do so (19:23-41).

With a schoolroom, the "Lecture Hall of Tyrannus" (19:9) as his headquarters, Paul labored in Ephesus for two or three years, speaking publicly and going door to door (20:20), day and night (20:30). He maintained himself by working at his own trade (20:34). He made many converts, especially among the Gentiles and had many friends among the leading people. His Ephesian ministry was one of the most important phases of his apostolic career. Referring to his ministry in Ephesus, Paul writes to the Corinthians, "But I will stay on in Ephesus until Pentecost, because a great door for effective work has opened to me, and there are many who oppose me" (I Cor. 16:8-9).

Having begun his work at Antioch, "east end of the backbone of the Roman Empire," now having done his greatest work at Ephesus, "center of the Empire's backbone,"[23] and having made known the story of Christ all over Asia Minor, Greece, and Macedonia, Paul now planned to complete his last tour by heading for Rome, the imperial capital (19:21-22). But first a very important charitable duty demanded his attention.

He had collected funds from the Gentile churches in Macedonia and Greece to help the poor Christians in Jerusalem. He wanted to take these funds to the Mother Church in Jerusalem. Leaving Ephesus, Paul headed for Macedonia and Greece, where he stayed three months (21:1-2). As he was setting out to sail to Syria, he learned of a plot by the Jews to kill him. So he changed his plans to return to Macedonia (20:3).

Several coworkers traveled with him to Philippi in Macedonia. Then they sailed across to Troas, where they stayed for a week. It was there that a man named Eutychus fell from the third floor of a building during Paul's lengthy evening discourse. He was picked up dead and miraculously restored to life by the Apostle (20:9-10).

Paul and his companions made their way down the island-studded coast of the province of Asia stopping at Assos, Mitylene, Samos, and finally at Miletus, which was about thirty-six miles from Ephesus. Paul called the Ephesian church elders to meet him at the little seaport of Miletus. There, Paul delivered a farewell speech, predicting his imminent imprisonment (20:17-38).

j. *Paul's Arrest in Jerusalem and Imprisonment in Caesarea* (21:1-26:32). Though warned of the danger, Paul was determined to preach the Gospel in Jerusalem (the capital of Judaism) and Rome (the capital of paganism) (19:21). From the start of the journey, he was warned of future persecution. In every city the Holy Spirit warned him that he faced persecution (20:23). The disciples in Tyre warned him (21:4). In Caesarea, while he was at Philip's house, the warning was repeated with graphic emphasis (21:10-11). Even Luke pleaded with him not to go (21:12).

As Luke had pictured Jesus turning his face resolutely toward Jerusalem (Luke 9:51), so he shows Paul doing the same thing.

Leaving Miletus, Paul now set off again toward the south, the boat making stops at the islands of Coos (Cos) and Rhodes. From Rhodes he and his party went to Patara on the Lycian mainland. Here they changed from a small coasting boat to a larger ship. The next stop was Tyre, a wealthy Phoenician seaport. After a week's stay, the ship continued to Ptolemais, and then to Caesarea. There Paul and his companions were entertained by Philip the Evangelist. It was here that a prophet named Agabus foretold that the Jews at Jerusalem would arrest him. Despite this, Paul could not be dissuaded.

Why was Paul so adamant in spite of a number of unmistakable warnings? There might have been many reasons. One reason was to deliver the offering of the money which he had gathered from the Gentile churches in Greece and Asia Minor for the poor Christians in Jerusalem (24:17; Rom. 15:25-26; I Cor. 16:1-4; II Cor. 9:1-15). The Apostle had spent over a year gathering this "crowning demonstration of the spirit of brotherly kindness, to encourage a feeling of Christian love between Jew and Gentile."[24]

Another purpose of the journey was to keep a vow (21:24). Still another could have been an express willingness on Paul's part to die in Jerusalem, in the same city where he himself had martyred many Christians.

Perhaps, too, Paul was impelled "to put forth a last, courageous effort to win over those of the Jerusalem leaders whose emissaries had opposed him for years, and thus to remove the chief obstacle to Christian solidarity."[25]

Paul and his companions finally arrived in Jerusalem and were welcomed by James and his fellow elders (21:17-19). The leadership of the Jerusalem church was grateful for the Gentiles' gift, but was concerned about rumors that Paul had encouraged Jewish Christians to give up their Jewish heritage, i.e. the observance of their ancestral customs. To offset these rumors, James "the Lord's brother," who held a preeminent position in the Jerusalem church, asked Paul to demonstrate his own continuing fidelity to Judaic customs by taking part with certain others in a Nazarite vow at the Temple (21:23-26). Paul must have followed the suggestion of James and the elders of the church, perhaps reluctantly.

After he had been in Jerusalem nearly a week, certain Jews recognized him and stirred up the whole crowd. They arrested him and dragged him from the Temple. Hostile mobs arrived from all directions. If the Roman tribune (commanding about one thousand soldiers) had not intervened, Paul would certainly have been lynched (21:30-32).

The tribune suspected that Paul was the Egyptian-Jewish revolutionary who, some time earlier, had marched on Jerusalem with four thousand followers in an attempt to take over Jerusalem.[26] Paul's Greek speech led the tribune to realize his mistake, and Paul was able to gain his consent to address the mob (21: 37-38).

On the stairway of the same castle where Pilate condemned Jesus about a quarter of a century earlier, Paul delivered a speech to the mob in which he told the story of Christ's appearance to him on the road to Damascus. They listened until he mentioned the words, "The Lord said to me, 'Go; I will send you far away to the Gentiles,' " at which the crowd broke !oose again (22:1-22).

The next day, Paul was brought before the Sanhedrin. Disclosing that he was a Pharisee, Paul succeeded in dividing the Jewish Council so that scribes of his party called for his release while the Sadducees and others denounced him (23:1-10).

Sometime during the following night Paul had another vision. The Apostle became convinced that "the Lord stood by him" and that he would indeed be given the opportunity "to testify in Rome," as he did in Jerusalem (23:11). But Paul's enemies sought to circumvent justice. Forty men planned to kill him, but the son of Paul's sister heard of the ambush and tipped him off (23:12-22). Under the cover of darkness the Roman officer, Claudius Lysias, transferred Paul to Caesarea, Roman administrative capital of Palestine. Also a letter was dispatched to the governor Antonius Felix, turning the whole matter over to him (23:23-35).

Despite violent allegations, Felix did not take the charges against Paul too seriously. He did defer judgment—hoping, according to Luke, to receive a bribe for acquitting him. While in prison, Paul enjoyed reasonable amount of freedom, with privilege of visitors, even. Occasionally, Felix and his Jewish wife, Druscilla, summoned Paul for religious conversation (24: 23-27).

In 59 A.D., Felix was recalled, and was succeeded by Festus. The new governor reopened the case. But when he spoke of holding the inquiry in Jerusalem, Paul became alarmed lest the new governor's inexperience might put him into the power of his enemies. Knowing that would certainly mean his death, Paul exercised his prerogative as a Roman citizen to appeal his case to Caesar (25 :1-12).

Before he could start on his way to stand trial in Rome, Paul was forced to appear before a visiting dignitary, King Herod Agrippa II (great-grandson of Herod the Great) and his sister and mistress, Bernice. Since Festus was married to Druscilla, another of King Agrippa's sisters, the Apostle confronted "a ruling family in which the power of Rome and Jewish royalty were combined."[27] Even Agrippa admitted that the prisoner had committed no crime and "could have been set free had he not already appealed to Caesar" (26: 32).

    k. *Paul's Voyage to Rome and His Ministry in Rome* (27 :1- 28: 31). Luke begins the final section of Acts with the dramatic details of Paul's adventurous voyage to Rome. Verse 1 of chapter 27 begins the last of the "we" sections of the book. Once again, the author impressively demonstrates his abilities as a story teller and historian.

It was apparently early in the fall of 60 A.D. that Paul started on this voyage. He made it in three different ships: one from Caesarea to Myra, another from Myra to Melita (Malta), and the third from Melita to Puteoli. After leaving Myra, they ran into fierce adverse winds, were driven off course, and, after many days, when all hope was gone, the Lord's angel assured them that not a single soul among them would suffer death (27:13-25).

As always in Acts, Luke is primarily interested in presenting Paul as a messenger to the Gentiles. In this tumultuous sea traveling experience Paul is looked at in the same light: although a prisoner perhaps destined for conviction and death, in time of danger Paul assumes leadership among 276 frightened crew and passengers aboard the ship, comforting and assuring them that eventually they will arrive to their destination safely. Indeed, as he had prophesied, they all survived the ordeal unscathed.

On his way to Rome, Paul did mission work for three months in the island of Melita (Malta), whose population proved to be most kind and hospitable. Paul performed many miraculous deeds of healing their sick and gained special honor with them (28:1-10). He also spent a week with a group of Christians in the port city of Puteoli (a few miles west of the modern city of Naples).

When, at long last, Paul arrived in Rome, he was kept under house arrest, but enjoyed considerable freedom to receive visitors and preach "without hindrance" (28:31). In Rome it was "to the Jews first" that he proclaimed the Gospel. In spite of all the hardships he experienced at the hands of his compatriots, three days after arriving in Rome Paul "called together the local leaders of the Jews" (28:17) and told them of his motive: "It is because of the hope of Israel that I am bound with this chain" (28:20). Unable to go to the synagogue, Paul encouraged the Jews to come to his house where "from morning to evening" he attempted "to convince them about Jesus" (28:23-24). Once again, there was a mixed reception. Some accepted Christ; others resisted the preaching of the Messiah. Ancient church traditions report that Paul wrote four of his letters during this period of imprisonment in Rome: to the Philippians, to the Colossians, to Philemon, and to the Ephesians.

Luke concludes his history of the early church with Paul's arrival in Rome, where he lived "for two whole years in his own rented house" under custody (28:30). We do not know why Luke's narrative stops here. The author does not reveal Paul's ultimate fate. Did his case come to trial, or was it allowed to lapse? Was he convicted or acquitted? One tradition states that Paul was acquitted and carried out his cherished plan to visit Spain (Rom. 15:24,28), "a trip to the West supported by a letter of Clement of Rome to Corinth in 96 A.D."[28] Others, referring to his presence in Crete and in Nicopolis and Asia Minor (Tit. 3:12), conclude that he returned to the East after his confinement in Rome.[29] According to many biblical scholars, he was executed about 62 A.D., following Emperor Nero's order to impose the death penalty on anyone suspected of undermining his supreme authority.[30] Some early church historians like Origen and Eusebius date Paul's death at about 64 or 65 A.D., and suggest that Paul was beheaded and Peter crucified during Nero's persecution.[31]

References

1   H. J. Cadbury, *The Making of Luke-Acts* (New York: The Macmillan Co., 1927), p. 2.
2   Stephen L. Harris, *The New Testament: A Student's Introduction* (Mountain View, California. Mayfield Publishing Co., 1988), pp. 180-181.
3   G.H.C. Macgregor, "Introduction and Exegesis of Acts," *The Interpreter's Bible* (New York and Nashville: Abingdon Press, 1954), Vol. 9, pp. 15-17.
4   Vernon A. Loescher, *The Needlepoint Panels—Book of Acts* (New York: F.C.C.) 1975, p. 4; Macgregor, p. 15; Cadbury, p. 3.
5   Loescher, p. 4.
6   Gordon D. Fee & Douglas Stuart, *How to Read the Bible for All Its Worth* (Grand Rapids, Michigan: Zondervan Publishing House, 1982), p. 92.
7   Macgregor, p. 31.
8   Harris, pp. 182-183.
9   James Price, *The New Testament* (New York: Macmillan Publishing Co., 1987), p. 70.
10 J. Jeremias, *Jerusalem in the Time of Jesus* (Philadelphia: Fortress, 1967), pp. 58-69.
11 Harris, p. 186.
12 I*bid*.
13 Henry H. Halley, *Bible Handbook* (Grand Rapids, Michigan: Zondervan Publishing House, 1959), p. 524.
14 Loescher, p. 2; Halley, p. 525.

15. F.J.F. Jackson and Kirsopp Lake, eds. *The Beginnings of Christianity* (London: Macmillan & Co., 1920-33), vol II, p. 154.
16. Price, p. 288.
17. W. M. Ramsay, *St. Paul the Traveler and the Roman Citizen* (London: Hodder and Staughton, 1896), p. 89.
18. Martin Dibelius, *Studies in the Acts of the Apostles.* Edited by H. Greeven. Translated by M. Ling (New York: Charles Scribner's Sons, 1956), p. 96.
19. Chamberlin and Feldman (Ed.) *The Dartmouth Bible* (Boston: Houghton Mifflin Co., 1961), p. 1037.
20. F.F. Bruce, *New Testament History* (Garden City, New York: Doubleday & Co., Inc., 1980), pp. 315-316.
21. Chamberlin and Feldman, p. 1038.
22. Jackson and Lake, p. 238.
23. Halley, p 530.
24. Halley, p. 531.
25. Chamberlin and Feldman, p. 1041.
26. *Ibid.*
27. Harris, p. 194.
28. Chamberlin and Feldman, p. 1041.
29. Halley, p. 535.
30. Harris, p. 195.
31. Bruce, p. 367.

PART 4

THE EPISTLES

A. MAJOR PAULINE EPISTLES

The twenty-one Epistles constitute almost a third of the New Testament. Although two-thirds of them are ascribed to Paul, the majority of scholars accept nine as unquestionably Pauline: Romans, I and II Corinthians, Galatians, Philippians, I and II Thessalonians, Philemon, and Colossians. Scholars are divided over the Pauline authorship of Ephesians and some believe that Titus, I and II Timothy were written after Paul's death by one of his followers.[1]

Paul was the first of the Christian leaders in the early Church to use epistles, or letters, to propagate the Christian faith. Paul was acquainted with excellent examples of letter writing, for the practice of writing letters was common in the Roman Empire. It was an established literary form.

Paul followed the accepted Hellenistic literary form. The Hellenistic letter writer typically began with a prescript, identifying the writer and the reader, and a greeting, wishing the reader well and commonly invoking the blessing of a god. As was customary in Graeco-Roman correspondence, Paul dictated either to professional penmen or to his own travel comrades, adding at the end a signature and a few words in his own hand. The scribe did not record the words precisely but merely paraphrased the gist of what was said (Rom. 16:21-22; Gal. 6:11; Col. 4:18).

In the light of the Epistles he wrote, Paul is revealed as a great theologian, a vigorous campaigner, a competent administrator, a powerful teacher, and a skillful debater. To his contemporaries his letters were "weighty and forceful" (II Cor. 10:10).

Paul's letters were to communicate his messages primarily

to the churches in Europe and Asia Minor. They were substitutes for his own presence; they were written communications in the absence of verbal ones, to meet specific needs in the churches, to instruct, to warn against, to inspire, and to scold.

Paul had no idea that the letters he wrote would some day be part of a collection of writings called the New Testament. He wrote them for specific purposes at specific times. They were incidental to his missionary work. They became authoritative Scripture many decades after his death.

Paul wrote letters so effectively that he made this literary category the standard medium of communication for many later Christian writers. Other New Testament authors imitated Paul by conveying their ideas in letter form.[2]

1. ROMANS

More like a theological argument than any other book in the New Testament, Romans was written from Corinth sometime between 56-58 A.D. Romans is generally regarded as the most important epistle Paul wrote. It is his most theological and doctrinal piece, and it is the first great theological formulation of Christianity. It had great influence on St. Augustine, one of the greatest church fathers, and all who, in turn, were influenced by Augustine. It has had enormous influence from the time of the early church to our present day.

In Romans Paul is revealed in three lights: a profound theologian, a man of great inner faith, and a great Christian statesman. He is revealed as a highly committed Christian who finds his vital roots in his personal relationship with Jesus Christ and who is striving to bring East and West, Jew and Gentile, together in the Kingdom of God.

Paul wrote this epistle for two reasons: First, it was meant to be a substitute for a personal visit to Rome. Paul's pioneer work in the East was pretty well completed. Churches had been founded in the Holy Land, in Asia Minor, and in Greece. The focal point of the Roman Empire was Rome, and Paul had set his sights toward Rome and westward. He intended to visit the Christians in the Imperial City, but his cherished dream was to be forgone, for he had to take the rather sizable offering for the poor back to Jerusalem (II Cor. 8:14). So instead of going to Rome, he wrote this letter.

Second, Paul remembered the problems which had plagued the churches in Galatia and Corinth—the misunderstandings, the abuses, and the divisions which had occurred—and he wanted the Roman Church and those churches which would be born in the West to avoid the mistakes of the Eastern churches.

Out of these motivations Paul wrote one of his longest and most comprehensive epistles of the new religion—a forceful doctrinal statement of the Christian Faith.

One of the basic themes of the Epistle is the revelation of a "righteousness from God" in the Gospel (1:16,17). God's righteousness is His spiritual character as well as His moral power. It is manifested in history and in the life of individuals, through such acts of grace as the sending of Jesus Christ and through such expressions of wrath as the punishment of sinners.

The Epistle to the Romans may be divided into the following eight parts:

1. Introduction (1:1-17)
2. The Evidence for the Need of God's Righteousness: Condemnation (1:18-3:20)
3. The Method of Attaining God's Righteousness: Justification (3:21-5:21)
4. The Method of Appropriating God's Righteousness: Sanctification (6:1-8:39)
5. The Explanation of God's Righteousness in Relation to Israel (9:1-11:36).
6. The Guidelines for Applying God's Righteousness: Christian Ethics and Conduct (12:1-15:13).
7. Paul's Future Plans and Personal Remarks (15:14-33)
8. Appendix: Letter Recommending Phoebe, a Christian Woman serving as deaconess of the Cenchreae Church (16:1-27)

1. Introduction (1:1-17) Paul opens his Epistle to the Romans with a long and formal salutation, including a creedal statement as well as an affirmation of his apostleship as the result of God's direct call (1:1-17).

After extending his customary thanksgiving, Paul introduces the theme of the letter: the revelation of the righteousness of God. Paul's term *righteousness (dikaiosyné) of God* refers to how God acts and relates to human history. God's righteousness is revealed and appropriated by faith.

2. The Evidence for the Need of God's Righteousness: Condemnation (1:18-3:20). After introducing his theme, the revelation of God's righteousness (1:17), Paul turns to the revelation of God's wrath (1:18). Both terms, *righteousness* and *wrath*, are eschatological. Within the eschatology of ancient Judaism, both righteousness and wrath were associated with a day of judgment, when God would bring human history to a climactic conclusion. What Paul says is that evil is self-destructive and judgment of evil is part of God's moral government of the universe.[3]

In this section, Paul first speaks of the unrighteousness of the Gentiles: the *reasons* for (1:18-23) and the *results* of (1:24-32) their condemnation. It is not as if the Gentiles had no access to knowledge of God, rather they lacked a proper acknowledgement, i.e., "they did not honor Him" (v. 21) and they "worshipped and served created things rather than the Creator" (v. 25).

Paul cites the example of homosexuality. He attributes the homosexual love affairs that characterized Greek and Roman cultures to the Gentile practice of idolatry. For him idolatry, serving and worshiping the creature rather than the Creator, is literally a perversion or an inversion of the natural order of things, a rebellion against the divine will.

Then Paul speaks of the unrighteousness of the Jews: *principles* (2:1-16) and *reasons* (2:17-3:8) of God's judgment. The idea that God shows no partiality (2:11) means that the Jew is brought to judgment on the same basis as the Gentile (2:12-16).

According to Paul, despite their advantage as the recipients and bearers of God's law, a fact that gives them an initial advantage over the pagans, the Jews have not lived to the Torah's high standards. They have not achieved justification before God any more than the Gentiles have.

Consequently, all men, both Jews and Gentiles, are sinners. Humanity stands in a state of universal sinfulness. People sin willingly. There is no distinction between the Jews and Gentiles in so far as their culpability is concerned, "for all have sinned and fall short of the glory of God" (v. 23).

3. The Method of Attaining God's Righteousness: Justification (3:21-5:21). Although God has every reason to punish humanity, he is a merciful and compassionate God. The evidence of this grace is Jesus Christ, whose Crucifixion reveals God's righteousness and his power for salvation (1:16).

Man is incapable of saving himself; redemption is possible only through the sacrificial death of Jesus Christ. The revelation of God's righteousness does not come through the law. Neither is this righteousness gained through works of the law. God's saving act in Christ is appropriated grace, unmerited love, which is received by faith. Faith is not the intellectual acceptance of a body of doctrine but receiving the grace of God in trust and self-commitment and accepting Christ as Savior and Lord. The end result is justification or salvation, which is God's act of acquitting man and releasing him from the bondage of sin. Elements of this process are *propitiation*, the blood offering of Jesus for the remission of sins, and *redemption*, the ransoming of mankind from sin, "like a benefactor's payment for the freedom of a slave."[4]

Speaking of justification by faith, Paul uses Abraham to illustrate his point. Abraham is the model of one justified by faith. Long before the Mosaic Law was given, faith was made the means by which God justified man. Indeed Abraham's faith in God "was counted to him as righteousness." Abraham is the progenitor not only of Jews but of believing Gentiles as well. Paul sees Abraham's faith as a "general prototype of specifically Christian faith and the righteousness reckoned to him as a model of that which the Christian receives by faith—that is, apart from works."[5]

Paul further explores his doctrine of justification by faith and its resulting freedom for the Christian. A believer's faith in the saving power of Christ's sacrificial death reconciles him to God. Reconciliation is the "peace of God" attained by man when, so long alienated by sin from God, he receives the indwelling Spirit.

Paul contrasts Adam, whose disobedience introduced sin and death into the world, with Christ, whose perfect obedience brings life to all who believe (5:12-21).

4. The Method of Appropriating God's Righteousness: Sanctification (6:1-8:39). In the first part of chapter six, Paul answers a question about God's grace. If the believer receives grace in proportion to the sin he commits, why should he not go on sinning to increase God's outpouring of grace? Apparently there were some Christians in Rome who were acting as if freedom from the Law entitled them to behave irresponsibly. Paul maintains that freedom imparted by God's grace does not confer liberty to continue sinning. A Christian must die to sin and rise to "newness of life" (6:8-11). That is what baptism is all about. Baptism symbolizes a believer dying to sin and thereafter freed from it. Of course, sin continues to exist as a reality, but the believer is no longer under sin's dominion.

Paul, therefore, exhorts his readers not to let sin reign over them (6:12), not to yield themselves to sin (6:13), but, rather, to yield themselves to God as instruments of righteousness (6:14).

Paul then answers a question regarding the place of the Law in a person's salvation. The question is: if we are no longer under the Law, then why was the Law given? Paul states that it was given as a preparatory measure to educate man to see his need of a Savior. The Law serves to increase man's consciousness of sin and need for grace. It makes him know the difference between right and wrong (7:7).

Paul then engages in a long discussion of the struggle between man's carnal and spiritual natures (7:7-25). His use of personal pronouns has given rise to an unsettled controversy. Is he remembering his old life under the Torah, or is he speaking of Christian experience as a whole? Perhaps both. He must have felt powerful impulses within his nature against which he had a continuous desperate struggle. Paul contends that life is a conflict between what is intended and what is actually accomplished (7:13,21).

Speaking of the new life in Christ, Paul discusses the indwelling Spirit of Christ in the believer's life (8:1-17). Delivered by faith from sin and death, the Christian lives by the Spirit, which makes him or her like Jesus, a child of God (8:14-17). In Christ, believers not only have their sins forgiven, but there is also an impartation of a new divine life from Christ born anew in our natural life from Adam!

In Paul's view the Spirit is both the life-giving power and the ethical guide for the believer's life. Those who live by the Spirit live out of God's resources rather than their own and are able to break free from the power of the flesh.[6]

Christians have an obligation to walk after the Spirit depending wholly on Christ and growing in Christ (8:12-17). This is what *sanctification* is all about—growth in grace, the continuing process in which "justified" and "reconciled" men increasingly approach Christlikeness.[7]

The whole creation, including ourselves, waits in eager expectation for a better order of existence, to be revealed in the day of God's complete redemption. It is a grand conception of the work of Christ (8:18-25).

Paul uses mystical language to describe not only human nature but the physical cosmos itself struggling and wailing, as if in childbirth, to be set free from the chains of mortality (8:22-23). Both the cosmos and the "children of God" have hope of regeneration through Jesus' redemptive sacrifice.[8] If they are Christ's, no power on earth or in heaven or in hell can separate them from the inviolable love of Christ (8:31-39).

5. The Explanation of God's Righteousness in Relation to Israel (9:1-11:36). Having explained his position on the Law, Paul explores the question of Israel's rejection of its Messiah. He discusses the problem of Israel's rejection (9:1-29), the reasons for Israel's rejection (9:30-10:21), and the restoration of Israel (11:1-36).

Paul is anguished that his Jewish compatriots, who were granted God's covenants, Torah, Temple, and promises, failed to recognize Jesus Christ. While some Jews had accepted Christ, the nation as a whole was not only unbelieving but bitterly antagonistic. The Jewish rulers had crucified Jesus. At every opportunity they had persecuted the Church. Paul then deals with the reasons for Israel's rejection. If Jesus Christ was really the Messiah of their own Scripture prophecy, why did the Jews reject him?

Paul argues that God never intended all Israelites to receive His promises. God's promises are based on the principle of election (9:5-26). Paul's assumption is that God predetermines the human ability to believe or disbelieve. The rejection of large numbers of Jews is predicted by the prophets Hosea and Isaiah (9:25-29). Thus God Himself had declared that it must occur.

Paul does not tell us how to reconcile the predestination of individuals to salvation or condemnation and the freedom of the human will.

Furthermore, the rejection of Christ by Israel can be found in her own misguided effort to please God. Israel did not understand that God's righteousness is to be received not by her own works (10:3) but by faith (9:30-33).

As for the future, what will be the destiny of the Jews? Paul believes that Israel's disbelief is temporary. God has not abandoned the Jews (11:2). In God's long-range plan, the Gentiles will first receive the Gospel and then the Jews. In an interesting analogy, Paul likens the Gentile believers to branches from a wild olive tree that have been grafted onto the cultivated olive trunk (Israel). When all Gentiles become believers, then the natural branches will be regrafted onto God's olive tree and all Israel will be saved (11:19-27). Then both the natural (Jewish) and grafted (Gentile) branches will grow together on a single tree. A faithful remnant of Israel has already accepted Christ, and Paul looks forward to the eventual conversion of the rest of the Israelites.

6. The Guidelines for Applying God's Righteousness: Christian Ethics and Conduct (12:1-15:13). Moving from theological to ethical considerations, Paul introduces a series of instuctions in chapters 12:1-15:13. He speaks of unselfishness in Christian relationships, checking Christian conduct, and love being the basis of all right relations among human beings. So closely do many of Paul's statements in this section parallel what Jesus said in the Sermon on the Mount, that these chapters are often called "Paul's Sermon on the Mount."

In chapter 12, Paul speaks about love within the church and love for all people. He states that God has created us all as individuals. It is God's purpose that men offer their unique gifts to His service. Everyone has something to offer. He also speaks of Christian qualities: humility, brotherly love, diligence, patience, joy, prayerfulness, hospitality, and sympathy. In short, the basis of Christian morality is love: love among fellow members of "the one body of Christ" (12:3-13), and love of everybody, including one's enemies (12:14-21).

Paul also advocates that Christians obey and cooperate with civil and governmental authorities, because "the governing authorities ... have been established by God" (13:1). His bold assertion is that there is no authority except from God, and those that exist have been instituted by God. Paul's advice of implicit obedience to the State poses the age-old issue of the obligations of the citizen to the government. Paul does not consider the ethical problem of a citizen's duty to resist illegal or unethical acts by the State.

It is difficult to understand the Apostle's counsel concerning the total subjection of Christians to the Roman government (13:1-8). One plausible explanation of this is that Paul expected the imminent Second Coming of Christ and considered resistance to government power an entanglement; the Christian era was moving on toward its consummation (13:11-14) and hence, why bother!

In chapters 14 and 15:1-14, Paul deals with specific problems, such as the abstention from certain foods and the observance of special days. Paul tries to reconcile some conflicts of conviction. He is critical of the arrogance of those who are judgmental. In his view, the principle to resolve these matters should be love. "None of us lives to himself alone and none of us dies to himself alone" (14:7). He affirms people's mutual interdependence: for better or worse Christians are bound together. Christians cannot rule their lives according to the dictates of their own interests. They live to the Lord, and their attitude toward other Christians should be that they are children of God and thus their brothers. To the Christian, the chief end of all is to glorify God.[9]

7. Paul's Future Plans and Personal Remarks (15:14-33). Paul's letter to the Roman Church virtually ends with this section. He expresses his appreciation to the faithful and commends them for being Christians "full of goodness, complete in knowledge and competent to instruct one another" (14:14)—marks of a strong church! Indeed, a healthy and a strong church is characterized by its "inward spirit of charity" and "outward activity of love," by its firm grasp of what faith really means, and by its ability to instruct one another.[10] He also mentions his "pride" in the work he has done for God—a pride not in himself but "in Jesus Christ" (14:17). Then he sketches out his plan to visit Rome and eventually go to Spain. First, however, he must carry a collection from the Gentile churches to the church in Jerusalem.

8. Appendix: Letter Recommending Phoebe (16:1-27). Most scholars believe that chapter 16, except for the closing doxology (16:25-27), represents a fragment of another Pauline letter, possibly to the Ephesians. It is a chapter of personal greetings to 26 of Paul's personal friends. It is also a letter of introduction—recommendation for Phoebe, a woman serving as deaconess of the Cenchrae church.

In conclusion, we might say that although Romans is the most difficult of Paul's epistles to read because of its theological intricacies, it is the most comprehensive statement of his teaching. It is primarily concerned with the *meaning* of Christ's appearance, death, and resurrection, and for the proper understanding of the relationship between God and humanity.

2. I CORINTHIANS

Paul wrote more to the Corinthian church than to any other church or individual. Further, he received a letter from them, the only letter Paul records receiving from a church.

While in the New Testament we have what we think of as two letters, I and II Corinthians, Paul actually wrote four letters to the Corinthians. These letters were written from Ephesus in Asia (I Cor. 16:8) and also from Macedonia (II Cor. 1:16, 2:13; 7:5) probably in the mid-fifties of the first century, during Paul's Third Missionary Journey.

I Corinthians was not Paul's first letter to the church at Corinth. In I Cor. 5:9 Paul mentions a previous letter he had written them from Ephesus and to a misunderstanding it had caused. Some scholars think that this letter is lost.[11] Others believe that a portion of the first letter is contained in II Cor. 6:14-7:1. These six verses that follow II Cor. 6:13 interrupt the train of thought, while II Cor. 7:2 ff. can be joined smoothly to 6:13. The teaching of this block, an appeal to shun pagan entanglements and to remain a separate group, seems to match Paul's description of his previous letter.[12] The canonical epistle called I Corinthians was probably the letter Paul wrote in reply to the letter he received from the Corinthians. The third letter called "The Painful Letter" was written from Ephesus, probably in 55 A.D. and may be partially preserved in II Cor. 10-13. The fourth letter Paul wrote to them, from Macedonia, is called "The Letter of Reconciliation" and is II Cor. 1-9 with the exception of the six verses of 6:14-7:1.[13]

Paul's correspondence with the Corinthian Church was not a one-way affair. In addition to writing to him, delegations from Corinth kept Paul in touch with the Corinthian community (1:11; 16:15-18; II Cor. 7:5-7).

The city of Corinth was so situated geographically that its importance as a center of culture and commerce was always assured. It was located across the Aegean Sea and was the capital of Achaia.

The original city was very ancient and had headed the

Achaean League during the Hellenistic period. That city was destroyed by the Romans in 146 B.C. It was rebuilt in 46 B.C. by Julius Caesar and was settled by former Roman soldiers who made it a Roman colony. This explains why Corinth was the only Greek city that had a Roman amphitheater. Shortly after the Romans, there came Greeks and other Middle Eastern people. The city grew rapidly. When Paul worked there it had a population of six-hundred thousand. It became a major city in Greece, second in importance only to Athens.

Corinth was a center of trade, lying on the narrow isthmus joining the Greek mainland to the southernmost island known as the Peloponnesus. It was the natural stopping place for sailors, businessmen, and merchants, and became the wealthiest city in Greece in Paul's time. The city accommodated new settlers from all over the Roman Empire, as well as their various religions, such as those of Isis, Seraphis, and Jupiter Capitolinus.

Corinth was the site of the famous pagan temple of Aphrodite (Venus) where thousands of priestesses served as sacred prostitutes. The city was also notorious as a place of vice and immorality (I Cor. 6:12-20). The Greeks had sayings and proverbs about Corinth; "to Corinthianize" (*korinthiazomai*) meant to engage in the most excessive forms of immorality; and the proverb warned, "Not for every man is the voyage to Corinth."[14]

Paul ministered in Corinth from the spring of 50 A.D. until the fall of 51 A.D., a period of about eighteen months. He had some success in his work. He won a number of prominent people to Christianity. He found superb helpers in Aquila and Priscilla, a Jewish couple converted to Christianity, who had been expelled with other Jews from Rome by an imperial edict. He won two leaders of the synagogue, Crispus and Sosthenes. But the bulk of his converts to the Christian faith were from the lower classes, primarily Gentiles—a mixed group, consisting probably of people from varied backgrounds. At the end of 18 months there was a thriving church in Corinth. Paul left for Ephesus, then on to Jerusalem, after which there came a missionary journey to Galatia and Phrygia, and back to Ephesus, where he preached the Gospel while he supported himself with his trade of tentmaking. It is from Ephesus that Paul began his correspondence with the Corinthians.

There was a good deal of travel between Corinth and Ephesus. One day, a group of people whom Paul calls "of the household of Chloe" (1:11) (who might have been servants, friends, or relatives) reported that there were some real problems in the Corinthian church.

They reported a number of things going on which caused Paul great distress: the church was splitting into factions, immorality was becoming rampant in the church, the Lord's Supper was degenerating into a kind of orgy, there were lawsuits among believers, and there were criticisms of Paul.

While Paul was receiving this report, three leaders of the Corinthian church—Staphanos, Fortunatus, and Achiacus—brought a letter from the church in which the Corinthians asked a number of questions (16:23).

Thus, the occasion of the letter was these problems, but the letter was only one stage in a lively dialogue between Paul and the congregation, a dialogue that had been in process for quite some time. Obviously Paul had received other reports about the situation (5:1), probably by letter (7:1). It is also evident that he had written a letter previous to I Corinthians (5:9).

I Corinthians may be divided into the following parts:
1. Introduction (1:1-9)
2. Admonitions Against Disorders in the Church (1:10-6:20)
    a. Admonition against factions and party-splits (1:10-4:21)
    b. Admonition against immorality (5:1-13)
    c. Admonition against lawsuits (6:1-11)
    d. Admonition against prostitution (6:12-20)
3. Answers to and Directives for the Church (7:1-15:58)
    a. The problem of marriage and celibacy (7:1-40)
    b. Christian freedom (8:1-11:1)
    c. Regulating behavior in church (11:2-14:40)
        — the conduct of women in church (11:2-16)
        — the Lord's Supper (11:17-34)
        — the use of spiritual gifts (12-14:40)

    d. The resurrection of the dead (15:1-58)
    e. The contribution for the saints (16:1-4)
4. Conclusion

1. Introduction (1:1-9). Paul's letter begins with his apostolic credentials, emphasizing his calling by Jesus Christ. In his customary salutation he unites two terms: *Grace* (unmerited goodness which men do not deserve) and *peace* (*shalom*, the Semitic term for God's salvation).[15] Then he expresses thanks to God for the Corinthian congregation because of God's "grace given you in Christ Jesus" (1:4).

2. Admonitions Against Disorders in the Church (1:10-6:20). Because of their grossly pagan background, the Corinthian church experienced a variety of problems. The spirit of the world was more prominent in the church than the Spirit of God. Paul addressed a variety of problems including factions, lawsuits, immorality, abuse of the Lord's Supper and other problems; he admonished them against these disorders and told them how to be a Christian in a non-Christian world.

In this letter he took up these problems in the following order:

    a. *Admonition against factions and party-splits* (1:10-4:21). Paul is concerned with division of parties in the church at Corinth. These factions were not over theological matters; they had arisen from a misguided loyalty attached to various leaders. It was a conflict over who was the best preacher!

After Paul left the church he had established in Corinth, there came a brilliant young preacher from Alexandria named Apollos. He was enthusiastically received everywhere he went. His language was polished. His style was in sharp contrast to Paul's rather halting and unpolished delivery. Apparently, some Corinthians were charmed by Apollos' style, and said they were Apollos' party. Others had championed Cephas (Peter). Some stuck with Paul, the founder of their church. Some others said that they got their directions from Jesus Christ and formed the "Christ-group." They may have been who Paul referred to in 12:3, the ones who saw the human Jesus as irrelevant and who were interested only in the divine Christ.

The result was that the church was split wide open. Its witness in the community had become ineffective.

Paul's point is that if the congregation is the body of Christ, then it is impossible for it to be split up into factions (1:13). To choose one preacher over the others is to make him their first loyalty rather than Christ. Preachers who serve them are not there as competitors, but as people supplementing each other in a common ministry (3:5-9). Moreover, Paul points out that if their prime loyalty is not to a preacher but to Christ, then they indeed have the ministries of all the preachers who have served them (3:23).

Paul recognizes that one of the serious causes of division may have arisen from the unequal social and educational backgrounds of the Corinthian congregation. Apparently, some members believed they were superior to their neighbors. There must have been a considerable group of people in the church who were prating about "wisdom," with evident desire to display their own brilliance in discussion while looking down on others.

In Paul's view, all believers are fundamentally equal. He believes that Christianity is incompatible with individual pride or competitiveness. He reminds the Corinthian Christians that human reason by itself did not succeed in knowing God but that God revealed His saving purpose through Christ as a free gift (1:21). Because all are equally recipients of the divine grace, no believer has the right to boast (1:21-31).

b. *Admonition Against Immorality* (5:1-13). Another problem reported to Paul was that of sexual misconduct. There was a case of incest. A man was living with his step-mother in an illicit relationship. It was not only the sin that shocked Paul but the condoning attitude of the Christian church.

Paul speaks rather sharply. Christians are not to accept that kind of immoral action or person. He points out that acceptance of that kind of thing acts like a destroying leaven within the Christian community and will result in the total disintegration of Christian nature (5:6-8). Paul directed that the immoral man was to be delivered "to Satan" (the devil-ruled world outside the church), that is, excommunicated from the church. The purposes of excommunication were to serve as an example, to keep the practice from spreading and to hopefully bring the party to repentance.

c. *Admonition against lawsuits* (6:1-11). Litigation between Christians in pagan courts was another scandalous phenomenon. Paul points out that asking a non-Christian court system to settle the differences of Christians had made the Corinthian church the laughing stock of Corinth. How can they talk about saving the world when they cannot resolve simple differences among themselves? He orders that such disputes be settled within the church community.

d. *Admonition against prostitution* (6 :12-20) . Aphrodite (Venus) was the principal deity of Corinth. Her temple in the city housed numerous priestesses—public prostitutes—for immoral sexual indulgence. Some of the Corinthian Christians, having been used to a religion that encouraged immoral living, were finding it hard to adapt themselves to their new religion which prohibited immoral activity.

Paul points out that Christians at Corinth should not take their standard of conduct from the morally corrupt Corinth. Rather, they should guide their moral conduct by the standard of Christ. He suggests that their orientation needs to be straightened out and that moral purity must be the character of their relations with each other. He reminds them that their bodies are "temples of the Holy Spirit," and therefore, their lives must be characterized by moral rectitude (16:19-20) .

3. Answers to and Directives for the Church (7:1-15:58). In this section Paul is answering questions addressed to him in a letter from the Corinthians.

a. *Problems of marriage and celibacy* (7:1-40). The first set of questions in chapter 7 concern human sexuality. What is the idea of marriage? Is it wrong to marry? Shall betrothed people marry? Paul's answers to these questions reveal that there were persons in the church who took the opposite position of libertinism. They were ascetics and considered that sex was inherently sinful.

Paul's preference is celibacy. He prefers a single life without any kind of sexual involvement. He begins this section by stating that "it is good for a man not to marry" (7:1). But if passion cannot be controlled, then people should marry. Marriage partners are to be totally faithful to each other. Women whose husbands have died are "better off" if they do not remarry. The whole chapter is dominated by the expectation of the imminent Second Coming of Christ and the end of the world (7:26, 29-31). He, therefore, believes that it is better to have freedom from sexual ties that bind one to the world, and devote oneself single-mindedly to the Lord's work because "the time is short" (7:29). Hence, all impediments and conflicts of interest subject to choice must be forestalled (7:31).

b. *Christian freedom* (8:1-11:1). An important question raised by the Corinthian Christians was whether or not it was right for them to eat meat that had previously been sacrificed to idols in Graeco-Roman temples. The meat, which was the best around, was sold in some of the meat markets which the Christians frequented. Some Christians were offended that their fellow church members, by buying and eating meat offered to pagan idols, condoned pagan idolatry. But those buying and eating this first-class meat were saying that there was no moral principle involved.

Paul argues that although Christians are free to do as they wish when their consciences are clear, they should not be a stumbling block to weaker brothers and sisters in the church who are trying to find their way into the new life. While Paul shared the convictions of the advocates of Christian liberty, he did not share their spirit. Thus, in Paul's view, a mature Christian should forfeit his right to eat sacrificed meat lest he "becomes a stumbling block to the weak" (8:9).

Paul interrupts his argument to insert two personal examples of his own practice, showing how he had waived his rights in the interest of building up the community: his right to be accompanied by a wife and his right to be supported by the churches which he served (9:1-23). He asks the Corinthians to imitate his selfless example (10:33-11:1).

c. *Regulating behavior in church* (11:2-14:40). Beginning with 11:2 and continuing through chapter 14, Paul treats a series of problems relating to the conduct of the Corinthians in their public assemblies. The issues he addresses include the veiling (head-covering) of women in leading public worship, the Lord's Supper, and the use of spiritual gifts.

— *The conduct of women in church* (11:2-16). This passage is open to a variety of interpretations. Paul insists that women cover their heads with veils (11:3-16). There are scholars who believe that Paul writes out of a background of the patriarchal Jewish family,[16] invoking what he assumed to be a divinely ordained hierarchy: as God is the head of Christ and as Christ is the head of mankind, so man is the head of woman (11:3). A woman attending church must veil her head "because of angels" (11:10) is an obscure phrase perhaps referring to angels who fell from heaven when attracted to women's beauty (Gen. 6:1-4). In other words, if women unveil their physical attractiveness, they may distract male onlookers.[17]

Other scholars insist that it was customary in Greek and Middle Eastern cities for women to cover their heads in public, except women of immoral character. Corinth was full of temple prostitutes who did not wear veils. Some of the Christian women, taking advantage of their new-found liberty in Christ, were laying aside their veils in church meetings. This did not please a number of modest people, and therefore Paul recommends certain restrictions on women's behavior.[18]

Still other scholars believe that the special problems in Corinth should not be seen as determinative for all the Pauline churches, and the programmatic sentence in Galatians 3:28 ("There is neither Jew nor Greek, slave nor free, male nor female, for you are all one in Christ Jesus") should not be forgotten. They think that this passage (11:2-16) is the interpolation of a later editor, added to make Corinthians agree with the non-Pauline instruction of I Tim. 2:8-15, 19.

It appears that Paul's directives to the Corinthian Christians do not stipulate universal requirements for all women, considering that the Apostle is dealing with the peculiar environment of Corinth, and considering his declaration that Christian equality transcends all distinctions among believers, including those of nationality, class, and sex (Gal. 3:28).

— *The Lord's Supper* (11:17-34). The Lord's Supper (known as *Communion*, *Mass*, or *Eucharist*), which was supposed to be the reenactment of Jesus' last meal with his disciples and a mystic communion between the Lord and his followers, was being abused. Before the Lord's Supper a common meal was held but not shared. The wealthy members, concerned only with the satisfaction of their hunger and thirst, came early and overate, overdrank, and left little for the poor latecomers. The communion meal had degenerated into a gluttonous orgy for some (11:17:22).

In response, Paul gives what is the earliest report we have in the New Testament of the Communion. (We must remember that Paul's epistles precede the writing of the Gospels.) He describes, in simplest language, the story of the first Lord's Supper and the symbolism involved. It was something given them which they did not create. It is in stark contrast to what they had made the Lord's Supper. For some, "the love feast" had become a time of eating, drinking, and merry-making—a shame and mockery!

The Lord's Supper has been interpreted in various ways throughout the ages. The ancient churches—Roman Catholic and Eastern Orthodox—believe in "The Real Presence" doctrine; they adhere to transubstantiation, believing that by a physical miracle the communion elements of bread and wine are transformed during the celebration of Mass into the actual (not symbolic) body and blood of Christ and that "his sacrifice is renewed."[20] Protestants in general believe Christ is spiritually present in the elements, although some of them regard the communion as just a commemoration of the Last Supper.[21]

Paul seems to point out the memorial character of the event when quoting Jesus' words "Do this in remembrance of me" (11:24,25), and when he insists "Whenever you eat this bread and drink this cup, you proclaim the Lord's death until he comes" (11:26).

Paul reminds the Corinthian Christians that it is possible for a person to partake of the Communion in a manner so unworthy as to make this partaking an act of judgment on himself or herself and an act which profanes the body of Christ (11:27-34).

— *The Use of Spiritual Gifts* (12:1-14:40). The assembly of Christians at Corinth led to other disorderliness. Like other early Christian communities, the Corinthian Church was composed of persons gifted with such abilities as prophecy, healing, working miracles, and speaking in tongues (12:7-10). These gifts and rivalries among those possessing them were yet another cause of diversion. One of these gifts particularly, that of *glossolalia*—speaking in unknown tongues—was very popular with the Corinthians. Some members of the church were interrupting the public worship services by breaking out in ecstatic speaking in tongues which no one could understand, including the speakers. Two things were happening. Those who spoke in tongues regarded those who did not as spiritually inferior, and those not speaking in tongues put down those who did.

Paul goes into a great deal of detail with the matter. He discusses it in chapters 12 and 14. He identifies with those who are speaking in tongues and states that he has on occasion done it himself, but only in private, not in a public meeting of worship (14:18;28). He suggests that no one ought to put it down, but then no one ought to think of himself as superior because he does it. He says that there are many gifts of the Spirit and speaking in tongues is by no means the greatest of the gifts of the Holy Spirit. He says the trouble with it is that worshipers cannot understand it, and it, therefore, disrupts corporate worship. Moreover, he indicates that if people do not understand what is being said, they will not know when to say "Amen" (14:13-17). He suggests that those who speak in tongues should pray for the gift of interpretation, so others can understand and "the church may be edified" (14:5). If there is no interpretation available, then they ought to remain silent in a service of worship. He says that he would rather speak five intelligible words in a public worship than ten thousand in a tongue that people cannot understand, for it is comprehensible instruction that strengthens the Church (14:18-28).

Reminding the Corinthian Christians that one indivisible Spirit grants all the gifts of prophesying, teaching, healing, working miracles, and speaking in tongues, Paul employs his famous metaphor of the Church's unity as the body of Christ having many differently functioning members. Although the members of the body are diverse in their functions, they all belong to a single body and are interdependent. Similarly, although blessed with diverse spiritual qualities, believers are all members of the same Church—the Body of Christ. Moreover, just as the physical organs of the body function corporately to achieve maximum benefits, so individual members of the Church must work together to benefit the Body of Christ (12:12-30).

In spite of all the brilliant gifts the Corinthian community had displayed, the church was still divided and ineffective. There just had to be a better way than that. Paul writes, "I will show you the most excellent way" (12: 31) . Then there follows what we know as "The Love Chapter" or "The Hymn to Agape"—one of the great bits of writing in all literature!

Excelling all other spiritual gifts is love. The word which is translated "love" is the Greek word *agape*. It is not to be confused with *eros*, romantic or physical love; nor is it to be confused with *philia*, family love or friendship. Agape, when applied to God, means God's unmerited grace toward men, His free and unconditional love. When applied to human relations, it means unconditional good will, the recognition of the sacredness of personality, and action consonant with good will and respect for personality.

In his famous chapter of I Corinthians 13, Paul deals with the superiority (vss.1-3), the nature (4-7), and the durability of love (8-13). Listing the most highly honored spiritually gifts—tongues, prophesy, knowledge, power, self sacrifice (vss. 1-3)—Paul states that without agapaic love they are meaningless. The characteristics of such love are that it is patient, kind, not envious, and not proud (v. 4); love is not rude, not self-seeking, not easily angered (v. 5); it does not delight in evil but rejoices with the truth (8-10); love is the greatest of the trio of Christian virtues—faith, hope, and love (v. 13).

Paul's recommendation to the Christians at Corinth is to "follow the way of love" (14:1).

d. *The Resurrection of the Dead* (15:1-58). In this section Paul deals with a very important theological concept—the Resurrection. Some Corinthian Christians, probably Greek in background, may have questioned the *bodily* form of life after death. The Greeks believed that after death the spirit entirely separates from the body, whereas the Jews did not think of spirit apart from body. To them, resurrection involved both soul and body.

To demonstrate that bodily resurrection is a reality, Paul

calls on the Corinthians to remember that Jesus rose from the dead (15:3-11). This was a fact attested by actual witnesses who had seen Jesus alive. He claims that he himself had seen Jesus on the road to Damascus. Besides a number of appearances to the Apostles, singly or in groups, Jesus had appeared to a crowd of five-hundred people at one time (15:3-4). The bodily resurrection of Christ, he insists, is absolutely central to Christian belief; if Christ be not raised from the dead, then all their preaching is in vain. If Christ did not rise, there is no basis for Christianity (15:16-19).

Then Paul contrasts Adam and Christ. Adam, God's first earthly son, brought death to the human race; but Christ, Adam's heavenly counterpart, brought life (15:20-28).

Paul next responds to the question of the nature of the resurrected body. In what form are the dead raised? While Paul agrees that "flesh and blood cannot inherit the kingdom of God" (15:50), he seems to believe that human beings cannot exist without some kind of body. The "natural body" is changed into a "spiritual body," identifiable and eternal. He uses the analogy of the seed. Life grows from buried seeds and existence takes different forms. The resurrected being will be clothed with an imperishable, immortal existence (15:50-54).

e. *The Contribution for the Saints* (16:1-4). In this concluding chapter, Paul speaks of the collection for the poor saints in Jerusalem. The mother church was in great need. Other churches had responded generously. He encourages the church in Corinth to follow their example, and set aside, "on the first day of every week," a sum of money (15:2). This systematic and disciplined giving is an excellent means to meet its moral obligation to the needy and sustain its Christian work.

4. Conclusion (16:5-24). Paul speaks of his travel plans. He closes with exhortation, greetings, and a benediction. It is customary for Paul to add a greeting in his own handwriting (Col. 4:18; Philem. 19). This served to authenticate the document (II Thes. 3:17). The letter ends with an Aramaic phrase *Marana tha* ("Come, O Lord")—a eucharistic prayer recited by the early Christians.[22]

3. II CORINTHIANS

People sometimes have some difficulty reading II Corinthians. It seems to be disjointed and contains extreme mood changes. It does not leave the impression of a unified document. The reason for this is that what we know as II Corinthians contains portions of three different letters Paul wrote to the Corinthians.

Chapter 6:14 through 7:1 (six verses together) constitute a portion of one letter. It deals primarily with the admonition that Christians at Corinth be not yoked with unbelievers.

The last four chapters of II Corinthians (chapters 10-13) are the so-called *"Severe Letter"* or *"Painful Letter"*—Paul's third letter to them. That letter is sharply written, has a flavor of sarcasm in it, contains a very cutting attack on the enemies and detractors of Paul and his work. It also contains that famous list of things which Paul has endured in the service of Christ.

When these two letters are separated from the remainder of what we call II Corinthians, we have Paul's fourth letter to them - *"The Letter of Reconciliation."* To the credit of the Corinthians they finally listened to Paul and the original warm relationship was reestablished. It is in that spirit that this fourth letter was written (II Cor. 1-9 with the exception of 6:14-7:1).

The present order of the chapters, then, could be rearranged so that chapters 10-13 (*"The Severe Letter"*) precede chapters 1-9 (*"The Letter of Reconcililation"*).

The outline of the contents of II Corinthians is as follows:
1. Introduction (1:1-11).
2. Paul's Ministry Described (1:12-7:16).
3. Paul's Collection for Needy Christians in Jerusalem (8:1-9:15).
4. Paul's Ministry Defended (10:1-13:10).
5. Conclusion (13:11-14).

1. Introduction (1:1-11). Paul begins his letter in the usual way of stating his authority as an apostle. Timothy, named as coauthor, had nothing to do with the actual dictation of the letter

(1:1). His name is mentioned probably because he was Paul's messenger and was associated with Paul.[23]

The letter was to be read not only in Corinth but to "all the saints throughout Achaia" (1:1), perhaps because Corinth was the capital of the Roman province of Achaia and the center of Christian life in that region.

Paul also expresses his thanks to God for the faith and comfort given him in all trials (1:8). He relates his recent deliverance from deadly peril (1:8-11). This passage may be called "The Comfort Passage." The verb or noun "comfort" is used ten times in the first ten verses. Paul points out that people committed to Christ can endure suffering and can be victorious in and through suffering. The reason they can is that they have the comfort of God strengthening them. Moreover, those who have been thus tried and comforted and built up in courage are able to give comfort, courage, and strength to others in their suffering.

2. Paul's Ministry Described (1:12-7:16). Here Paul defines his integrity (1:15-22). He explains his change of plans was not due to fickleness. The stern letter was sent in lieu of another painful visit. He delayed his visit because he did not want to visit them again "in grief" (2:1-3). After writing I Corinthians, he had visited Corinth to correct the condition there and was not treated amicably. That was a painful visit (also referred to in 12:14 and 13:1-2). At that time he had promised to return soon, but later he decided to delay his return. This is the change of plan for which he was criticized and which he is now defending. He sent Titus to Corinth with "The Severe Letter," for he could not face another painful visit (2:1-4).

After Titus visited Corinth and delivered Paul's stern letter, Paul came to see him somewhere in Macedonia. Their meeting was joyful as Titus had good news about Corinth.

This section of Paul's letter includes the following important passages:

a. *"Jesus the Living 'Yes to God' Passage"* (1:19-20). Paul's view here is that at the very heart of the universe, at the heart of life is no negative, but a great living positive. Jesus is the living "Yes" of God at the heart of all things. To find him at the heart of our lives is to have a "yes" in our attitudes, responses, and lifestyles.

b. *"The Letter of Recommendation Passage"* (3:2-3). In the ancient world it was a common practice for a traveller going to a strange place to carry letters of recommendation, to introduce him and to testify to his character. Romans 16, for example, is such a letter of introduction-recommendation for Phoebe.

Paul, using this custom as a background, says that the Christians at Corinth are letters of Christ to be known and read by those who see them. Christ is judged by the quality of his followers!

c. *"The Freedom Passage"* (3:12-18). The background of this passage is the contrast between slavery to the law and freedom through commitment to Christ. It is the theme which Paul elaborates in his Epistle to the Galatians.

The secret of freedom is found in the power of the indwelling Spirit. Through him men find both guidance as to what they ought to do and the power to do it.[24] This is what Paul means when he says, "where the Spirit of the Lord is, there is freedom" (3:17).

d. *"Courage in Ministry Passage"* (4:1-15). In this message Paul describes his apostolic ministry. In some respects his ministry is an imitation of that of Jesus. The fact that he is doing God's work makes him no less subject to human limitation: "We have this treasure in jars of clay" (4:7). His own afflictions demonstrate this (4:8). But such afflictions (4:8-9) do more than show that Paul is human; they recapitulate the death and resurrection of Jesus (4:10-11). To suffer as Paul does is to carry in the body the death of Jesus, through which the life of Jesus becomes manifest (4:11). Because of Paul's living martyrdom the Corinthians experience life, even as through Christ's death human beings gain life. Paul's "offering is therefore vicarious, on behalf of others."[25]

e. *"The Immortality Passage"* (5:1-10). Paul uses the analogy of "the earthly tent we live in" (5:1) as he speaks about immortality. He uses the figure of the human body as a house or tent used by man's spirit and contrasts it with the "eternal house in heaven." One day the human body will be discarded, but it will be replaced by a finer instrument for one's spirit to continue to serve and adore God as a person with his own identity (5:6-8).

f. *"The Reconciliation Passage"* (5:11-6:2). In this passage

Paul says that to be committed to Christ is to become a new creature, to have a new outlook, a new lifestyle.

A person who really encounters Christ is a different person from what he was before (5:17).

The "new creation" is viewed by Paul against the background of man's revolt. God is declared to be the Reconciler. He reconciles us to Himself, which is not to say that God has to be reconciled to us. There is no God who has to be appeased at the heart of the Christian faith. Rather, the God of Christ is the God who reached out to his creatures, not to reconcile himself to them but they to him. Although Paul does not offer the Corinthians any theory of atonement, it should be pointed out that chronologically these few verses (5:11-18) are the first declaration of Paul's interpretation of the death of Jesus Christ as God's plan for the atonement for sin and redemption of mankind. He returns to this central theme in other letters, especially the Letter to the Romans.[26]

When we are reconciled to God, he gives us ministry among our fellow human beings. As God's major work of love in Christ is our reconciliation to him, so our major work as Christians is the reconciliation of people who are at odds with themselves, with God, and with each other. Our ministry is a ministry of reconciliation (5:18). That makes us ambassadors for Christ. An ambassador is a representative in whose hands is the welfare of the nation he or she represents. Similarly a Christian is a representative of Christ, and in the Christian's hand is the effectiveness of Christ's ministry of love and reconciliaton among men (5:19-20).

In chapter 6 Paul continues to vindicate his ministry. He describes how steadfastly he has fulfilled his mission in the face of many odds against him - "hardships, afflictions, calamities, beating, imprisonmments, tumults, labors, watching, and hunger" (6:4-5). Then he lists qualities and divine gifts that mark his ministry: "purity, understanding, patience, kindness" (6:6).

In 6:14-7:1 the appeal for mutual love is suddenly interrupted and a new subject matter is abruptly introduced. It is a warning that Christians should not be yoked with unbelievers. Apparently, there had been some intermarriages with non-believers and these were causing some real trouble in maintaining the faith in full strength. So Paul advises against such marriages, which would tend to weaken the faith and witness. Some scholars believe that 6:14-7:1 is a non-Pauline fragment on the basis of both ideas and vocabulary, and it may represent the opinion of Paul's opponents; its ideas are very much characteristic of the Qumran community.[27] Other scholars believe that it is a part of a separate Pauline letter that somehow was interpolated in II Corinthians.[28] There are also some other biblical students who believe that Paul's letters simply contain such digressions, especially the Epistles to the Corinthians, written during a greatly disturbed period.[29] It may be that 6:14-7:1 is a portion of the first letter he wrote. Because of their background in paganism, Paul warns the Christians at Corinth against pagan influences lest those would turn them from their Christian way of life. He insists that "we are the Temple of the Living God" (6:16). A temple must be kept clean because God dwells in it. Therefore, when and where loyalties conflict, the Christian's first loyalty is to God (6:17).

3. Paul's Collection for Needy Christians in Jerusalem (8:1-9:15). Chapters 8 and 9 seem to repeat each other and may once have been separate missives before an editor combined them at the end of Paul's "Letter of Reconciliation."[30] They both deal with the collection for needy Christians in Jerusalem. It appears that this project had been interrupted by the recent revolt of some competitors against Paul. To resume and complete this project would cement their new loyalty to Paul, deepen their Christian stewardship, and help to bind Jewish and Gentile Christians together in a band of brotherhood.[31]

Paul first seeks to challenge the Corinthian Christians by citing the example of the churches of Macedonia (8:1). He also cites arguments to move them to respond worthily in their giving: the example of others—the Macedonian churches (8:1-6); the example of Christ who, "though he was rich, yet for your sakes he became poor" (8:9); their own past record of giving (8:11); the necessity of putting fine feelings into fine actions (9:6-8).

Paul also outlines the basic principles of generous giving: No one ever lost because he was generous; God loves the happy, cheerful giver; God can give a person both the substance to give and the spirit in which to give it; giving is to be systematic, proportionate, and cheerful (9:6-11).

Furthermore, Paul points out that giving does wonderful things for the needy, for the giver, and for God (9:12-14).

All of this, Paul asserts, grows out of the wonder of the gift of God to us in Jesus Christ.

4. Paul's Ministry Defended (10:1-13:10). The last four chapters of II Corinthians are not part of the "Letter of Reconciliation" or as some scholars call it "The Thankful Letter," but rather a part of the *"Severe Letter"* or the *"Painful Letter"* - the third letter in the series. This section contains vigorous self-vindication on Paul's part. In defending himself and his ministry, Paul engages in ironic boasting to show how foolish the Corinthians were for listening to the false charges and exaggerated claims of his enemies. The Apostle bitterly reproaches the Corinthian church for believing "the false apostles" - those Jewish-Christian itinerant preachers, recently arrived in Corinth (11:4, 22), who claimed apostleship (11:5, 13) and preached a different Gospel with a "Jesus other than the Jesus we preached," (11:4). Those "false apostles" questioned Paul's credentials to be an apostle (10:8), seeking proof that "Christ is speaking through Paul" (13:3). They accused Paul of weakness, which to them would be incompatible with apostleship. Paul, therefore, assumes that role gladly and develops his theology of "weakness" and suffering after the pattern of Christ the Crucified, beginning his words with "By the meekness and gentleness of Christ, I appeal to you" (10:1). He declares that he can be stern if necessary but prefers not to be so, and he asks the Corinthians to change their attitude toward him so that he need not be (10:2).

Paul challenges his critics to compare themselves to him by every standard: as a loyal Hebrew, as an effective worker for Christ, he had done more than all of them put together (11:22-23). As a sufferer for Christ, his whole career as a Christian Apostle had been an unbroken story of living martyrdom (11:24-29).

Paul's standard of what constitutes a true apostle of Jesus Christ differs from those who considered themselves "super apostles" (11:5). He is concerned about the welfare of the Church and keeps to his own field (10:12-18) and seeks to move the Corinthian Christians to repent (12:19-21).

Paul anticipates a third visit to Corinth, in which he hopes things will go well, although he is apparently wary (13:10). He appeals to them to repent before his visit so that he need not be severe (13:5-10).

5. Conclusion (13:11-14). The final exhortations and greeting are brief and friendly. He ends his letter on a note of encouragement. There will be harmony in the church if they "live in peace, and be of one mind" (13:11).

Paul tells them to "greet one another with a holy kiss" (13:12). The practice of exchanging a holy kiss, a mark of brotherhood in the one faith, was evidently widespread in the early church (Rom. 16:16; I Cor. 16:20; I Thess. 5:26).

Finally, Paul ends his letter with one of the most elaborate and popular biblical benedictions—"May the grace of the Lord Jesus Christ, and the love of God, and fellowship of the Holy Spirit be with you all" (13:14). This threefold experience supports the doctrine of the Trinity. Although the term "trinity" is not found in the New Testament, the church formulated the Trinitarian doctrine as the standard creed of Christian orthodoxy in the fourth and fifth centuries.

4. GALATIANS

Galatians, like Romans, defines Christianity's relationship to Judaism. Paul asserts that Christians are free of the Mosaic law. He uses the Hebrew Bible to demonstrate Christianity's declaration of independence from Judaism.

Galatians is called the *Magna Charta* of Christianity, the document of Christian freedom.[32] It revolutionized the development of Christianity. By sweeping away all the Torah requirements and insisting on the abandonment of all Mosaic observances, Paul opened the doors of the Church to the Gentile converts. These Gentile Christians were granted full equality with Jewish Christians. One of the factors of this swift transformation was Paul's epistle to the Galatians.[33]

There are no hints within the letter itself regarding date and place of writing. Also, there are no hints concerning its destination. The identity of the Galatian churches Paul addresses is uncertain. Two theories have been proposed:

a. *"The North Galatia Theory"* claims that the letter may have been directed in the north-central plateau region of Asia Minor (near present-day Ankara, Turkey). The cities in that area were Pessinus, Ancyra, and Tavium.[34]

b. *"The South Galatia Theory,"* upheld by many scholars, insists that Galatians was addressed to a group of four churches in the province of Galatia - Antioch of Pisidia, Iconium, Lystra, and Derbe. These were churches founded by Paul on his first missionary journey.[35]

It is not necessary to solve these critical problems in order to appreciate the essential meaning of this letter.

The occasion and the purpose of Galatians is twofold:
a. To defend Paul's apostolic right and authority;
b. To defend the true gospel of grace which replaces works of Law.

Christianity started within Judaism and, of course, the first Christians were Jews. Then came an influx of Gentiles converted to Christianity. In the early days, there was some conflict between the groups. There was a strong party in the church who held the view that to receive the spiritual blessings which Jesus brought, one had first to become a Jew, since the promise was to the descendents of Abraham. Therefore, all Gentile male converts had to be circumcised before they could become Christians. They had to become ritual Jews and observe all the ritual laws to know the blessings of Jesus. It was this group, known as Judaizers, that had come into Galatian churches and were fighting Paul's presentation of the Gospel, in which he had declared acceptance for all people, Jews and Gentiles alike. It was the conflict over whether Christianity was to be a universal religion in which there were no Jews or Gentiles, but one people in Christ.

Paul, who had stood against the Judaizers in the Council of Jerusalem in 49 A.D., once again took an adamant stand. He wrote this epistle, probably around 52 A.D., to explain to the Galatians that while circumcision had been a necessary part of Jewish national life, it was not a part of the Gospel of Christ and had nothing whatever to do with one's being a Christian.

Not only were Paul's opponents trying to reverse his free and open Gospel, but they were also attacking him personally. They declared that he was not a fit teacher to be trusted because he was neither one of the Twelve original disciples, nor was he authorized by one of the Twelve.

Much as Paul would have liked to meet them face to face, he could not, so he wrote a blistering letter to them - a letter which is both a defense of himself and his credentials and a maginificent presentation of the freedom from ritual, law, and class which Christ gives to those who receive him.

Galatians may be divided into five parts:
1. Introduction (1:1-9)
2. Paul's Defense (1:10-2:21)
3. Faith Over Law: Justification by Faith (3:1-4:31)
4. The Consequences and Obligations of Christian Freedom (5:1-6:10)
5. Summary of Paul's Argument (6:11-18)

As Paul defends his apostolic right and authority and as he defends the gospel of grace, he stresses the supremacy and sole sufficiency of Christ. He argues that if justificaton were possible by law, Christ's death was unnecessary.

1. Introduction (1:1-9). The letter is addressed to "churches," suggesting its circulation to the congregations where problems were developing as a result of Judaizers' activities. The precise location of these churches is problematic because of the term "Galatia," which originally denoted an old Celtic tribal kingdom in north-central Asia Minor but after 25 B.C. became a Roman province whose borders were extended southward to include part of Phrygia.

Normally Paul's letters include a customary note of thanksgiving for the faith and life of the addressees; in this case he launches immediately into an attack on those who are disturbing that faith and life, anathematizing them for advocating what to him is "false gospel" (1:6-9).

2. Paul's Defense (1:10-2:21). This section includes a personalized historical account of events relevant to the Galatian situation. It offers invaluable autobiographical information on Paul's initial movements in mission. Paul expresses dismay to the Galatian churches which had questioned his authority as an apostle. He defends his personal autonomy and apostolicity and claims that he is an apostle by direct commission of the resurrected Christ and does not derive his authority from any human agency. Then Paul gives the story of his spiritual pilgrimage. He tells of his spiritual experience with Christ on the road to Damascus. He tells of how he had changed from persecutor of Christians to an evangelist for Christ. He says that after three years in his new life, he had met with Peter and learned that the Gospel he was preaching matched that which Peter was preaching. Fourteen years later he went to Jerusalem and told the Apostles what he understood the Gospel to be and was welcomed and approved (1:1-2:10).

Chapter 2:11-21 deals with Paul's confrontation with Peter. Verse 11 indicates that the congregation at Antioch was made up of Jews and Gentiles. Before Peter's visit the congregation had already practiced free table fellowship without observing the Jewish dietary laws. When Peter came to Antioch, he initially participated in the communal meals; however, when "certain men came from James . . . he began to draw back and separate himself from the Gentiles, fearing the circumcision group" (2:12). Paul's comment in verse 17 is programmatic: if Christ leads us to freedom from the Law, to fellowship with "Gentile sinners" (2:15) - and if such fellowship is now sinful, "is Christ an agent of sin?" There was only one answer.

3. Faith Over Law (3:1-4:31). This section is a carefully constructed example of Pauline exegesis and offers ample insights into the force of his logic. Paul asks the Galatians whether the new existence to which they were introduced by his missionary preaching was based on the works of the law of faith. Obviously, Paul is convinced it is based on the Spirit and faith, not the law (3:1-14). Paul tells of two alternatives: the Galatians received the Spirit *either* through works of law *or* through hearing with faith. It is an either-or, not both (2:21-25). This alternative is steadfastly carried through the rest of the letter with consistency.

Paul is astonished that the Galatians should so soon be turned away from the true Gospel of Jesus Christ. He calls them "You foolish Galatians!" and asks, "Who has bewitched you?" He tells them that they did not receive the Holy Spirit when keeping the law but only when they trusted the message of Christ.

The Judaizers made much of the covenant with Abraham, that his descendants should receive God's blessing and be a blessing to the world. The constituent part of that covenant was the requirement of circumcision, described in Genesis 17:13 as "everlasting." Meeting this argument on its own terms, Paul argues from Genesis 15:6 and 12:3 that the covenant actually began and was in effect before the requirement of circumcision, and that it began when God announced the Gospel in advance to Abraham (3:8). The promise of the gospel was received by Abraham through *faith*. Abraham's faith in God's call "was counted to him as righteousness" (Gen. 15:6). Paul points out that God made a covenant long before the Mosaic Law was given and long before the ritual law developed and therefore it follows that one does not have to observe the law to become a descendant of Abraham. One becomes a descendant of Abraham by faith, for justification is by faith. Those who now strive to keep the Law labor under a delusion; attainment of righteousness before God is a divine gift, not a reward for good works.

If the Law cannot really help anyone, why was it given? What is its role? Paul's answer is that the Law was a temporary device intended to teach human beings that "they are unavoidably law breakers, whose efforts cannot earn divine favor."[36] Using an analogy, Paul compares the Law to the work of the *paidogogos* (the Greek word translated by "custodian" in the R.S.V. and "schoolmaster" in the King James Version, neither of which is adequate), who in Roman society was the slave in charge of disciplining boys between ages 6 and 16; he was not necessarily a teacher and was neither loved nor respected, only feared.[37] Just as the Law had a beginning in history (430 years after the promise to Abraham), so it also had an end in history, namely when Christ came (3:17).

All those who come to Christ in faith and trust are the spiritual descendants of Abraham, and the freedom they find in Christ overcomes all barriers of nationality and class, for in Christ "there is neither Jew, nor Greek, slave nor free" (3:28).

Paul concludes his argument by citing an allegory, the biblical story of Abraham's two sons. Ishmael, son of Abraham's Egyptian slave woman Hagar, represents the Judaism of Paul's day, in bondage to the Law. Conversely, Isaac, the son of Abraham's free wife Sarah, symbolizes the "heavenly Jerusalem," the spiritual church whose members are also free. Thus, those who try to force God's promise through works of law are children of slavery (4:21-31).

4. The Consequences and Obligations of Christian Freedom (5:1-6:10). In this section Paul speaks of the responsibilities of freedom; he confronts the issue of the free Christian's moral responsibility. There are dangers in freedom. It can degenerate into license. Freedom is no excuse for what Paul calls "acts of the sinful nature": "sexual immorality, impurity and debauchery, idolatry and witchcraft, hatred, discord, jealousy, fits of rage, selfish ambition, dissension, factions and envy, drunkenness, orgies, and the like" (5:19-21).

The Spirit-led Christian will not only control baser impulses of his sinful nature, but will bear "the fruits of the Spirit": "love, joy, peace, patience, kindness, goodness, faithfulness, gentleness, and self-control" (5:22-23).

Then Paul gives a series of practical counsels on how Christians should deal with each other. He reminds them that the entire law is summed up on a single command: "love your neighbor as yourself" (5:14). He speaks of bearing one another's burdens for in this way they will "fulfill the law of Christ (6:2). He urges them that "each should test his own action . . ." without comparing himself to somebody else (6:4-5). Finally, he reminds them that they will reap what they sow, concluding his advice with these words: "Let us not become weary in doing good, for at the proper time we will reap a harvest if we do not give up. Therefore, as we have opportunity, let us do good to all people, especially to those who belong to the family of believers" (6:9-10).

5. Summary of Paul's Arguments (6:11-18). This section is like a postscript written not by his secretary but in his own hand where he reiterates his principal arguments, stressing the futility of circumcision (6:12-13), and reminding the Galatians of his suffering for Christ (6:14-17). He closes with the benediction: "The grace of our Lord Jesus Christ be with your spirit, brothers. Amen." (6:18).

5. *EPHESIANS*

Scholars are divided on the authorship of Ephesians. There are those who claim that the author of Ephesians is Paul. Others question Paul's authorship and claim that one of Paul's disciples or sympathizers composed this letter in his name and spirit.

On the other hand, there is strong evidence that Ephesians is a Pauline Epistle. According to tradition, Paul wrote Ephesians from his Roman prison. Ephesians was one of four prison epistles; the other three were Colossians, Philippians, and Philemon. The Epistle carries in the introduction the name of "Paul, an apostle of Christ Jesus" (1:1). Again, chapter 3 begins "For this reason I, Paul, the prisoner of Christ Jesus . . ." (3:1). Furthermore, in 6:21-22, the mention of Tychicus in the same manner as Col. 4:7-8 suggests that the author of the two letters is Paul.

Since the nineteenth century, however, scholars have increasingly doubted Paul's authorship and have regarded the epistle as the work of an anonymous member of a Pauline school of thought.[38] Those scholars also maintain that Ephesians was not even written for the church at Ephesus, because several of the best manuscripts omit the address "at Ephesus" in the opening verse of the letter. Moreover, the absence of greetings and specific references to persons and places is conspicuous.[39] Furthermore, many scholars question Paul's authorship of Ephesians on the following grounds:

a. There are differences in the literary style of Ephesians and those of the unquestionably genuine letters of Paul. Ephesians contains long and convoluted sentences, in contrast to Paul's usually direct and forceful statements.[40]

b. There are differences of vocabulary. More than ninety words that are not found elsewhere in Paul's letters appear, and this novel vocabulary is akin to Christian writings after Paul.

c. There are theological differences. In I Corinthians, Paul wrote that "no other foundation can anyone lay than that which is laid, which is Jesus Christ" (I Cor. 3:11). In Ephesians, "the apostles and prophets" are called the foundation of the Church (Ephes. 2:20).

d. In Ephesians, *church (ecclesia)* invariably means the one universal church, in sharp contrast to Paul's normal use of the word to mean the individual gatherings of believers (Gal. 1:2; I Cor. 11:16; 16:19).[42]

e. In Ephesians there is no suggestion of the Second Coming of Christ, while in other Pauline letters the emphasis is conspicuous.

Some scholars also insist that Ephesians is not really an epistle, but rather a tract, a circular, or a "cover letter" to accompany an early collection of Paul's epistles. It is like an essay that is shaped in letter form.[43]

The letter has been accepted from early in the second century as an authentic work of apostle Paul.[44]

Paul founded the church at Ephesus while returning from his Second Missionary Journey (Acts 18:19-21). On his Third Missionary Journey he spent three years in Ephesus (Acts 19:1-20:1). On the way back to Jerusalem, he stopped again in Ephesus and gave an emotional farewell address to the Ephesian elders at Miletus (Acts 20:17-38).

Ephesus was the religious and commercial center for Asia Minor (present northwestern Turkey). It was famous for the temple of Diana (Roman) or Artemis (Greek). The temple was one of the seven wonders of the ancient world. The conversion of significant numbers of people to Christianity precipitated a riot led by the silversmith Demetrius because of the economic threat of people turning away from worshipping Artemis (Acts 19:23-41).

Ephesians is the most complete summarization and ultimate development of the thinking of Paul about God, Christ, creation, and the Church.

Compared to all other writings of Paul, the style is grand and overflowing. The sentence structures are often very complex, and the sentences are very long, sometimes running on for several verses. It leaves the impression that language was not adequate to express what the writer was trying to put into words.

The letter, undoubtedly, is highly theological. It represents the author's completely developed theology. It has something in it from all Paul's previous letters, yet goes beyond any and all of them in the heights of theological development and implication.

There is a very close relationship between Ephesians and Colossians; of the 155 verses in Ephesians, 53 are identical and another 22 include phrases found in Colossians. But there are differences between the two letters. In Colossians, Paul expresses the supremacy, adequacy, all-sufficiency, and glory of Christ as the head of the Church. In Ephesians, the thought goes further to emphasize the authenticity and universality of Christ's Church. In Colossians, there is a note of controversy. The ideas are developed in opposition to heresies which were dominant in the area. In Ephesians, there is no note of controversy. The sovereignty and supremacy of Christ and the work and nature of the Church are developed for their own sake.

Paul wrote Ephesians probably sometime between 60-64 A.D. from his Roman prison cell. In the leisure he had in prison, he composed this, the devotional and theological crown of all his work.

The diverse contents of Ephesians may be subsumed under the following headings:

1. God's Plan of Salvation Through the Unified Body of the Church (1:13:21).
2. Instructions and Exhortations for Living in the World While United to Christ (4:1-6:20).

The first three chapters of Ephesians are doctrinal in nature, beginning and ending in prayer. The last three chapters are hortatory. The author's theme is that the unity of the universe through Christ (chs. 1-3) must be reflected in the unity of the Church, which is the earthly manifestation of the divine oneness (chs. 4-6).

1. God's Plan of Salvation Through the Unified Body of the Church (1:13:21). The letter's introduction has been likened to a "hymn of praise," taking up and elaborating the characteristic Pauline thanksgiving.[45] In this section it has been argued that the apostle Paul, though he is thus named in the salutation, cannot have been the author of the epistle, because the earliest manuscripts omit the address "at Ephesus" in verse 1. It is also argued that whereas the typical thanksgiving makes contact with the concrete situation of the church Paul is addressing, the Ephesian thanksgiving does not. It can be argued, however, that Ephesians was intended as a circular letter to the Asian churches. Tychicus, a loyal helper and companion of Paul, accompanied Paul through the Roman province of Asia on his Third Missionary Journey and delivered his letters to the Colossians (Col. 4:7-9) and Ephesians (Ephes. 6:21), with space for each city to insert its own name. This would account for its lack of personal greetings, with which most of Paul's letters abound.

Paul says although the human race had become alienated from God, God's redemptive act in Jesus' death and resurrection has brought "all things in heaven and on earth together under one head, even Christ" (1:10).

Paul looks upon himself and others and sees within each person a world of conflict, tension, disharmony, and disunity. He looks upon the world and sees in it violence and disharmony (2:1-3). Paul then says that Christ, in whom the fullness of God is present, is the one in whom all things are to be united in harmony.

The Church as Christ's Body brings to completion the purpose conceived by Christ. According to His preordained plan, God has made Christ the head of the Church, and through Christ God dwells in the Church (1:22-23), and brings about reconcilialtion and harmony among formerly hostile segments of humanity (2:11-17). God's age-old secret is now understood: "The Gentiles are heirs together with Israel, members together of one body, and sharers together in Christ Jesus" (3:6).

2. Instructions and Exhortations for Living in the World While United to Christ (4:1-6:20). The last three chapters of the letter are of hortatory nature. Having discussed God's ultimate purpose in creation and the significance of the Church in that purpose, Paul brings out the ethical implications of living properly in the world while remaining united to Christ. Paul explores four areas in which the Spirit imparts unity:

a. The first area is the Church, where all believers are to promote the unity of the Church. Being composed of many members of diverse talents and tempers, the fundamental requisite to its proper functioning is a spirit of humility and mutual forebearance of the members one toward another (4:2).

Unity in the Church is not expressed through uniformity or unanimity, but by diversity of gifts (4:7-16). The real unifying power of the Church is its Head, Jesus Christ. The Church unified in him is to be his Body through which Christ continues to do his work of reconciliation and unification.

b. The second area in which the Spirit imparts unity is the pagan world. In this section, there is a vivid description of Christian behavior as the opposite of pagan immoralities (4:17-5:20). Paul appeals to his readers not "to grieve the Holy Spirit of God . . . and get rid of all bitterness, rage, and anger . . . and be kind to one another, forgiving each other, just as in Christ God forgave you" (4:30-32). Furthermore, he tells them to abandon their heathen ways: sexual immorality, impurity, obscenity (5:3-4), drunkenness, debauchery (5:18), and "be filled with the Spirit . . . and submit to one another out of reverence for Christ" (5:19-21).

c. In the third area, the Spirit permeates in the household. Home life is to be as reverent and orderly as behavior in the church. The relation between husband and wife is here represented as being a counterpart of the relation between Christ and the Church (5:22-32). According to Paul, marriage is a holy union like Christ's mystical bond to his Church. Based on this concept the ancient churches—Catholic and Orthodox—consider marriage a Sacrament.

Children and parents have their duties and obligations. Children are to honor those who gave them life: their parents (6:1-4). Fathers are cautioned against being too severe with their children.

Slaves and masters have mutual obligations (6:5-9). Slaves must obey their earthly masters (6:5), and masters must treat their slaves humanely. In Christ masters and slaves stand in the same footing (6:9).

Paul's injunctions to slaves to be obedient to their masters have been criticized by some. But they are neither "approval or condemnation of the institution of slavery in itself, but are based upon the matter-of-fact recognition that it constituted the sociological framework within which many members of the Christian community found their lives actually cast."[46]

d. The Spirit offers protection against powers in the unseen world (6:10-20). Using the analogy of Christians armed like Roman soldiers, Paul urges Christians to arm themselves against evil. Truth, righteousness, peace, faith, salvation, the Word, and prayer are weapons that ward off the darts of the unseen enemy.

The injunction to put on the whole armor of God indicates that Paul expects a long fight; unlike his earlier letters, he no longer expects the imminent return of Christ and the end of the age.

6. PHILIPPIANS

Philippians is one of Paul's four "Prison Letters;" the other three are Ephesians, Colossians, and Philemon. It was written around 61-62 A.D. to the church at Philippi, the first church Paul founded in the continent of Europe.

The city of Philippi was named after Philip of Macedon, the father of Alexander the Great, in the fourth century B.C. It became a Roman colony in 168 B.C. It was strategically located on the great East-West highway between Rome and Asia and was a center of world travel and commerce. Many Roman soldiers and their families retired in Philippi.[47]

The founding of the church at Philippi is recorded in Acts 16. There Luke mentions three converts who represent different classes and races of people - Lydia (a Jewish proselyte), a slave girl (Greek), and a prison official (Roman). Being the first church founded by Paul in Greece, the Philippian church was the spearhead of Paul's thrust into Europe.

Philippians is a letter of warm thanks written by Paul in response to the generosity of the church at Philippi. The congregation had sent a generous gift to the Apostle through Epaphroditus (4:18). Epaphroditus not only brought the gift but personal greetings from the Philippians. While in Rome, Epaphroditus became ill and almost died (2:25-30). After his recovery, Epaphroditus carried the epistle to the church at Philippi.

Philippians contains Paul's expression of appreciation for the Philippians' concern and support (4:10-19). It is also a letter of personal witness to what Christ meant in Paul's life, a testimony to the joy Christ brings into a life wholly committed to him. It is a warning against certain people trying to aberrate the Gospel, and a plea for unity in the church — a unity born of a common commitment to Christ, who transcends all personal differences and draws his followers into a common purpose and mind.

Paul enjoyed affectionate relationship with Christians at Philippi. His epistle to them is the warmest and most personal of all his letters. The Philippians were in a special way his special people, his dearest group of friends. He calls them "my brothers . . . whom I love and long for, my joy, and my crown" (4:1).

There is no note of rebuke, no "boasting" and no threats to the recipients in this letter as there is in some letters Paul wrote.

There is no presentation of his apostolic credentials, as in the opening of most of his other letters. Such a thing was not needed with these people. There was something else unique in this relationship. Paul reminded the other churches that he had always supported himself and never asked for any financial support from them. The Philippian church was the only Christian community who offered, and from whom Paul accepted, financial help.

This letter is known as the "lovely" letter because of the warmth and affection of the relationship it reveals. It is the "letter of joy," for joy and rejoicing are the constantly repeated theme in it. Paul encourages joyfulness in the Christian life. Though he is imprisoned and subjected to suffering he rejoices. Rejoicing is mentioned in every chapter.[48]

Like some other Pauline letters, Philippians reveals the author's quick changes of mood, ranging from a meditation on his imprisonment and impending death to a severe attack on his opponents.[49] These abrupt and sharp changes in tone have led some scholars to believe that Philippians, like II Corinthians, is a composite work, containing parts of different missives.[50]

On the other hand, other scholars insist that this is an intensely personal letter. There is no attempt to produce a unified, carefully-organized argument; in a personal letter the viewpoints and contents may change suddenly.[51]

Philippians may be outlined in the following way:
1. Salutations and Thanksgiving (1:1-11)
2. Personal Reminiscences and Reflection (1:12-30)
3. Exhortation to Humility, in Imitation of Christ's Example (2:1-18)
4. Plans to Dispatch Emissaries: Timothy and Epaphroditus (2:19-30)
5. Warning and Denunciation of Evil Workers (3:1-4:9)
6. Expression of Thanks and Conclusion (4:10-23)

1. Salutations and Thanksgiving (1:1-11). The letter opens with greetings from Paul and his co-laborer Timothy "to all the saints . . . together with their overseers" at Philippi (1:1). In no other letter does Paul describe his readers in such affectionate terms, calling them partners in his mission and partakers in his imprisonment (1:3-11).

2. Personal Reminiscences and Reflection (1:12-30). Paul explores the significance of his prison experience. (An account of his arrest and imprisonment is found in Acts 22-28.) Despite his unfortunate circumstances, he emphasizes the positive results of his imprisonment. His coming to Rome as a prisoner had turned out to be a help rather than a hindrance in making Christ known in Rome (1:12-18).

Moreover, his imprisonment advanced the spread of the Gospel by inspiring other Christians "to speak the word of God more courageously and fearlessly" (1:12-14). But not all of his fellow Christians supported him; they used his confinement as a means of stirring up trouble for him. Paul, however, is confident of his ultimate vindication (1:19). He is not worried about the future, for to him, "to live is Christ and to die is gain" (1:21). He desires to face either life or death with courage, so that Christ will be honored in his body. Because of the continuing needs of the Philippians, Paul regards it as more urgent that he continue to live (1:24).

3. Exhortations to Humility, in Imitation of Christ's Example (2:1-18). In this section Paul appeals for unity. He points out that selfishness and self-conceit have threatened the unity of the church. He counsels the Philippians to avoid rivalry, have the attitude of Christ and cultivate humility as Jesus had. To enable his readers to share the same attitude and experience as Christ, Paul presents here his fullest statement of what is known in Christian theology as the Doctrine of Incarnation.[52] In the famous passage of chapter 2:5-11, Paul tells the Philippians that Jesus Christ was so humble that, being God "he did not consider equality with God something to be grasped" (2:6), but instead lowered himself to become a human being. He then humbled himself further to die on the Cross, for which act of obedience "God exalted him to the highest place and gave him the name that is above every name" (2:9). Christians should seek the same

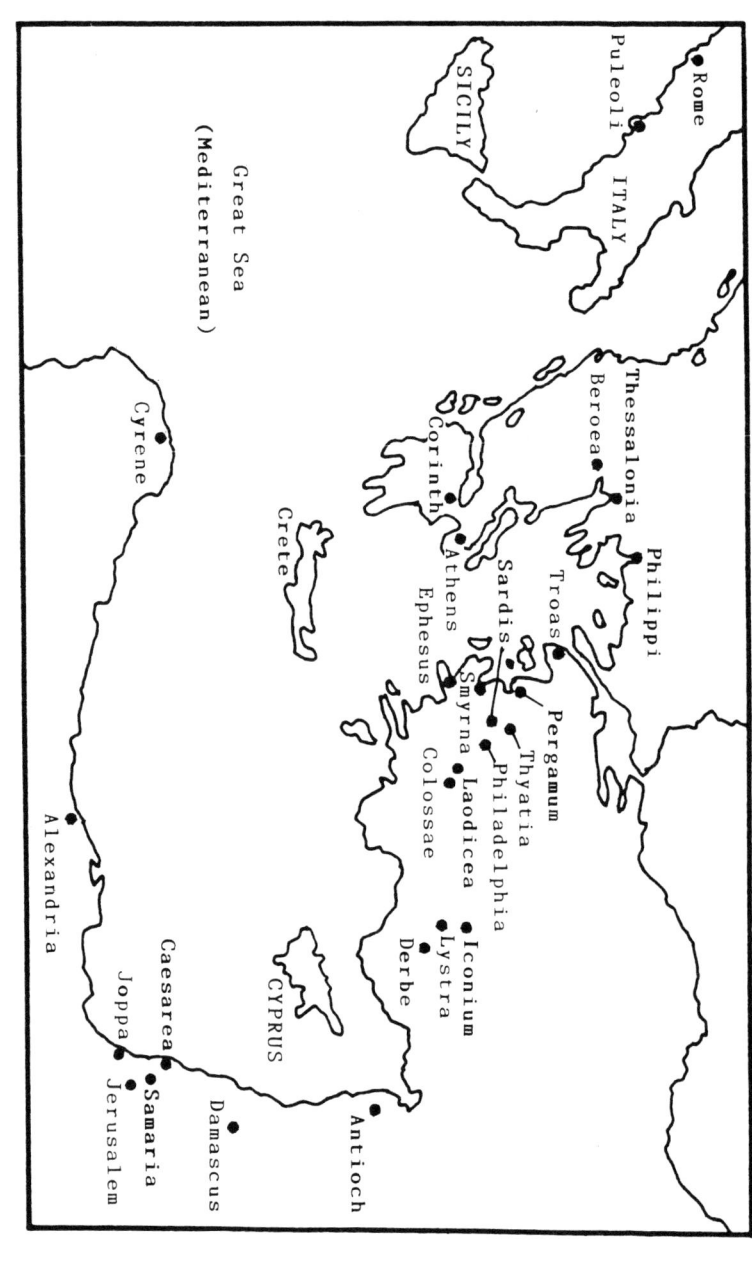

Locations of some of the Middle Eastern cities Paul visited during his three missionary journeys (between 47-56 A.D.) He established most of the churches in Western Asia Minor as well as in Greece.

attitude, working out their salvation, "with fear and trembling" (2:12-13).

4. Plans to Dispatch Emissaries: Timothy and Epaphroditus (2:19-30). In this part of the letter, Paul speaks of the arrangements he is making for the church at Philippi. He wanted very much to visit them, but could not, because he was a prisoner, so he is sending two of his favorite companions to represent him: Timothy, whose name appears as courtesy co-author of this letter (1:1), who shared Paul's positive attitude toward Gentile converts, and Epaphroditus, whom the Philippians had sent to assist Paul in prison. These two emissaries of Paul were to act with his full authority.

5. Warning and Denunciaton of Evil Workers (3:1-4:9). Here, the shift to a sterner tone, particularly from 3:1-21, leads some scholars to suggest that this passage represents an earlier memorandum attacking Judaizers who insisted on circumcising Gentile converts.

Paul describes, in violent language, the danger of Judaizers, "Watch out for those dogs, those men who do evil, those mutilators of the flesh" (3:2).

Then Paul relates his own experience in this regard. Despite his exemplary credentials - a Benjaminite, a Pharisee, "Hebrew of Hebrews," a persecutor of the church, and "faultless" keeper of the Law - he regards his heritage "rubbish" compared with the new experience in Christ (3:4-11).

In the verses that follow (3:12-15), Paul pictures himself as in a race in which his present life is a period of struggle and aspiration; he is striving to be Christlike, which is still far beyond him. In this race he says, "one thing I do: forgetting what is behind and straining toward what is ahead, I press on toward the goal" (3:13-14). His advice to the Philippians is to follow his example in pursuit of the vibrant and victorious Christian life: focusing in on Christ, forgetting those things that are passed, and forging on to their Christian life.

Following the analogy of his never-ending race, Paul warns against those who distorted his message of a Christian's freedom from Law and interpreted it as a sanction for self-indulgence or moral indifference (3:18-19). He tells the Philippians not to fix their "minds on earthly things" (3:19), but to ever remember their "citizenship is in heaven" (3:20).

In chapter four, Paul again deals with a troubling situation. Two quarrelsome women, Euodia and Syntyche, leaders of the church, were allowing their personal differences to become an annoyance to the church. Paul does not suggest that they be shut up or kicked out of the church, but he pleads with the church "to help these women" (4:2-3).

6. Expression of Thanks and Conclusion (4:10-23). Before he closes his letter, Paul once again thanks the Philippians for their kindnesses and their financial support. Then he undergirds all that he wrote in the words, "rejoice greatly in the Lord" (4:10). That is the recurring theme in the whole letter. Eleven times in this short letter he uses the word "rejoice," and six times he uses the word "joy."

Paul tells his Philippian friends that the secret of his contentment and joy "whatever the circumstances," even when bound with chains is Christ himself, for in his words, "I can do everything through him who gives me strength" (4:13).

7. COLOSSIANS

There are arguments for and against the Pauline authorship of Colossians. Those biblical scholars who dispute Paul's authorship of this letter base their arguments on the following points:

a. Differences in language and style from the undisputed Pauline epistles. There are 34 words that occur in Colossians but not elsewhere in the New Testament. There are long, verbose sentences which are quite uncharacteristic of Paul.[53]

b. Theological differences. There is a lack of concepts particularly dear to Paul: righteousness, law, salvation, revelation.

On the other hand, there are concepts which are more developed than those in undoubtedly Pauline letters. For example, the sacrament of baptism is viewed as a Christian version of the Jewish rite of circumcision in which Christians symbolically experience dying with Christ and arising with him (2:12; 3:1). Another well developed concept is the idea of the office of the ministry as a divine office (1:25).[54]

c. The close relation both in style and thought to Ephesians which, according to these New Testament critics, was the work of a later Paulinist rather than of Paul himself.[55]

d. The Christology of Colossians is more developed. There are concepts in the letter which have their roots in pre-Pauline Christianity.[56]

e. Paul did not found and never visited the church at Colossae, and therefore would not write a personal letter to a church which he had not organized.

On the other hand, many scholars insist that Paul was the author of Colossians because of a few important observations:

a. The letter begins with Paul's greetings: "Paul, an apostle of Jesus Christ" (1:1), and the salutation is in the characteristically Pauline style.

b. The Letter to the Colossians was included in the collection of Pauline letters from the time that they were first brought together; it is listed in the Muratorian canon,[57] that list of scriptural books which as early as the third century offered a list of the New Testament books. It is also included in the Chester Beatty codex of the Pauline epistles, which was made in Egypt toward the end of the second century.[58]

c. The early church fathers, such as Irenaeus, Tertullian, and Clement of Alexandria, quote from the letter and consider it a typical Pauline letter.

d. The verbal parallels of similarities between Colossians and earlier letters by Paul suggest that Paul wrote Colossians.[59]

e. Colossians was composed at about the same time as Philemon, to which it is closely related. In both letters Paul writes from prison including his friend Timothy in the salutation and adding greetings from many of the same persons, such as Onesimus, Archippus, Aristarchus, Epaphrus, Mark, and Luke.[60]

The majority of New Testament scholars tip in favor of Pauline authorship.

Colossae, located in the Lycus Valley about one hundred miles east of Ephesus, was one of three cities in the valley. The other two were Hierapolis and Laodicea. The area was rich in mineral deposits, and the city may have been named after one of the deposits (*Colossus* means large statue).[61]

Apparently the founder of the churches in the Lycus Valley was Epaphras (1:17), who probably owed his conversion to Paul.

Epaphras came to visit Paul in prison, in Rome, and reported on the religious situation in Colossae. He brought the good news that there were faithful people who were working there and that they held Paul in their affection and respect. He brought some news that was not so good. Some of the faithful were being confused by false teachings. There was a heresy being presented to them. The situation had not yet reached epidemic proportions, but it was like a cloud on the horizon presaging a storm to come.

To head off and counteract what might develop, Paul wrote this letter to the Colossians sometime between 60 and 62 A.D. The letter was delivered by Tychicus and Onesimus. Onesimus was the runaway slave of Philemon of Colossae whom Paul had converted to Christianity and reconciled to his master (Philem. 8:21; Col. 4:7-9). It is believed he carried a second letter from Paul to Philemon, the owner of Onesimus.

We do not know exactly what the heresy was which was developing in Colossae. We know that the area was filled with all kinds of mystery religions and pagan cults. Syncretism, the practice of taking a bit of each of the variety of religions, was rampant. There were elements of Neo-Platonism. There were the elements of what later became Gnosticism against which the Gospel of John was written.[62] The net effect of this spiritual climate was that the people were losing what Christ had brought them—a new and transforming insight into God and the meaning of life.

The general structure of the epistle may be outlined as follows:

1. Introduction (1:1-14).

2. The Person and Work of Christ - *Doctrinal* (1:15-23)
3. The Apostleship of Paul - *Pastoral* (1:24-2:5)
4. Warning Against Erroneous Teaching - *Polemical* (2:6-23)
5. Moral Instruction and Exhortation - *Practical* (3:1-4:6)
6. Conclusion: Friends of Paul - *Personal* (4:7-18)

Paul writes to show that Christ is preeminent and that believers are totally complete in Jesus Christ. Believers need to know the cosmic significance of Christ as the "image of invisible God" and as the Creator of all in heaven and on earth (1:15-16), as well as the all sufficient head of the Church (1:18).

1. Introduction (1:1-14). The epistle begins with the usual salutation and an extended thanksgiving. In the introduction Paul mentions Epaphras. Verses 5-7 suggest the possibility that Epaphras founded the Colossian church. Paul strongly supports Epaphras in his position and assures the church that Epaphras is preaching the same Gospel as Paul.

It is surprising that Paul, although he neither founded the church nor even visited it, indirectly claims the right to control it. By supporting Epaphras's authority, Paul's authority for the commissioning of other men in ministry is affirmed. Here we can see the beginning of a solution to a problem faced by the church as the first apostolic generation died off: how can apostolic authority be preserved in the absence of an apostle, particularly after his death? Is "succession" to be based on teaching or on direct descent from the original apostles? This is a question faced by the church on its way from being a movement to being an institution.[63]

2. The Person and Work of Christ—Doctrinal (1:15-23). Paul here discusses his Christology. He first writes about the Person of Christ. Christ is the "image of the invisible God . . . and the first-born of all creation" (1:15). The phrase, "first-born of all creation" is a title of dignity and function. It does not imply Christ is himself a part of the creation. The first-born in Jewish tradition is heir and destined ruler of all. Christ as first-born "is accorded in respect of the created universe that place of honor that belongs to the eldest son in the household or in the kingdom."[64] Christ is the maker and mediator of the created universe with all its spiritual inhabitants (1:16-17).

Paul then turns to Christ's role in human life and human history. Christ comes into human history to redeem it and launch into it the church, a body of believers. He is the head of the body (1:18), and "is conscious of the experience of every member, and prompts and guides the actions of every member." [65]

Peace between God and the alienated and sinful mankind has been made through the blood of Christ, shed on the Cross (1:20). Paul points out that the former state of the Colossian Christians was also one of alienation. Now God "has reconciled them through Christ" (1:21).

3. The Apostleship of Paul—Pastoral (1:24-3:5). In this passage there is a discussion of Paul's apostolic office. The apostle justified his intervention into the affairs of a church which he had not founded. He is not seeking to win them to a new loyalty, having already reminded them that Epaphras, who brought them the Gospel, came to them under his direction. But he appeals to them because of his divine commission, which is worldwide in scope (1:25), and because of his personal interest and care for them (2:1-15).

4. Warning Against Erroneous Theology—Polemical (2:6-23). In this section Paul warns the church of Colossae against the dangers of some heresies which the Colossians had apparently amalgamated with the Christian gospel. There was an astrological element (2:8). The Colossians were being led to seek the guidance of the spirits of the stars and the planets.[66]

There was also a philosophical element, what Paul calls "hollow and deceptive philosophy" (2:8). The false teachers were detracting from the gospel by saying it was too simple and people needed to have a more sophisticated approach.

Moreover, there was an ascetic element in the heresy (2:16; 2:21) which laid down strict rules about eating and drinking. There was a whole series of prohibitions: "touch not, taste not, handle not."[67]

This synchronistic heresy in the Colossian church tended to foster loose morals among the people. It gave a large place to the worship of angels as intermediaries between God and man, setting Christ aside as the only Mediator. Furthermore, the Colossian heresy tended to create spiritual and intellectual snobbery—an elite, in-group, who had the special knowledge—shutting out the common person. Above all, the most devastating aspect of the heresy was the down playing of Jesus Christ.

In answer to the effects of the heresy on the position of Jesus, Paul makes the strongest statement in all his writings of the superiority, preeminence, and adequacy of Christ.

5. Moral Instruction and Exhortation—Practical (3:1-4:6). In this section Paul deals with some ethical matters. He states that the Colossians are to be so committed to Christ that the spirit of Christ is incarnate in them, and their conduct must follow from Christ living in them. They are to put on "the new man" created in the image of Christ. That means they have to "put to death whatever belongs to earthly nature: sexual immorality, impurity, lust, evil desires, greed . . . anger, rage, malice, and slander" (3:5-8).

This gospel and ethic is universal. It is for all people. It breaks down old barriers of Greek and Jew, Barbarian, Scythian, slave or free (3:11).

There is a second table of rules for the Christian household in the section 3:18-4:1. Paul advises that wives must submit to their husbands and husbands must love their wives (3:18-19). His views on marriage relations, however inadequate we may regard them to be, actually represent a marked advance over the then current view and practice. In the ancient Jewish, Roman and Greek world, women had very little if any rights at all. Paul introduces the principle of mutuality into marriage; Paul says that women have rights too, that husbands have obligations towards their wives as well as wives toward their husbands. Those mutual relations are to be governed by and to express love and kindness.

About parents and children Paul states: "Children, obey your parents in everything, for this pleases the Lord. Fathers, do not embitter your children, or they will become discouraged" (3:20-21).

Again, Paul makes a marked advance over the societal norms. The old law in the Ten Commandments simply said, "Honor your father and mother that your days may be long upon the earth." Nothing was said there about whether parents were worthy to be honored by their children. Paul suggests that obedience is to the worthy parents. He is also suggesting that parents, if they are not careful, can alienate children by constant criticism and overpowering demands to excel. Here again, Paul is injecting the principle of mutuality, of mutual obligations, and of mutual devotion between parents and children.

The same principle applies to slaves and masters. Slaves must obey their earthly masters (3:22), but masters must provide their slaves "with what is right and fair," because they should know that they "have a Master in heaven" who is the Father of all (4:1).

6. Conclusion (Friends of Paul) - Personal (4:7-18). After making general exhortations which apply to all alike—"to continue steadfastly in prayer with thanksgiving" (4:2) and after giving some instructions on Christian behavior toward pagans (4:5-6), Paul closes his epistle to the Colossians with an interesting series of greetings. Among those listed are Onesimus (4:9) who is the subject of his letter to Philemon; Mark (4:10) who had incurred Paul's displeasure by deserting the mission in Pamphylia (Acts 13:13) but who now had apparently regained the confidence of Paul; and Luke, "the beloved physician" and the author of the third Gospel and the Acts (4:14). The Letter to the Colossians ends with the brief benediction: "Grace be with you" (4:18).

8. *I THESSALONIANS*

First Thessalonians is Paul's earliest surviving letter and thus the oldest Christian document in existence. It was written about 50 A.D. to the newly formed church in Thessalonica, founded by Paul in cooperation with his companions, Timothy and Silas (Silvanus).

Thessalonica, today named Saloniki, was already in Paul's time a large and thriving seaport city, serving as both the capital of the Roman province of Macedonia and the seat of the proconsul. As one of the crossroads on the Egnatian highway, connecting the eastern and western regions of the empire, it was economically and militarily important.[68]

The Church in Thessalonica was founded on Paul's Second Missionary Journey (Acts 17:1-9). Although Luke implies that Paul stayed three weeks and was involved with Jews (Acts 17:1-18:5), Paul's Letter to the Thessalonians indicates a much longer visit and an association mainly with Gentiles (I Thess. 1:9).[69]

After their beating and imprisonment at Philippi (Acts 16), Paul and his companions traveled about 100 miles southwest in Macedonia to Thessalonica (Acts 17:1). Thessalonica was predominantly Greek in culture, but enough Jews lived in the city to establish a synagogue. Accompanied by Timothy and Silas, Paul went straight to their synagogue and began preaching the messiah-ship of Jesus. The effect of Paul's preaching was great among the Gentile proselytes in the synagogue, occasioning the jealousy and hostile reaction of the Jews. As in Philippi and later in Corinth (Acts 19), this led to an eruption of feeling, and Paul and his companions were hauled before the city magistrate and accused of disturbing the peace and causing insurrection. Jason, their host, had to pay a fine, and they were then released (17:5-9). As soon as it was night, the Thessalonian church members sent Paul and Silas away to Berea.

Finally, Paul went on to Athens and then on to Corinth where he preached the Gospel and was engaged in his trade of tent making to support himself (Acts 17:16-18:3).

Paul could not forget the church at Thessalonica whom he left after such a short stay. He was plagued by the question of whether the seed he had planted and which had sprouted so promisingly, continued to grow, or as the people felt pressure from those about them, had it withered and died? He was also concerned about what kind of impression had been left by his hasty departure. Further, could the Gospel be established in a place in a relatively short period, or did it take long residence in a place to get it firmly established? The answer to that had great implications for Paul's future work. What he wanted was a report. Hence, Paul sent Timothy to Thessalonica to bring him a report.

Timothy went, found out what was going on, and reported back to Paul. The news was generally good, and Paul was very pleased. There was also some not-so-good news that Timothy brought and Paul deals with those matters as well.

Thus, I Thessalonians is a substitute for a face-to-face meeting with Paul's recent converts, and it is an expression of the author's earnest desire to see them again that he may "supply what is lacking" in their faith (3:10).

The epistle may be outlined as follows:
1. Address and Greeting (1:1)
2. Thanksgiving (1:2-3:18)
3. Exhortation and Encouragement (4:1-5:22)
4. Conclusion (5:23-28)

The theme of the epistle is the Second Coming of Christ. This subject is mentioned in each chapter (1:10; 2:12, 19; 3:13; 4:13-18; 5:11, 23). Paul corrects some beliefs about Jesus' Parousia and the Resurrection.

1. Address and Greeting (1:1). The letter begins with a characteristic form of salutation. It is a Christianized form of the Hellenistic letter—author's name listed first, then the addressees, then a greeting. It is noteworthy that Paul includes his co-workers' names (Timothy and Silas).

2. Thanksgiving (1:2-3:13). Like most of his letters, Paul begins with a thanksgiving, setting a positive tone and recalling the good associations he has had, using them as a basis for his current concerns.

Paul begins by telling the church members of his uncontainable joy at Timothy's report of their steadfastness and faithfulness. He rejoices in the good news he had received about them.

Chapter 2 deals with Paul's defense of his mission. There were those in Thessalonica who were speaking slanders about Paul, trying to discredit him to the Christians by accusing Paul of being mercenary and vain. Paul answers these matters by reviewing his conduct among them and his relations with them. He had not sought praise; he had asked no money; his conduct had been exemplary.

3. Exhortation and Encouragement (4:1-5:22). Along with his encouraging words, Paul reminds the Christians in Thessalonica that they should conduct themselves in terms of certain Christian moral standards. The Apostle's admonitions include sexual purity (4:3-8) and continuing growth in the practice of Christian love (4:9-12). Paul writes that self-control and chastity are necessary to attain a wholesome life.

Then Paul drives to his principal reason for sending the letter - a clarification of teachings about the end time (4:13-5:11). Apparently, some Thessalonians believed that the Parousia would occur so swiftly that all persons converted to Christ would live to see his Second Coming. The Thessalonians were confused at the death of some in the congregation who had come to believe in Jesus and to look forward to the return of Jesus before their death. Now they assumed that those who had died would not participate in the joys of Jesus' return.

Paul reassures his readers that those members of the Christian community who have died in faith are not lost, but will share in the glory of Christ's return (4:14-16). When Jesus returns, the "dead in Christ" will rise and together with those who are left alive will ascend to meet the descending Lord in the air (4:17). Thus the deceased will participate in the Parousia. Therefore, they may "encourage each other with these words" (4:18).

In the second part of this rather long discussion of the coming of Jesus (5:1-11), Paul states that "the day of the Lord," the Judgment Day, will come suddenly "like a thief in the night" (5:2). Its coming will be a cause of dismay for those who have not believed or are not prepared (5:3-4). But Christians need not be afraid, for they are safe from eternal wrath. They should keep awake, armed with faith and love, active in good works. They should maintain a tranquility of mind, not meddle in others' affairs, be joyful, and hold on to the good (5:12-22).

4. Conclusion (5:23-28). The epistle ends with a characteristically Pauline version of the typical Graeco-Roman conclusion and final greetings.

9. II THESSALONIANS

Some biblical scholars question the authenticity of II Thessalonians; many others regard it as genuinely Pauline.

Those who dispute the authenticity of the letter claim that it is a pseudonymous writing, a writing whose author wrote in Paul's name "to preserve his influence and apply his stature and spirit to new problems in the church that developed after the apostle's death."[70] According to these scholars, two problems that the church had to face are evident from a close reading of II Thessalonians. First, the writer of II Thessalonians is part of a church experiencing official persecution. Second, his church was to come to grips with the delay of the Parousia. This latter problem is treated in terms of a scenario, listing a number of things that must first happen before the final End can occur (2:3-12). This, according to these critics, is far different from I Thessalonians 4:13-17, in which Paul seems to expect the End to come within his own lifetime (4:15,17). Moreover, II Thessalonians 1:5-10 states that at the Judgment God will reward the persecuted and will destroy their persecutors; such an idea is not found in Paul's undisputed letters and is more representative of the generation after Paul (Rev. 16:5-17; 19:2), which suffered severe persecution under the Emperor Domitian.[71] Furthermore, these critics indicate that if Paul composed II Thessalonians, why does he repeat—almost verbatim—so much of what he had already just written to the same recipients?[72]

The majority of biblical scholars, however, insist that II Thessalonians was written by Paul. They state that Paul claims that he wrote the epistle (1:1; 3:17). They also explain the author's apparent change of attitude toward the Parousia. In the first letter Paul stresses the tension between "the shortness of time the world had left and the necessity of the believers' vigilance and ethical purity as they await the Second Coming."[73] In the second letter Paul writes to correct the misconception of the Christians at Thessalonica about the nearness of the end time.[74] The theme is identical in the two letters: the Lord's coming (1:7; 2:1).

The occasion of II Thessalonians is that a few weeks after he had sent his first letter to Thessalonica, Paul learned that his preaching on the Parousia had been misunderstood. He had suggested in his first letter that the Second Coming of Jesus was imminent but not as soon as previously expected. Some believers were claiming that "the day of the Lord has already come," (2:2) and they had given up work and supporting themselves.

Thus the purpose of II Thessalonians is two-fold:

a. To correct a misconception that "the day of the Lord" had already arrived (2:2);

b. To insist believers who lazily awaited the end must work to support themselves (3:6-15).

The letter may be outlined as follows:
1. Salutation (1:1-2)
2. Thanksgiving (1:3-12)
3. Placing Christ's Second Coming in Perspective (2:1-17)
4. Admonition Concerning the Idle (3:1-15)
5. Conclusion (3:16-18)

1. Salutation (1:1-2). The opening address and greeting of this second letter follows closely that of I Thessalonians. The names of Paul, Silvanus, and Timothy are mentioned here, too, as well as those to whom the letter is written - "the church of the Thessalonians" (1:1).

2. Thanksgiving (1:3-12). As customary in his letters, Paul begins this letter with thanksgiving. He commends the believers' faith, love, and endurance under persecution (1:3); he encourages the afflicted and warns those who "do not obey the Gospel of our Lord Jesus" that they will be punished (1:8-9).

3. Placing Christ's Second Coming in Perspective (2:1-17). In his first letter to the Thessalonians, Paul had encouraged the new believers to remain steadfast in the hope of Christ's Second Coming (I Thess. 4:13-18). Apparently, many Christians at Thessalonica misunderstood Paul. They believed that the Parousia, the day of the Lord, had already come (2:2) and thus they abandoned all work and worldly responsibility (3:6-13). Paul in this section deals with correcting inaccuracies concerning Christ's Second Coming, giving instructions about: a. disturbing reports (2:1-2); b. being deceived (2:3-12); c. being distracted (2:13-17). He outlines certain events or "signs" that must occur before "the day of the Lord" comes. Specifically, it cannot come "until the rebellion occurs and the man of lawlessness is revealed, the man doomed to destruction" who will proclaim himself "to be God" (2:3-4).

Paul's portrayal of the anticipated events of the future is painted in apocalyptic language, similar to such books as Daniel, Revelation, and the Qumran War Scroll.[75] Some have held that "the man of lawlessness" refers to an emperor or agent of Rome. Others interpret Paul as referring to Judaism. Still others believe that Paul is making reference to Satan's agent or activity. With the coming of the day of the Lord, the lawless one is to be slain as a result of the cosmic conflict.[76]

Although his original audience may have understood Paul's explanation, modern readers are puzzled by it. One thing, however, is clear: those who believe and serve "the Lie" will be destroyed (2:11-12).

4. Admonition Concerning the Idle (3:1-15). Connected with these erroneous beliefs about the Parousia was an existential problem: idleness. Some people had given up working and lived off the charity of other Christians (3:11-13). Paul warns against idleness. His admonition is "If a man will not work, he shall not eat" (3:10). He cites himself as one who works hard. He reminds them that when he and his associates were among them, they "worked night and day, laboring and toiling so that we would not be a burden to any one" (3:8). He urges them to follow his example of self-sufficiency.

5. Conclusion: (3:16-18). Paul concludes his letter with a final prayer, farewell, and benediction. At this point Paul once again takes a pen and writes in his own hand, verifying his personal signature.

10. PHILEMON

The Epistle to Philemon is Paul's only surviving personal letter to be included in the New Testament. It is the eighteenth book in the present canon of the New Testament and comes after the pastoral letters of First and Second Timothy and Titus, but because it is a genuine Pauline document, we shall review it here. Philemon is not addressed to a congregation, but to an individual Christian, Philemon, whose slave, Onesimus, had absconded with some money.

In this brief letter of twenty-five verses Paul makes no bold theological affirmations and does not develop any theological formulations. There is no attack on enemies of faith. There is no presentation of Paul's apostolic credentials or authority. There is no defense of himself. It is an intimate, courteous, personal plea for forgiveness by Philemon, one of Paul's converts, of Onesimus, another of Paul's converts. It is a letter filled with warmth, deep personal feeling, grace, charm, and courtesy. Besides Philemon, it is addressed to "Apphia our sister" and "Archippus our fellow soldier," perhaps the chief recipient's wife and son. The family may have been leaders in the church that met in their home before which the letter was probably intended to be read (vss. 1-2).

Philemon was a resident of Colossae (Col. 4:9, 17; Philemon 1,2). His house was apparently large enough to serve as a meeting place for the church (vs. 2) and he may have been the leading elder in the church (vs. 1).

The Epistle to Philemon, like those of Ephesians, Philippians, and Colossians, is said to have been written by Paul from prison (Eph. 3:1; 4:1; Phil. 1:12-18; Col. 4:10; Philemon 1, 3).

In spite of biblical reference that the letter was written from Rome, there are some scholars who champion an Ephesian origin of the letter. Their claim is that Philemon lived in Colossae, a town in the Roman province of Asia, about one hundred miles inland from Ephesus. When Onesimus escaped, where would he most likely have run? To Ephesus, rather than faraway Rome, say the proponents of this theory. Moreover, if Paul were at Ephesus, then his request to Philemon that a guest room be prepared is a reasonable one. But if Paul were in Rome (planning a mission in Spain) what would have been the point of such a request? Finally, two of Paul's friends, sending greetings to Philemon, were with him in Ephesus.[78]

The Letter to Philemon provides no compelling reasons for adopting the Ephesian hypothesis. Some passages are better suited to an imprisonment at Rome.[79] Paul had known Onesimus long enough to become attached to him as a "father," and as Paul wrote he needed him for a longer service during his time "in chains for the Gospel" (10, 13).

The one-chapter letter may be outlined as follows:
1. Introduction (1-3)
2. Paul's Thanksgiving (4-7)
3. Paul's Plea for Onesimus (8-22)
4. Conclusion (23-25)

1. Introduction (1-3). Paul begins his letter with "Paul, a prisoner of Jesus Christ," meaning a prisoner for Christ's sake. His greetings and salutations are addressed to Philemon, Apphia, and Archippus. Most probably these three persons were a husband, wife, and son, though there is no real evidence for this.

2. Thanksgiving (4-7). Paul expresses his gratitude for Philemon's Christian witness (4-6) and states that Philemon's benefactions have brought Paul "great joy and encouragement" (7).

3. Paul's Plea for Onesimus (8-22). Perhaps after stealing money (v. 18), Onesimus, a slave, ran away from his wealthy Christian master, Philemon (v. 5). He fled to Rome, perhaps hoping to get lost in the teeming populace of the capital city. However, there he met Paul, and there he became a believer in Jesus Christ.

Paul manifestly wished to keep Onesimus with him, after Onesimus had become Paul's close friend and was very helpful to Paul in his imprisonment. Yet, Paul felt honor-bound to return the run-away slave to his owner, Philemon, also a very good friend of Paul.

Paul knew that there was a great risk in returning a run-away slave to his owner. In those days, the master held absolute power of life and death over his slaves. Yet he is willing to take the risk because he believes Philemon to be a different kind of person than the average slave holder. Thus, Paul instructed Onesimus to return to Philemon, but he wrote this epistle urging him to receive Onesimus not as a slave but "as a brother in the Lord" (v. 16). Paul even promised to pay any debts that Onesimus had incurred (v. 18).

Then Paul makes a kind of pun with the name Onesimus. The name means "useful" or "profitable." Paul says that Onesimus, who had been useless and unprofitable, has now become useful and profitable to both of them because of what had happened to him (v. 11). Onesimus has come to live up to the meaning of his name. The letter urges Philemon to receive Onesimus with the same kindness he would show to the apostle Paul (v. 17).

4. Conclusion (21-25). Expressing confidence that Philemon will do even more than he asks (v. 21), Paul ends his letter telling him about his plans for a visit and with his customary salutations and benediction (vss. 23-25).

This letter has raised the question of Paul's attitude toward slavery. Why doesn't he use this opportunity to speak against that social institution? Some see vss. 15-22 as a suggestion to Philemon that he is to stop treating (Christian?) people as slaves.[80] Others see the letter as no objection to the institution itself. However, we must not read Paul's intentions here in the light of modern socio-ethical concerns. The issue here is the power of Christian faith and love (vs. 5-7). The issue is not slavery but the master and his slave. The phrase "in Christ" occurs no less than five times in this short letter and forms the basis of Paul's charge to Philemon (v. 20). Just as Paul as a criminal before God was accepted and was called to be a servant of the accepting God, criminal Onesimus must be a recipient of Philemon's acceptance and love.[81]

Paul has often been criticized for not attacking the whole institution of slavery. But we need to see Paul in the perspective of his day. In his time, the whole social order was built on a base of slavery. Christianity at this point was about thirty years old. It was a minority. It was under attack. To have made a frontal attack on the base institution of society would not have succeeded. It could only have brought severe retribution to the slaves encouraged to revolt and could have resulted in the widespread extermination of the small minority of Christians.

Moreover, Paul expected the imminent end of the current social order with the return of Christ and the setting up of his Kingdom. He was convinced that before Christ's Second Coming, the task of all Christians was to spread the saving power of Christ, not necessarily to readjust society.

Most importantly, however, Paul brought a new dimension into the whole matter of slave-master relations when he pointed out both Philemon and Onesimus had a new master, Christ. Thus they were spiritual brothers-equals in Christ, who breaks down the old barriers between master and slave.

Finally, a word about the preservation of this letter: it is something of a mystery as to how this short, private letter was preserved and became part of the New Testament. Tradition states that about fifty years after Paul sent his letter to Philemon, Ignatius, an early church father and great Christian martyr, was being taken by the authorities from his church in Antioch to Rome to be executed. As they traveled, Ignatius wrote letters to various churches in Asia Minor, of which a number survived. While he and his guards were stopping in Smyrna, Ignatius wrote a letter to the church in Ephesus. In it he has much to say about their wonderful bishop, Onesimus. Ignatius made the same pun on the name "Onesimus" as Paul did and referred to Onesimus as the profitable and useful one by both name and nature.[82] The possibility and the likelihood is that Onesimus, the run-away slave, became the greatly respected and beloved bishop of Ephesus.

The first collection of Paul's letters was made at Ephesus about the turn of the century. There Paul's letters were collected, edited, and published. It was at the time that Onesimus was the bishop of Ephesus. It is possible and likely that Onesimus insisted that this personal letter of Paul, written from his Roman jail around 61 A.D., be included in the collection,[83] so that all might know what the grace of God had done for him—a run-away slave, a thief, who owed his life to Paul and his changed character to Christ—so that even the shame of his youth might add to the glory of God's love expressed in Christ.

References

1. Stephen L. Harris, *The New Testament: A Student's Introduction* (Mountain View, California: Mayfield Publication Co., 1988), p. 203; Chamberlin and Feldman (Ed.), *The Dartmouth Bible* (Boston: Houghton and Mifflin Co., 1961), p. 1045.
2. Harris, p. 204.
3. C.H. Dodd, *The Epistle of Paul to the Romans* (London: Hodder and Stoughton, 1932), pp. 23-24.
4. Chamberlin and Feldman, p. 1089.
5. Robert A. Spivey and D. Moody Smith, *Anatomy of the New Testament*, 4th Ed. (New York: Macmillan Publishing Co., 1989), p. 337.
6. F.W. Beare, "The Letter to the Romans," *The Interpreter's Dictionary of the Bible*, Vol. 4, (New York and Nashville: Abingdon Press, 1962), pp. 115-120.
7. Chamberlin and Feldman, p. 1089.
8. Harris, p. 233.
9. Gerald R. Cragg, "The Epistle to the Romans," *The Interpreter's Bible*, Vol. IX, (New York & Nashville: Abingdon Press, 1954), pp. 619-621.
10. *Ibid*, pp. 642-643.
11. Robrt A. Spivey and D. Moody Smith, p. 299.
12. James L. Price, *The New Testament: Its History and Theology* (New York: Macmillan Publishing Co., 1987), p. 315; also, Chamberlin and Feldman, p. 1060.
13. Chamberlin and Feldman, p. 1078.
14. Richard L. Jeske, *New Testament: Toward a Historical Understanding* (Lawrence, Kansas: The University of Kansas, 1977), p. 101; Spivey and Smith, pp. 298-299; Cragg, pp. 3-10.

15. Clarence R. Craig, "The First Epistle to the Corinthians," *The Interpreter's Bible*, Vol. X, (New York & Nashville: Abingdon Press, 1954), p. 18.
16. Craig, p. 124.
17. Harris, pp. 217-218.
18. Henry H. Halley, *Bible Handbook* (Grand Rapids: Zondervan Publishing House, 1960), p. 548.
19. Jeske, p. 102.
20. Chamberlin and Feldman, p. 1075.
21. Chamberlin and Feldman, p. 1076.
22. Harris, p. 220.
23. Floyd N. Filson, "The Second Epistle to the Corinthians," *The Interpreter's Bible*, Vol. X, (New York & Nashville: Abingdon Press, 1954), p. 280.
24. James Reid, "The Second Epistle to the Corinthians," *The Interpreter's Bible*; *Ibid*, p. 312.
25. Spivey and Smith, p. 306.
26. Chamberlin and Feldman, p. 1086.
27. Jeske, p. 105.
28. Dieter Georgi, "Second Letter to the Corinthians," *The Interpreter's Dictionary of the Bible*, Supplementary Volume, op. cit., pp. 183-185.
29. Price, pp. 327-28.
30. Harris, p. 222.
31. Filson, p. 363.
32. Raymond T. Stamm, "The Epistle to the Galatians," *The Interpreter's Bible*, Vol. X, (New York & Nashville: Abingdon Press, 1954), p. 429; Wayne Meeks, *The Writings of St. Paul* (New York: Norton, 1972, pp. 435-436.
33. Harris, p. 225.
34. David Magee, *Roman Rule in Asia Minor to the End of the Third Century after Christ*, Vol. I, (Princeton: Princeton University Press, 1950), pp. 453-67.
35. Harris, p. 226; Spivey and Smith, p. 289; Chamberlin & Feldman, p. 1053.
36. Harris, p. 228.
37. Jeske, p. 97.
38. F.W. Beare, "Introduction and Exegesis of Ephesians," *The Interpreter's Bible*, Vol. XI, (New York and Nashville: Abingdon Press, 1953), p. 597.
39. E.J. Goodspeed, *The Meaning of Ephesians*, (Chicago: Univesity of Chicago Press, 1933), pp. 7-10; Price, pp. 382-383; Harris, pp. 250-252.
40. Price, pp. 383-384.
41. G. Johnston, "Letter to the Ephesians," *The Interpreter's Dictionary of the Bible* (Nashville: Abingdon Press, 1962), Vol. II, pp. 108-114.
42. Price, pp. 382-383; Harris, p. 250.
43. Norman Perrin, *The New Testament: An Introduction* (Harcourt Brace Jovanovich, Inc., 1974), pp. 130-138.
44. Goodspeed, p. 7; Jeske, p. 122; Harris, p. 251.
45. Spivey and Smith, p. 363.
46. Beare, p. 732.
47. Francis Wright Beare, *A Commentary on the Epistle to the Philippians* (New York: Harper and Row, 1959), pp. 4, 101.
48. Ernest F. Scott, "The Epistle to the Philippians," *The Interpreter's Bible* (New York and Nashville: Abingdon Press, 1955), Vol. XI, p. 12.
49. Harris, p. 239.

50 Bruce D. Rahtjen, "The Three Letters of Paul to the Philippians," *New Testament Studies*, 6, (1959/60), pp. 167-168; H. Koster, "The Purpose of the Polemic of a Pauline Fragment (Philippians III) *New Testament Studies*, 8, (1962), p. 317.
51 Halley, pp. 566-67; Harris, p. 239.
52 Chamberlin and Feldman, p. 1119.
53 Ed Parish Sanders, "Literary Dependence in Colossians," *Journal of Biblical Literature*, 85, (1966), pp. 28-29.
54 H.C. Kee, *The Origins of Christianity: Sources and Documents* (Englewood Cliffs: Prentice-Hall, 1973), pp. 52-53.
55 Jeske, pp. 117-118.
56 Eduard Lohse, *Colossians and Philemon* (Philadelphia: Fortress Press, 1971), pp. 8-12.
57 Francis W. Beare, "The Epistle to the Colossians" *The Interpreter's Bible* (New York and Nashville: Abingdon Press, 1955), Vol. XI, p. 143.
58 Beare, *The Epistle to the Colossians*, p. 143.
59 Price, p. 370.
60 Harris, p. 243.
61 B. Reike, "The Historical Setting of Colossians," *Review and Expositor*, 70, (1973), pp. 430-431.
62 Charles Guignebert, *The Jewish World in the Time of Jesus*, tr. S.H. Hooks, Book IV, ch. 2 "The Judaeo-Pagan Syncretism," (London: Keegan Paul, Trench, Trubner and Co., 1939), pp. 238-52.
63 Jeske, p. 121.
64 Beare, *The Epistle to the Colossians*, p. 164.
65 Lewis Bostock Radford, *The Epistle to the Colossians and the Epistle to Philemon* (London: Methuen & Co., 1931), p. 182.
66 Spivey and Smith, pp. 359-360.
67 Price, p. 373.
68 Howard Clark Kee, *Understanding the New Testament*, 3rd Edition (Englewood Cliffs: Prentice Hall, 1973) pp. 145-148.
69 R.C. Briggs, *Interpreting the New Testament Today* (Nashville: Abingdon, 1973), pp. 142-43; Harris, pp. 209-210.
70 Jeske, p. 115; Kee, pp. 231-235.
71 Jeske, p. 116.
72 Harris, p. 211.
73 *Ibid.*
74 *Ibid.*
75 Spivey and Smith, p. 288.
76 Price, p. 314.
77 Harris, p. 242.
78 George Steward Duncan, *St. Paul's Ephesian Ministry: A Reconstruction With Special Reference to the Ephesian Origin of the Imprisonment Epistles* (London: Hodder and Stroughton, 1929), p. 188; Price, pp. 362-363.
79 Pirce, p. 369.
80 Frederick Fyvie Bruce, *Paul: Apostle of the Heart Set Free* (Exeter: Paternoster, 1977), p. 406.
81 Jeske, pp. 76-77.
82 John Knox, "The Epistle to Philemon," *The Interpreter's Bible*, Vol. XI, (New York & Nashville: Abingdon Press, 1955), pp. 557-559.
83 Knox, pp. 559-160.

B. THE PASTORAL EPISTLES

I and II Timothy and Titus are commonly called "The Pastoral Epistles." They are also called *Pastorals* (from *pastor*, shepherd, or spiritual leader) because they stress pastoral and ecclesiastical (church-related) concerns.

There are diverse views about the authorship and date of these letters. The traditional view is that they were written by St. Paul between 64-67 A.D.[1] Others claim that these epistles are a product of genuine fragments of Paul's correspondence used by a second-century writer.[2] Still others reject Pauline authorship and put their date between 90-140 A.D.[3]

Those who insist on Pauline authorship claim that the biblical evidence suggests that Paul was the author of the Pastorals. They state that the writer claims to be Paul (I Tim. 1:1; II Tim. 1:1; Tit. 1:1). They also say that the writer's relationship with Timothy and Titus is consistent with what is known about Paul's life (I Tim. 1:8; Tit. 1:4). Moreover, they maintain that the personal references in the epistles are of Paul's known acquaintances (II Tim. 4:19-21).[4]

The name "Pastoral Epistles" has been used since the eighteenth century because the addressees, Timothy and Titus, are addressed as ministers with pastoral responsibilities. The name does not describe the epistles fully because they contain exhortations for the whole Church and not only for pastors. Furthermore, we see from the contents that they are not really addressed to a specific situation or location but are to be used as tracts, guidelines for correct ministerial practice, suggesting Paul himself (or even Timothy or Titus) as the prototype.[5]

Those scholars who question the Pauline authorship of the Pastoral Epistles base their views on a number of considerations:

a. On *historical-canonical* grounds. The earliest available manuscript of the Pauline letters known today, Papyrus 46, does not include them.[6] Marcion, (the early Gnostic Christian who attempted to establish a Christian Scripture distinct from the Jewish Bible and whose canon included the Pauline letters (ca.150 A.D.), does not include the Pastorals. He either did not know about them or simply rejected their Pauline authorship.[7] The Muratorian fragment (ca. 220 A.D.) places them after Philemon, which suggests that only then were they coming to gain a place within the Pauline corpus and that they were still being treated as a kind of appendix to it.[8]

b. On *grammatical-linguistic* grounds. The language of the Pastorals is markedly different from the other Pauline letters. According to a critical study of the vocabulary of the Pastorals, there are 306 words that are not found elsewhere in Paul. Of these 306 words, 175 do not occur elsewhere in the entire New Testament, while 211 are part of the general vocabulary of the Christian writers in the second century.[9] Scholars go so far as to say that the vocabulary of the Pastorals is "closer to that of popular Hellenistic philosophy than it is to the vocabulary of Paul or the deutero-Pauline letters."[10]

c. On *theological* grounds. The theology of the Pastorals differs from that of the other letters, particularly where the same words and concepts are used. For example, *faith* in most Pauline letters means the acceptance of God's grace, trusting what He has done in Jesus (Romans 3:21-31; 4:1-25). It refers to a believing, faithful relationship. In the Pastorals, however, *faith* means primarily the content or object of belief and loyalty to church traditions. Thus the author can speak of "the faith" (I Tim. 3:9; 4:1; II Tim. 4:7) meaning a body of doctrine.[11]

There are other biblical critics who claim that the author of the Pastorals did not know what Paul meant by the Law. It also seems that he forgets the central value which Paul attaches to the Cross and he has nothing to say of the conflict between the flesh and the Spirit.[12]

d. On *ecclesiastical* grounds. The Pastorals appear to reflect a second-century Church with an advanced organization in which "bishops," "elders," and "deacons" have precisely delineated functions, a situation which did not prevail in Paul's day.[13] There is also an interesting observation in Philippians 1:1 where Paul speaks of "bishop*s*" (plural) in the church there, whereas in the Pastorals "bishop" is always singular, in contrast to deacon*s* and presbyter*s*. In the Pastoral letters the bishop emerges as the chief office holder in the church, very much as in the letters of Ignatius (the Apostolic Father and martyr, bishop of Antioch, who lived from c. 35-107 A.D.). Such hierarchical order was not developed during Paul's lifetime. So the date of the writing must be placed into the second century.[14]

e. On *doctrinal* ground. A survey of the content of the Pastorals reveals the preoccupation of the author with doctrinal matters, particularly attacking false teachings. It can be argued that Paul attacked heretical teachings in his other letters. But the author of the Pastorals, unlike Paul in undisputedly Pauline letters, resorts to name-calling and even ridicule (I Tim. 1:9; 3:8; 4:1, II Tim. 1:13). There is "a very different spirit" in the Pastorals than that revealed in the Pauline letters.[15]

Based on the internal evidence, we can say that we cannot be sure exactly who was the author of the Pastorals. The weight of argument tilts toward the idea that these three letters are deutero-Pauline compositions. There is here a problem of pseudonymity —the practice of creating new works under the identity of a well known deceased person. Intending to honor an esteemed figure of the past rather than to deceive the reading public, both Jews and Christians produced a large body of pseudonymous literature. They wrote about contemporary issues as they believed their leader would have, had he still been alive.[16] The majority of scholars believe that the Pastorals are deutero-Pauline works. Writing to Timothy and Titus as symbols of a new generation of Christians, an anonymous disciple (known as the Pastor) warns his readers against the prevailing heresies of the time and urges them to adhere to the original apostolic teachings.[17]

Those who insist that the Pastorals are genuine Pauline epistles state that Paul addresses these letters to Timothy and Titus, his fellow workers, who are mentioned frequently in other Pauline letters. Timothy was the son of a Greek father and Jewish mother (Acts 16:1; II Tim. 1:5) from Lystra; he became a Christian under Paul's ministry: Paul called him "beloved son" (I Cor. 4:17; I Tim. 1:2-28; II Tim. 1-2). To please the Jews, Paul circumcised Timothy before taking his Second Missionary Journey (Acts 16:1-4; 20:1-4). Paul later sent him to Macedonia (I Thess. 3:6) and from there to Corinth to quiet the dissension (Acts 19:22; I Cor. 4:17; 16:11), which he was unable to do (II Cor. 7:6, 13-14; 8:6).

Titus, a Greek whom Paul converted, became a companion of Paul on his missionary journey (II Cor. 8:23; Gal. 2:1-3; Titus 1:4). Titus effected a reconciliation between the Corinthians and Paul (II Cor. 7:5-7; 8:16-24; 12:18).

The Pastorals describe both Timothy and Titus as young and present them as the ideal of the young pastor who needs help and guidance. As ordained ministers of the church, Timothy and Titus are urged to practice correct behavior in order to be above moral reproach. The false teachers, as bad examples, should be avoided. The Pastorals are thus to be viewed as tracts issuing general guidelines for the church and its ministers in any location.

1. *I Timothy*

The first two Pastorals are addressed to Timothy. In terms of chronology, I Timothy was written first, then Titus, and then II Timothy.

I Timothy may be outlined as follows:
1. Introduction (1:1-2)
2. Instructions Concerning False Teachings (1:3-20)
3. Instructions Concerning Public Worship (2:1-15)
4. Instructions Concerning Church Leaders (3:1-13)
5. Instructions Concerning the Ministry (3:14-4:15)
6. Instructions Concerning Special Groups (5:1-6:19)
7. Conclusion (6:20-21)

1. Introduction (1:1-2). An important feature in the introduction is the use of the words "God our Savior," which are not paralleled in the main Pauline epistles and reflect the language of the post-apostolic Church.[18]

2. Instructions Concerning False Teachings (1:3-20). In this section, there is an exhortation concerning teachers of false doctrine (1:3-11), and encouragement to teach sound doctrine (1:18-20). The precise nature of the false teaching warned against is difficult to determine, but verses 4 and 7, along with verses 8 and following, seem to suggest it was the heresy of Gnosticism, a cult of secret "knowledge" (*Gnosis*), mentioned in 6:20.

Hyenenaeus and Alexander were the two ring-leaders of the false teachers from whom church membership was withdrawn ("they were handed over to Satan").

3. Instructions Concerning Public Worship (2:1-15). In the first part of this section, the author speaks on prayer. Prayers and intercession should be made for bad rulers as well as good (2:1-8). The second part deals with women. Women should not be permitted to teach (2:12). They are by nature transgressors and easily deceived, by temperament too garrulous (II Tim. 3:6). Here is another difference between Timothy and the main Pauline letters. Whereas Paul recognized women as prophets and speakers (I Cor. 11:5), the Pastor does not, seemingly because the first woman, Eve, was weak-minded and tempted her husband to sin (2:13-14).

4. Instructions Concerning the Church Leaders (3:1-13). The author gives the qualification of bishops, overseers, elders, and deacons. They are the leaders of the church and must be people of blameless character and able to work with others. Also, they must have no doubts concerning the "deep truths of the faith" (3:6-9).

5. Instructions Concerning the Ministry (3:14-4:15). The writer regards the institution of the Church as "the pillar and foundation of the truth" (3:15). Only right-thinking, morally irreproachable people can successfully resist the false teachers who infiltrate it. The best way to combat erroneous doctrines is by unceasing reiteration of simple Gospel truth.

6. Instructions Concerning Special Groups (5:1-6:19). This section contains specific guidance for dealing with various groups in the church: widows, elders, deacons, slaves, and masters. A Christian who would not support his own dependents is worse than an unbeliever (5:8). The church as a family has an obligation to care for the material wants of those who are in need.

Then the Pastor speaks of the remuneration, discipline, and selection of elders (5:17-22). Elders who do their duties well should be considered as deserving twice as much as they get (5:17). However, their primary motive should not be profit but service.

Slaves are instructed to submit to their masters. A Christian slave who has a Christian master must serve all the better, knowing that the one who benefits by his services is a fellow Christian (6:1-2).

The rich and the powerful should share their wealth (6:17-19). The author's advice to people ambitious to wealth is "the love of money is a root of all kinds of evil" (6:10).

7. Conclusion (6:20-21). In closing, Timothy, the prototype of the wise church supervisor, is told "to guard" the doctrine entrusted to him and to combat "what is falsely called knowledge" disseminated by heretics (6:20). The letter ends with a very short benediction: "Grace be to you." (6:21).

2. II TIMOTHY

II Timothy is also concerned with refuting false teachings. There are a couple of passages which leave the impression that the author feels abandoned by former associates (1:15; 4:9-11). The epistle, however, mingles hope with despair. The writer feels lonely and deserted (4:16), but he has not been defeated. In the face of death he looks forward to a safe arrival in heaven (4:18).

II Timothy presents the concept of Christian discipleship (2:2). It declares the inspiration of Scriptures and their total sufficiency for equipping the people of God (3:16-17). The author emphasizes the preaching of the Word (4:14) and the perpetuation of the Christian faith as the responsibility of every generation (2:2).

According to scholars, of the three Pastorals, II Timothy most closely resembles Paul's genuine letters. It is more in the spirit of Paul than the other letters.[19]

The outline of the epistle is as follows:
1. The Introduction (1:1-2)
2. Exhortation to Witness Based on the Example of Paul (1:3-2:13)
3. Exhortation to Good Behavior (2:14-4:5)
4. Paul's Farewell (4:6-22)

1. Introduction (1:1-2). The epistle opens with a normal Pauline salutation. It corresponds in form to Paul's letters. The formal greeting suggests public rather than private letter style and "emphasizes the authoritative position of the author as over against those addressed."[20]

2. Exhortation to Witness Based on the Example of Paul (1:3-2:13). The true minister is called to testify to the crucified Christ (1:8). He is supposed to preserve and promulgate the teaching originally received by Paul. The writer instructs Timothy to "guard the good deposit entrusted to him" (1:11, 14). The minister is called to be Christ's soldier on duty; he has neither time nor interest for ordinary "civilian affairs;" he has to please his commanding officer, i.e. Christ (2:4).

The author uses another metaphor, that of the professional athlete, who must play "according to the rules," to illustrate that the minister must practice self-discipline (2:5).

3. Exhortation to Good Behavior (2:14-4:8). The emphasis here is on the every day personal behavior of the ideal minister. There are things to do and things to avoid, with special reference to promoters of controversy. The Pastor's recommendation is to avoid "foolish and stupid arguments" because they give rise to quarrels and division (2:26). Timothy must "avoid godless chatter" which can infect the church "like gangrene" (2:16-18).

The good minister keeps the received faith. In his hands the Word of God will break down opposition and hold the Church in its true course (2:22-26).

There will be godlessness in the last days. People will be selfish, "lovers of money, boastful, proud, abusive, ungrateful, unholy... unforgiving, slanderous, brutal, treacherous" (3:2-4). False teachers will preserve "a form of godliness but [deny] its power" (3:5).

The greatest antidote against apostasy and the church's corruption is the "holy Scriptures" (3:14-16). Timothy is to hold fast to the Scriptures, inspired by God (3:16).

4. Paul's Farewell (4:6-21). Readers will not agree concerning the letter's farewell. Some will insist that Paul certainly wrote it. Others will consider that these words are the Pastor's loving tribute to his hero.[21] In either case this final passage is like a triumphant valedictory. The battle-scarred old warrior of the cross, looking retrospectively over a long and hard struggle writes: "I have fought the good fight, I have finished the race, I have kept the faith. Now there is in store for me the crown of righteousness, which the Lord, the righteous Judge, will award me on that day - and not only to me, but also to all who have longed for his appearing" (4:7-8).

Switching abruptly to practical matters, the author asks the recipient to remember to bring his cloak and his scrolls (4:12).

Finally, he expresses confidence that he will be kept safe until the Parousia (4:18).

3. TITUS

Although it is the shortest of the Pastorals, Titus has the longest prescript.

Those who accept the Pauline authorship of the letter state that the historical Titus, like Timothy, was a young minister who was very helpful to Paul's ministry. He is not mentioned in Acts, but is frequently referred to in Paul's epistles. Paul sent him on some important mission and held him in high regard (II Cor. 7:4-7, 13-14, 8:6; 16:23; Tit. 1:5; II Tim. 4:10).

Again, those who do accept Paul's authorship state that the occasion of the letter is as follows. On his journey to Rome, Paul's ship stopped briefly at Crete. Since Paul's stay was too short for him to have started a church, it is probable one already existed, perhaps begun by converts from Pentecost (Acts 2:11). After his release from prison, Paul visited Crete and left Titus there to deal with the problems in the church and complete the work of organizing the church (Tit. 1:15). Paul wrote to encourage Titus to exhort the Cretan believers to conduct themselves in a way worthy of the Gospels.

Those who reject Paul's authorship insist that like the "Timothy" of the other Pastorals, "Titus" also represents the post-apostolic church leadership, the prototype of those preserving the Pauline traditions.[22]

The epistle deals with some of the same subjects as addressed in I Timothy—heresy, pastoral qualifications, conduct of social groups.

One of the characteristics of the letter is that the phrase "good works" is used six times (1:16; 2:7-14; 3:1, 8, 14). This suggests the believers had neglected their responsibilities in this regard.

The letter's chief purpose is to outline the requirements and duties of church elders and bishops (overseers).

Titus can be divided into four sections:
1. Introduction (1:1-4)
2. Qualifications for the Christian Ministry (1:5-2:15)
3. Christian Conduct in a Non-Christian World (3:1-11)
4. Conclusion (3:12-15)

1. Introduction (1:1-4). The letter opens with a longer than usual introductory salutation. In the genuine Pauline letters, Paul always refers to himself as "a servant of Jesus Christ" (Rom. 1:1; Phil. 1:1), while here he calls himself "a servant of God" (1:1). The introduction also emphasizes the loyalty of "Titus" to the

Pauline faith by addressing him as "my true son in our common faith" (1:14).[23]

2. Qualifications for the Christian Ministry (1:5-2:15). The author states that he left "Titus" in Crete that he "might straighten out what was left unfinished and appoint elders in every town" (1:5). The writer also gives some directives on how ordained ministers should conduct themselves. Here in this section, the offices of the "elder" and "bishop" seem to be used synonomously (1:5, 7). Such persons must be "blameless, husbands of but one wife, and fathers of children who are believers" with good reputations and under parental control (1:6). In addition to possessing these domestic qualifications, elders/bishops must be hospitable, right-minded, temperate, just, devout, and self-disciplined (1:7-8).

Significantly, one of the paramount functions of the ministerial office is "to hold firmly to the trustworthy message as it has been taught, so that he can encourage others by sound doctrine and refute those who oppose it" (1:9).

The author then assails false teachers (1:10-16). The false teaching referred to here apparently had something to do with Crete (1:12) and certainly with Judaism (1:14). The Cretans had a notorious reputation as liars. To "cretanize" meant to lie. The sixth-century B.C. Cretan poet, Epimenides, is quoted, "Cretans are always liars, evil brutes, lazy gluttons" (1:12).[24] "Titus" is told to rebuke such persons sharply and to counteract the "Jewish myths" (Gnostic speculations based on the Hebrew Scriptures).[25]

In contrast to false teachers, "Titus" as pastor is commanded to teach "what is in accord to sound doctrine" (2:1). He has to teach a) Older men to be temperate (2:2); b) Older women to be reverent in behavior (2:3-4; c) Younger women to be sensible, chaste, domestic, kind, and submissive to their husbands, (2:5); d) Younger men to be as self-controlled as "Titus" who is to "set them an example by doing what is good" (2:6-8); e) Slaves to be subject to their masters (2:9-10).

3. Christian Conduct in a Non-Christian World (3:1-11). The author reminds his audience that as Christians in a pagan world they must live exemplary lives of obedience and submission to governmental authorities (3:1).Then, the author contrasts the negative personality traits that many believers had before their conversion with the new life in Christ (3:3-8). In their pre-Christian life they were "foolish, disobedient, deceived, and enslaved by all kinds of passions and pleasure . . . [they lived] in malice and envy, being hated and hating one another" (3:3). But when they became Christians they were saved by the washing of regeneration and renewal in the Holy Spirit and became heirs in hope of eternal life (3:5-7).

Finally, the writer urges believers "to devote themselves to doing what is good," for Christian faith manifests in works, not words (3:8-11).

It is interesting to note that in this epistle there is strong emphasis on "good works." Not that men are justified by good works, but "by his mercy" (3:5) and "by his grace" (3:7). But good deeds are the natural fruits of one's relationship with Christ. Thus believers are "eager to do what is good" (2:14); they are "ready to do whatever is good" (3:1); they devote themselves "to doing what is good" (3:8); they must always "devote themselves to doing what is good, in order that they may provide for daily necessities and not live unproductive lives" (3:14).

4. Conclusion (3:12-15). The letter ends with personal services requested (3:12-13). The importance of "good deeds" is stressed again (3:14). Then there is final set of greetings with a brief benediction (3:15).

References

1 Ernest F. Scott, *The Pastoral Epistles* (New York: Harper and Bros., 1936), pp. 8-12; Henry Halley, *Bible Handbook: An Abbreviated Bible Commentary* (Grand Rapids: Zondervan Publishing House, 1960), p. 580; William H. Marty, *Surveying the New Testament* (Dubuque: Kendall/Hunt Publishing Co., 1987), p. 136.
2 B.W. Bacon, *An Introduction to the New Testament* (New York: The Macmillan Co.), p. 128; P.N. Harrison, *The Problem of the Pastoral Epistles* (London: Oxford University Press, 1921), pp. 15-17.
3 Stephen L. Harris, *The New Testament: A Student's Introduction* (Mountain View, California: Mayfield Publication Co., 1988), pp. 250-254; James L. Price,

The New Testament: Its History and Theology (New York: Macmillan Publishing Co., 1987), pp. 388-389.
4   R.S. John Parry, *The Pastoral Epistles* (Cambridge: Cambridge University Press, 1920), pp. 52-66; Marty, p. 136.
5   Howard Clark Kee, *Understanding the New Testament*, 3rd Ed., (Englewood Cliffs: Prentice-Hall, 1973), pp. 256-267.
6   Richard L. Jeske, *New Testament: Toward a Historical Understanding* (Lawrence, Kansas: The University of Kansas, 1977), p. 135.
7   Price, p. 388.
8   Jeske, p. 135.
9   Harrison, pp. 19-80.
10 Norman Perrin, W*hat is Redaction Criticism?* (Philadelphia: Fortress Press, 1969), p. 264.
11 Robert A. Spivey and D. Moody Smith, *Anatomy of the New Testament* (New York: Macmillan Publishing Co., 1989), p. 372.
12 Ernest Findley Scott, *The Pastoral Epistles* (New York: Harper and Bros., 1937), p. 21; Burton Scott Easton, *The Pastoral Epistles: Introduction, Commentary and Word Studies* (New York: Charles Scribners Sons, 1947), pp. 22-23.
13 Stephen L. Harris, *Understanding the Bible*, 2nd Ed. (Palo Alto and London: Mayfield Publishing Co., 1985), p. 340.
14 Jeske, pp. 135-136.
15 Price, p. 389.
16 Harris, *The New Testament*, p. 251.
17 Ibid., p. 250.
18 Price, p. 390.
19 J. Benton White, *From Adam to Armageddon*, 2nd Ed., (Belmont, California: Wadsworth Publishing Co., 1986), p. 175.
20 Fred D. Gealy, "The First and Second Epistles to Timothy and the Epistle to Titus," *The Interpreters Bible*, Vol. XI (New York and Nashville: Abingdon Press, 1955), p. 460.
21 Price, p. 394.
22 Harris, *The New Testament,* p. 256.
23 Gealy, pp. 522-24.
24 Marty, p. 143.
25 Gealy, p. 531.

C. GENERAL (CATHOLIC) EPISTLES

Several relatively short writings in the New Testament have been known as *General (or Catholic) Epistles*. The term "Catholic Epistles" refers to the idea that these epistles are addressed to a general audience rather than to any particular congregation or individual. They are "catholic," meaning *universal*, or *general*, or *open* letters.

Scholars differ as to which epistles are General. Some claim that eight letters comprise the Catholic Epistles: Hebrews, James, I Peter, II Peter, I John, II John, III John, and Jude.[1] Others insist only seven letters have been known as General Epistles since the early fourth century: all the above mentioned letters with the exception of Hebrews.[2] Still others consider only four of these letters (James, I & II Peter, and Jude) as Catholic Epistles.[3]

The General Epistles were written to encourage Christians who were threatened by persecution and false teaching. Another common feature of these writings is their collective struggle to be included in the New Testament canon. Although I John, I Peter, and James were known in some Christian churches at a relatively early date, the others were not mentioned until amost 200 A.D.[4] They were not totally accepted as Scripture until well after the beginning of the fourth century, partly because of the controversy surrounding their origins.[5]

Most New Testament scholars believe that all these letters were written very late in the New Testament period, although there is no consensus on either date or authorship.[6] There are others who do not share this view, and insist that almost all of these General Letters were written during the Consolidation Period of the Christian Church (A.D. 62-96). Moreover, they claim that all the authors of these letters can be identified. All are attributed to prominent leaders of the original Jerusalem church. Six are ascribed to the three Jerusalem "pillars" - Peter, James, and John (Gal. 2) - the seventh, Jude, is purportedly by James' brother.[7] Hebrews is attributed to Paul.[8]

1. HEBREWS

The Epistle to the Hebrews is not an epistle or letter in the usual sense. There is no personal salutation or greeting as in Paul's letters. It is rhetorical and hortatory in spirit. It is much more like a sermon or an oration than a letter.

It is one of the most closely reasoned, detailed, and highly theological writings in the New Testament, so much so that some think it was written by a scholar to a small group of scholars. Some contend that the author ranks with John and Paul as one of the most original theologians in the New Testament.[9]

Hebrews is written in the finest Greek in the New Testament by one who knew Greek grammar and syntax and could employ all the nuances of the language.[10] It is certainly one of the most difficult books in the New Testament for a modern to read and understand.

There is no book in the New Testament which more completely and profoundly emphasizes equally the total humanity and divinity of Jesus.

It was a long time before Hebrews became an unquestioned part of the New Testament. The first list of the New Testament books in 170 A.D., the Muratorian Canon, does not mention it. Not until the middle of the fourth century A.D. was Hebrews definitely accepted as part of the New Testament.[11]

The authorship, date, and destination of the book have been enigmatic. Thus there have been controversies concerning the book in the following areas:

A) *Authorship.* The authorship of Hebrews is debatable, even though the King James Version lists Paul in the title. The American Revised Version and many other versions do not include an author because in the oldest manuscripts the author is not named.

The Eastern Church accepted its Pauline authorship from the beginning. Clement of Alexandria held that Paul had written it in Hebrew and that Luke had then translated it into Greek.[12] Origen attributed its authorship to Clement of Rome.[13] Tertullian called it the Epistle of Barnabas.[14] It was not until the fourth century that Pauline authorship was generally accepted which, undoubtedly, became an important reason for its admission into the canon. During the time of the Reformation, Erasmus, Luther, and Calvin disputed the traditionally accepted view of Pauline authorship. Martin Luther suggested that Apollos might have written the book (cf. Acts 18:24 ff). Other reformers suggested Barnabas,

Philip, or Silas. As a reaction to such critical investigation, the Council of Trent demanded acceptance of the Pauline authorship. In 1914, however, the Papal Biblical Commission determined that "one need not believe that Apostle Paul gave the letter its present form."[15]

Appeal is made to the reference to Timothy in 13:23 as evidence for Pauline authorship. On the other hand, however, evidence against Pauline authorship seems to be stronger. Paul's name is not mentioned as it is in his other epistles. Also, the style and vocabulary are vastly different from Paul's. In conclusion, we must agree with the third century theologian Origen who wrote," "Who it was that really wrote the epistle, God only knows."[16]

B. *Date and Place of Composition of the Book.* The date and place of composition of Hebrews are also unknown. Various scholars suggest Rome, Alexandria, Antioch, and Corinth, with the time of writing estimated between 61 and 96 A.D.[17]

Scholars who insist that Hebrews was written for a second-generation Christianity which was experiencing severe persecution set the date sometime between 81 and 96 A.D. at the time of the terrible wave of persecution which took place during the reign of Emperor Domitian.

Other scholars contend that the ordeal in question had occurred during an earlier time, perhaps Nero's, in 64-65 A.D. They argue that because of the numerous references to sacrifices, the epistle was written sometime prior to the destruction of Jerusalem in 70 A.D.[18]

C. *Destination.* Because the book's title, "to the Hebrews," is not part of the original text, and because the author does not identify its recipients, scholars are also unsure of its intended destination.[19]

Some scholars believe that the recipients of the letter were primarily Jewish converts. They were tempted either to return to Judaism or join a Jewish sect.[20]

Other biblical critics believe that this letter is addressed to all Christians, regardless of their background. Some passages, in fact, seem to suggest a Gentile readership.[21]

In the Epistle to the Hebrews there are also five "Warning

Passages" or "Danger Passages." They are: a. the Danger of Neglect (2:1-4); b. the Danger of Unbelief (3:7-9); c. the Danger of Immaturity (5:11-6:8); d. the Danger of Drawing Back (10:26-29); and e. the Danger of Refusing God (12:25-29). Are these passages directed to Christians, to Jewish Christians, or only to nomimal Christians? Scholars differ in their views.

Hebrews may be divided into five sections:
1. Introductions (1:1-3)
2. The Superiority of Christ's Person (1:4-7:28)
3. The Superiority of Christ's Work (8:1-10:39)
4. Application: The Necessity of Faithfulness (11:1-12:29)
5. Epilogue (13:1-25)

The theme of the book is Christ's superiority to all other beings. The theme is developed by the use of the word "better" or "greater," which is used thirteen times (1:4; 6:9; 7:7, 9, 22; 8:6; 9:23; 10:34; 11:16, 35, 40; 12:24).

1. Introduction (1:1-3). The epistle opens with a powerful and magnificent sentence which is the theme of the book: Jesus Christ is God's Final Word, superior to all. God has spoken (1:1), and He has spoken to us by a Son (1:2), who reflects the glory of God (1:3).

2. The Superiority of Christ's Person (1:4-7:17). Stressing his theme of Christ's superiority to all others, the author begins by contrasting earlier revelations with God's final revelation through the person of Christ. Christ is superior to the Hebrew prophets (1:3), to the angels (1:4-14), to Moses (3:1-4:13), and to the Aaronic priesthood (4:14-17).

Christ is exalted in heaven as he reigns above all the angels, that is, above all earthly and heavenly powers. The exaltation of Christ is grounded in his preexistence and role in creation (1:2). Moreover, not just the heavenly exaltation of the Son, but also the earthly ministry comes into view (2:5-9). As a perfectly obedient Son, Christ is greater than Moses (3:1-6). He leads us to our heavenly homeland.

To demonstrate that Jesus is greater than the Levitical priests who administered the temple, the passage cites the story of Melchizedek and Abraham (Gen. 14:17-20). According to his story, Abraham, returning from a successful war, paid Melchizedek, king of Salem (Jerusalem) and priest of "God Most High," a tenth of his victor's spoils. Because the account mentions neither Melchizedek's ancestors nor descendants, the author concludes that his priesthood is without beginning or end. As king of righteousness and peace and an eternal high priest, Melchizedek is the prototype of Christ. Jesus lives and works at God's right hand as superior high priest after the order of Melchizedek (5:10; 6:19-20). Moreover, because Melchizedek blessed Abraham and accepted offerings from him, the writer argues that the king-priest is naturally Abraham's superior. He is also superior to Abraham's Levitical and Aaronic descendants, the Jewish priests. Sinless and deathless, Christ's priesthood is forever (7:1-28).

In this section are three of the five "warning" or "danger" passages:

a. *The Danger of Neglect* (2:1-4). It may also be called "Warning to Pay Attention." Christians must pay more attention to what they have heard, so that they do not drift away.

b. *The Danger of Unbelief* (3:7-9). Christians must guard against falling into unbelief and disobedience. The example is cited of the Israelites who, after being delivered out of Egypt with mighty signs and wonders, fell into the sins of unbelief and disobedience and perished in the wilderness.

c. *The Danger of Immaturity* (5:11-6:8). Christians are "to go on to maturity" (6:1). They must guard against falling away from Christ. For those who remain faithful and true to Christ, the hope of salvation is sure and steadfast.

3. The Superiority of Christ's Work (8:1-10:39). Christ brought to mankind a New Covenant. The first covenant, centered around the Tabernacle and the Ten Commandments, had served its purposes (9:1-5). Its laws were written on tables of stone (9:4). Christ's laws would be written on our hearts (8:10). The first covenant was sealed with the blood of animals. Christ's covenant was sealed with his own blood (10:29). It was a better covenant, with better promises.

"Better" is one of this epistle's favorite words: better covenant (8:6), better promises (8:6), better hope (7:9), and better possession (10:34).

To sum up, the author maintains that the superiority of Christ's word is manifested in the following ways:

a. Christ serves in a better tabernacle (8:1-5; 9:1-5, 23-24).
b. Christ mediates a better covenant (8:6-13; 9;15-22).
c. Christ made a better sacrifice (9:6-10; 9:11-14, 25-28).

This section ends with a fourth warning, a warning against the Danger of Drawing Back (10:26-39), similar to that mentioned in 6:1-8. Christians should loyally adhere to the true religion because the Day of Judgment is near. There has been one sacrifice for sin. There will never be another. If people willfully sin and alienate themselves from God stubbornly, they should remember that Christ cannot die for them a second time (10:27-31).

4. Application: The Necessity of Faithfulness (11:1-12:29). Christians must maintain their faith while awaiting the Second Coming of Christ. The author reaches the climax of his rhetorical masterpiece in chapter 11, which is the famous "Hall of Fame" or "Cloud of Witnesses" passage. In encouraging Christians to keep their faith, he gives twenty-two examples of Old Testament heroes of faith. This parade of the faithful culminates in Jesus as the pioneer and perfecter of faith (12:2).

In chapter 12, the author is making the following three appeals to the Christians:

a. To lay aside every hindrance (12:1-2);
b. To endure hardships as discipline (12:3-12); and
c. To make every effort to be holy (12:14-24).

Following this three-fold appeal is the writer's fifth and final warning: the Danger of Refusing God (12:25-29). He tells his readers "to worship God acceptably with reverence and awe, for our God is a consuming fire" (12:28-29).

5. Epilogue (13:1-25). Urging believers to lead blameless lives, the author closes his epistle with gracious exhortations to his readers to be loyal to Christ and to follow him in all the ways of life, especially in brotherly love and kindness. He reminds them that "Jesus Christ is the same yesterday and today and forever" (13:8), and that Christians have no permanent home on earth and should seek the unseen city above as their goal and destination (13:14).

2. JAMES

The Epistle of James is a sermon, or a homily, published as a letter. Like a typical sermon of the period, it is not developed around one theme. It goes in quick procession from one subject to another and contains a lot of imperatives and rhetorical questions. It has no coherent plan of development. It is as a string of pearls, a series of separate pronouncements on a variety of subjects strung together like a necklace.

James was very late in getting into the New Testament canon. It was not accepted until toward the end of the fourth century A.D. It finally got in because of its high ethical tone, and because the mention of James was read as a reference to the Apostle James.

Some scholars argue whether there is really anything uniquely Christian about James. In it Jesus' name is mentioned only twice (1:1; 2:1). There is nothing about the atoning work of Christ—his incarnation, his atonement, or his resurrection. If the two references to Jesus were eliminated, there is nothing in the letter with which an orthodox Jew of the period could not agree.

The emphasis of the contents of the book is on teaching material rather than proclamatory material, and in this way James resembles collections of the teachings of rabbis and such books as Proverbs and Sirach.[22] The nature of teaching in the book has to do with every day godly living. In spirit, the contents are close to the old Hebrew prophets and to the moral teachings of the Gospel of Matthew—often very close to the Sermon on the Mount. The author was also acquainted with some of the letters of Paul and closely parallels some of their ethical teachings.[23]

James is written in very good Greek, employing various Hellenistic Greek rhetorical devices (cf. 2:18-26; 5:13-15). It also contains some wordplays and alliteration, recognizable in the Greek text of 1:1-2; 2:4; 3:5; and 4:14.[24]

The author's style is graphic, terse, and forceful, mingling scorn and humor. It abounds in imperatives. There are 54 imperatives in its 108 verses.[25] While the book is not a theological treatise and does not deal with the theological content of the Christian faith, it certainly deals with the kind of conduct which is supposed to result from that faith.

The authorship of the book is controversial. It was originally attributed to James, the brother of Jesus, a leader of the early church in Jerusalem. Most scholars, however, who insist that though the author does not identify himself specifically, the most logical choice is James, the half-brother of Jesus. Although James was not a believer during Christ's earthly ministry (John 7:5), after the Lord's resurrection he became a believer (Acts 1:14).[26]

In the New Testament there are five different men who carry the name "James":

a. James, the brother of the Lord—I Cor. 15:7; Gal. 1:19, 2:9; Mark 6:3 and parallels; Acts 12:17; 15:13; and 21:18.

b. James, the son of Zebedee—Mark, 1:19 and parallels; Acts 1:13 and 12:2.

c. James, the son of Alphaeus—Mark, 3:18 and parallels; Matt. 10:3; Acts 1:13.

d. James the Less, son of Mary—Mark 15:40 and parallels, 16:1.

e. James, the father of the Apostle Jude—Luke 6:16; Acts 1:13.

If the first verse of the Letter of James refers to one of these five, then it can only mean James, the brother of Jesus. The Zebedean James was executed in 44 A.D., and of the other three only their names are known. Only Jesus' brother James would have been so well known and respected to have been able to so authoritatively address "the twelve tribes scattered among the nations" (1:1).[27]

There are, however, the following considerations that cast

doubt on the claim that the author who calls himself "James, a servant of God and the Lord Jesus Christ" is Jesus' brother:

a. If the author is Jesus' brother, it is strange that he rarely mentions Christ and never refers to Jesus' teachings.

b. If the author is Jesus's brother, it is difficult to understand that the letter of such a highly respected church leader is not mentioned in the Muratorian Canon; rather it waited for centuries to receive canonical status.

c. If the author is Jesus' brother, it would have been odd for a figure so dominant in the early Christendom not to leave his imprint of religious philosophy. James, the brother of Jesus, is well known for his insistence on the strict application of the Law among the Gentiles, but in this letter there is no such emphasis.

Similarly, there is no unanimity among biblical critics with regard to the date and place of the letter.

Some scholars believe that the epistle was written from Jerusalem in the early fifties, making it one of the earliest epistles.[28] Others claim that it was written probably about 60 A.D., near the close of James' life, after a thirty-year pastorate of the Judean Church.[29] Many scholars, however, insist that the book is an anonymous work composed between 80 and 100 A.D. The place of writing is unknown.[30]

The purpose of the letter was to recall Christians from worldliness and misconceptions of Christianity to the moral demands of their faith. Also, to urge Christians to maintain a balance between faith and works in the Christian life. Without a discernable central theme, the epistle deals with ethical conduct and pragmatic morality.

Although the Letter of James does not lend itself to clear structuring, the following outline might be helpful as an overview:

1. Introduction (1:1)
2. The Nature of Trials and Temptations (1:2-27)
3. On Partiality: Respect for the Poor (2:1-13)
4. Faith and Works (2:14-26)
5. On Controlling One's Tongue (3:1-12)
6. Clusters of Sayings (3:13-5:20)

1. Introduction (1:1). James is addressed to "the twelve tribes scattered among the nations," which probably refers not to the Israelites of the diaspora but "Israelites in the new dispensation," Christians dispersed throughout the world.

2. The Nature of Trials and Temptations (1:2-27). The author states that in the Christian life there are all kinds of trials and testings. But, says the author, these trials and testings provide the occasions by which one grows in character and becomes strong.

There is a difference between trial in the sense of testing and trial in the sense of being tempted to do wrong. It is very important to have a proper response to trials. A trial can be either

a. a test of faith—the response that leads to endurance and life (1:2-12), or

b. a temptation to sin—the response that leads to evil and death (1:13-18).

God's righteousness is produced in us through trials when we respond by being "quick to listen, slow to speak and slow to become angry" (1:19-20). Then James speaks about the marks of true religion: helping people in distress (such as orphans and widows) and keep oneself from being polluted by the world (1:27).

3. On Partiality: Respect for the Poor (2:1-13). In this section, the author denounces all social snobbery. He criticizes the evil of showing partiality to the rich and discriminating against the poor. Christians are to keep "the royal law found in Scripture: Love your neighbor as yourself" (2:8), for in the Christian fellowship all are "neighbors" regardless of the social and economic distinctions of society.

4. Faith and Works (2:14-26). Perhaps this section is the most famous pasage of James. The author speaks of the necessity of showing faith through good works, for "faith without deeds is useless (dead)" (2:20).

Martin Luther, among others, described James as an argument against Paul's doctrine of justification by grace through faith. He called the Letter "an epistle of straw," arguing that

James is an attack on Paul's viewpoint.[31] Rather than viewing the book as a refutation of Paul, we can view it as an affirmation of Paul. Actually Paul and James are complimentary. Paul says justification before God can only come through faith, but he rejects works as a condition for justification. James looks at works ("good deeds") as an indication of genuine faith. James emphasizes that the person who has been justified before God will demonstrate his faith in works before men. This is also consistent with what Paul teaches (Eph. 2:10).

5. Controlling One's Tongue (3:1-12). In this section, James stresses the importance of self-control in speech. He speaks of the power of words to heal or hurt; the power of gossip to destroy; the power of praise to heal. He scolds us for the opposite kinds of things that can come from the same mouth - the praising of God and the cursing of our fellows by the same tongue (3:9-10).

6. Clusters of Sayings (3:13-5:20). In this final section James deals with a number of sayings and admonitions:

a. *Two kinds of Wisdom* (3:13-18). There is a heavenly wisdom which is peaceloving, considerate, merciful, impartial and sincere; there is an earthly wisdom which is contentious and demonic.

b. *World-mindedness* (4:1-12). The author speaks of covetousness as the origin of wars (4:1-2); then, he speaks of friendship with the world and alienation from God—an expansion of Jesus' statement that a person cannot serve God and Mammon (Matt. 6:24).

c. *Boasting* (4:13-17). James is critical of those who are boastful of their financial successes and are forgetful that their continued existence depends on God's mercy.

d. *Warning Against Rich Merchants* (5:1-6). James condemns the rich and materialistic merchants who exploit the poor, thereby condemning themselves to destruction.

e. *Patience in Suffering* (5:7-12). The author urges the Christians to be patient in suffering until the day of the coming of the Lord.

f. *The Prayer of Faith* (5:13-20). James ends his homily-letter on a positive note of the power of prayer: prayer can heal the sick and effect forgiveness of sin.

3. I PETER

The First Epistle of Peter belongs to what is called "persecution literature." It is one of a number of New Testament writings created while the Christians were being persecuted and needed to be encouraged and undergirded. The dominant message of the book is hope.

I Peter is highly pastoral in tone. It is filled with a pastor's concern for people. It is affectionate, loving, and humble in its spirit.

Whereas Hebrews is one of the most difficult letters to read and understand, I Peter is one of the easiest to read and understand.

In I Peter there is a strong emphasis on the Second Coming of Christ. According to the author, the day of his visitation is near. Christians will soon rejoice with Christ. They will receive a crown of glory from the Chief Shepherd himself.

The First Epistle of Peter was long attributed to the Apostle Peter, although it did not appear on all the lists until late in the canonical period. In 1:1 the author is presented as "Peter, an apostle of Jesus Christ," and in 5:1 as "a fellow-elder and a witness of Christ's suffering," yet scholars are divided on the authorship of the epistle. Many accept the tradition that the Apostle Peter composed it in Rome before he was executed during Emperor Nero's persecutions of Christians (64-65 A.D.).

Some biblical scholars question the Petrine authorship and base their objections on the following points:

a. The superb Greek of I Peter raises the question whether the Galilean fisherman, whose native language was Aramaic, could have written it.[32]

b. The use of the Septuagint (the Greek translation of the

Old Testament) in all Old Testament quotations and allusions point to someone other than a Palestinian.[33]

c. The theology of I Peter is Pauline. The epistle contains Pauline motifs and ideas, especially the concept of Jesus' death atoning for sin and affecting righteousness (1:18-21; 2:24). There is a striking similarity between the view expressed in 2:14-21 and the attitude commended by Paul in Romans 13:1-7. Did the author of I Peter know the Pauline letters? If he knew the collected Pauline letters, this could imply that I Peter was written perhaps a generation later and could not be the work of Peter, who is reported to have died in the sixties in Rome.[34]

d. I Peter contains no indication of acquaintanceship with the historical Jesus. One cannot imagine that one of the intimate disciples of Jesus would not demonstrate his close relationship in his writing.[35]

e. If the Apostle Peter composed I Peter, it is surprising that the epistle is addressed to churches in Asia Minor (1:1), since official persecution was then confined to the imperial Rome.[36]

Furthermore, the greetings from "she who dwells in Babylon," (5:13) gives an indication that the letter was written after the destructon of Jerusalem in 70 A.D. "Babylon" became the Christian code for Rome after Titus destroyed Jerusalem. So, "the painful trial" referred to by the author in 4:12-13 may not have been the persecution under Emperor Nero, but possibly under Emperor Domitian in 95-96 A.D. or Emperor Trajan in 112 A.D.

Some eminent scholars believe that I Peter is a pseudonymous work (written anonymously in the name of a well-known figure), composed between 80-112 B.C. The place of writing is called Babylon (5:13)—a cryptic reference for Rome.

The author writes to churches scattered throughout Pontus, Galatia, Cappodocia, Asia, and Bithynia. These churches were located in northern and central Asia Minor.

The writer's primary purpose is to exhort Christians to hold fast their integrity during intense persecution and to promote Christian ethics. A common theory among modern biblical scholars is that I Peter was originally a baptismal sermon, preached on the initiation of Gentile converts to delineate both the privileges and the dangers involved in joining the Christian community.[38] The author states his purpose in 5:12: "I have written to you briefly, encouraging you and testifying that this is the true grace of God. Stand fast in it."

I Peter may be divided into the following five sectons:
1. Introduction (1:1-2)
2. The Privileges and Values of the Christian Calling (1:3-2:10)
3. The Duties of Christians in the World (2:11-4:11)
4. The Trials of Christians in the World (4:12-5:11)
5. Conclusion (5:12-14)

1. Introduction (1:1-2). The author salutes Christians scattered throughout Asia Minor. The Christians are referred to as "God's elect, and strangers in the world," which means that Christians are sojourners, pilgrims, citizens of another world, living for a little while in this world, away from home, journeying along toward their homeland.

2. The Privileges and Values of the Christian Calling (1:3-2:10). In this section the author stresses the value of the Christian faith recently transmitted to them. They must regard their present trials as a test that will render their faith worthy of honor when Jesus comes again (1:6-7). By remaining faithful they will attain salvation (1:9-12). Christians are exhorted to be holy in their conduct (1:13-2:3). They must rid themselves of "all malice and all deceit, hyprocrisy, envy, and slander of every kind . . . and crave pure spiritual milk . . ." now that they have "tasted that the Lord is good" (2:1-3).

Then the writer speaks of Christians as a "chosen people . . . a holy nation . . . a royal priesthood" (2:9-10). They who had been "no people" are now "a people" with identity and purpose. This is one of the major roots of the Protestant doctrine of the "priesthood of all believers"—that each person is his or her own priest before God, and that each person, by the Christian quality of his or her life, is a priest for others.

3. The Duties of Christians in the World (2:11-4:11). This section concentrates on the duties and moral conduct of Christians who should "live such good lives among the pagans that . . . they may see [their] good deeds and glorify God" (2:12). Like Paul (Rom. 13), the author advises peaceful submission to government authorities (2:13-15). Slaves and servants are subject to their masters (2:18), as well as women to their husbands (3:1-2).

The author reminds Christians to exemplify the supreme virtue of life: Christian love. This virtue should be manifested in terms of living in harmony with one another, being sympathetic, and loving one another as brothers (3:8-12).

4. The Trials of Christians in the World (4:12-5:11). In this section the author examines the ethical meaning of suffering for the faith. Christians are under persecution because they are Christians, and they are to persevere in hope under affliction. When they suffer innocently because of their Christian faith, then that is a great credit to them and they will have their reward. Such suffering has a meaning beyond its pain (4:12-16). In these persecutions and afflictions they are to remember that Christ, too, suffered innocently. As they identify with his suffering, their suffering can be redemptive; they will also share in Christ's glory and triumph.

5. Conclusion (5:12-14). The author concludes his letter by appealing to his readers to trust and glorify God. He exhorts them to be humble, self-controlled, and watchful, and "greet one another with a kiss of love" (5:14).

4. II PETER

There is no unanimity among biblical scholars concerning the authorship, date, and place of writing of II Peter.

Some scholars insist that II Peter was written by the Apostle Peter from Rome around 67-68 A.D. Their claim of Petrine authorship is based on the following three points of the author's testimony:

    a. The opening verse (1:1) specifically claims the epistle to be the word of Simon Peter;

    b. The writer represents himself as having been present at the Transfiguration of Christ (1:16-18);

    c. The author also claims to have been warned by Christ of his impending death (1:14).

Most scholars, however, believe that II Peter was written by an anonymous writer in Rome sometime in the second century. They base their arguments on the following reasons:

    a. The similarity of II Peter and Jude (the latter having been written in the second century). Most of the material of Jude is quoted almost verbatim in the second and third chapters of II Peter (cf. II Peter 2:18 and 3:1-3 with Jude verses 4-18).

    b. The author's acquaintance of a collection of the Apostle Paul's letters which he refers to as "Scriptures" (3:16). Paul's letters did not attain canonical status until the mid-second century.

    c. The author's apparent knowledge of the Synoptic Gospels (cf. 1:17-18), as well as John's Gospel (1:14; 21:18), which were written long after the Apostle Peter's martyrdom in about 64-65 A.D.

    d. The problems of the canonicity of the book. If the book had apostolic origins, it would have been listed as an "approved" book in the early church; it would not have had a hard time gaining entrance into the New Testament.[39]

According to independent scholars, the author assumes an apostolic identity for the purpose of giving weight to the epistle's contents as embodying true apostolic doctrine and authority as he fights against the "false teachers" (2:1) who pervert apostolic traditions.[40]

The epistle does not locate the readers, but they were probably Christians along the northern coast of Asia Minor.[41] The author writes to remind believers that there is no substitute for the knowledge of Christian truth for growth (chap. 1), for combating false teachers (chap. 2), and for certainty of the Lord's coming (chap. 3).

The book is an urgent plea to preserve and hold to the true

Christian faith in the face of heresies. Although the heresies are not named in this letter, we get some idea what they were because of the denunciations and accusations made in attacking them. It was the time when Gnosticism was a prevailing heretical movement. The Gnostics sharply divided spirit, which was wholly good, from matter, which was wholly evil. It was also the time of Docetism, which denied both the incarnation and humanity of Jesus. It was the time of Marcionism, which held that the Old Testament scriptures were of no value. It was the time of the Aninomians who perverted Paul's doctrine of grace. They held that spiritually one was saved by God's grace, but one's spirit was wholly disassociated from one's body. Spiritually, they were without sin, and it did not make any difference what they did with and through their bodies. So they practiced every kind of lust; moral conduct became a shambles.[42]

II Peter may be divided into the following five sections:
1. Introduction (1:1-2)
2. Knowledge for Christian Development (1:3-21)
3. Condemnation of False Teachers (2:1-22)
4. The Coming of the Day of the Lord (3:1-13)
5. Concluding Exhortation (3:14-18)

1. Introduction (1:1-2). II Peter is addressed to Christians without reference to their place of residence. The addressees of the epistle are those who "have received a faith as precious" as that of the apostles. The author is concerned with the relationship of the ordinary Christians to the apostles. Their faith is of equal standing. A faith at variance with the apostolic standards would not be an orthodox faith.[43]

2. Knowledge for Christian Development (1:3-21). In this epistle faith is a set of doctrines, a body of knowledge, to be defended and adhered to against all attempts to pervert it or dilute it. The key word is "knowledge." In this letter it occurs sixteen times. Knowledge is the means of growth, the antidote to heresy, and the key for watchfulness in the last days. The author asserts that the "knowledge of Christ" enables Christians to combat all heresies. He urges the believers to remember the truth, for they grow by remembering and applying God's word (1:12-21).

Along with knowledge, there is a strong emphasis on the kind of ethical conduct required of believers in contrast to the conducts of the heretics. Christians are to make every effort to supplement their faith with virtue and their godliness with brotherly affection and love (1:5-7).

3. Condemnation of the False Teachers (2:1-22). The author cautions the church to guard against apostasy and heresy. He speaks of false teachers and their destructive ways (2:1), their greed (2:3), the corrupt desire of their sinful nature (2:10), their "beastly conduct" (2:12), their "eyes full of adultery" (2:14), and their slavery to depravity (2:19). Those who lead others astray will surely face the judgment of God.

4. The Coming of the Day of the Lord (3:1-13). Here the author deals with the problem of the delayed Parousia. One of his major concerns is the defense of "the promise of Jesus' Second Coming." His primary goal is to reinstate the early Christian apocalyptic hope.[44] Skeptics may point out that those apostles who promised Christ's early return have all died and yet the world continues on exactly as before. They ask, "Where is this coming he promised?" (3:4).

The author answers the questions raised by the so-called scoffers on the basis of Scripture. First, he maintains that all things have not continued as they were from the beginning of creation (3:4) and point to the destruction of the world by flood in the days of Noah as proof. Then he reiterates that a fiery judgment is still to come (3:7). He goes on to state that God does not measure time by the same standards as people do, because with him "a day is like a thousand years, and a thousand years are like a day" (3:8). Moreover, if the Lord seems slow, it is just another manifestation of his great mercy; he merely exercises patience so that as many people as possible will be saved.

The author summons his readers to holy living and offers words of encouragement and hope. He affirms the early Church's hope that Jesus would soon return to establish his kingdom with divine justice. While they await the Lord's return, Christians "ought to live holy and godly lives" (3:11-13).

5. Concluding Exhortation (3:14-18). The author concludes his letter by again criticizing the false teachers in a famous reference to Paul's letters (3:15). While admitting that the Pauline letters contain unclear passages, he condemns the distortions of the critics (3:16).

With a final warning and admonition "not to be carried away by the error of lawless men," he closes his letter with a doxology (3:17-18).

5. *I JOHN*

Although the three letters of John (I, II, and III John) are traditionally ascribed to the Apostle John, most scholars believe that he wrote none of them. Biblical scholarship is divided: Who wrote these epistles? When were they written? Where were they written? To whom were they written?

According to the majority of modern biblical scholars, the three letters of John probably have a common authorship and presuppose similar circumstances. While none of the three directly identifies its author, the second and third letters say they are from an "elder."

Those who subscribe to the traditional view insist that I John was written by the Apostle John, one of the Twelve. Tradition places John in Ephesus in his latter years, where he lived until the reign of Trajan, which began in 98 A.D. Since the letter was written after the Gospel of John (85-90 A.D., according to the traditionalists), the Epistle is dated between 90-95 A.D.[45]

Again, according to tradition, Apostle John wrote this epistle as a circular letter to the churches around Ephesus, to emphasize the main essentials of the Gospel, to give assurance to those who have believed in Jesus Christ, and to encourage them to walk in fellowship; also, to warn these churches against "incipient heresies which later produced a corrupt and paganized form of Christianity."[46]

As far as the background of these letters is concerned, the following are noteworthy observations:

a. The Church is, at this period, not under persecution.

b. The enthusiasm of the first-generation Christians had waned. The thrill of the new discovery in Christ was not as dramatic as at first. Christianity had become something taken for granted, and something of the original wonder and awe were lacking.

c. The strong ethical demands of faith were becoming burdensome to some. The quality of moral life had begun to deteriorate. Many were taking their premises of conduct from the world rather than from Christ.

d. A heretical movement, subversive of the Christian faith, had crept in the church. It was known as Gnosticism. Gnosticism taught that salvation was gained through special knowledge (gnosis) and was the property of an elite few who had been initiated into its mysteries.[47]

The language and style of I John indicate a close involvement with the "Johannine School" (John 21:23), which attempted to update the original concerns of the Fourth Gospel in terms of the church's situation at the end of the first century and the beginning of the second.[48]

I John may be divided into the following four sections:
1. Introduction (1:14)
2. The Nature and Essence of Christianity (1:5-3:24)
3. The Criteria for Certainty and Assurance Among the Faithful (4:1-5:12)
4. Conclusion (5:13-21)

1. Introduction (1:1-4). The book begins with no epistolary salutation, without the usual expression of good wishes. It is a Christian manifesto in which the author declares that his purpose in writing the epistle is to proclaim the message of the reality of God revealed in Christ.[49]

2. The Nature and Essence of Christianity (1:5-3:24). Those who have fellowship with God are those who walk in the light and live according to the truth and who are cleansed from all sin (1:5-7). Those who are free from sin are those who confess sin, relying on Jesus, the expiation for sins (1:8-2:2). Only those who keep God's commandments know him (2:3-5), and have overcome the Evil One and the world; they walk with Christ and love their brothers (2:6-17).

The author goes on to say that the children of God are those who have personal experience with Christ. Nine times he states "by this we know" (2:3, 5; 3:16, 19, 24; 4:2, 6, 13; 5:2). In other words, personal experience with Christ is the final test.

3. The Criteria for Certainty and Assurance Among the Faithful (4:1-5:12). In this section, the author treats two basic themes: Christian love and Christian faith. He admonishes Christians to test the spirits: the spirit of truth and the spirit of error (4:1-6). The spirit of error manifests itself in antichrist and false prophets. The criterion for distinguishing the Spirit of God from that of the antichrist is in one's positive affirmation and proclamation that Jesus actually came in the flesh (a human being) and is the Son of God. Believing this is the means to eternal life.

Then, the author introduces a second major motif. Being born of God is joined to the exhortation to love. He who loves is born of God. The command to love is based on the revelation of love (4:7-12). God is love, and a Christian love grows out of God's love (4:15-21). Thus, the real Christian, as distinguished from the pretender, is the one who believes in Jesus and practices love (4:19-5:4).

4. Conclusion (5:13-21). In his concluding remarks, the author once again reaffirms what has already been said: a declaration of sound doctrine and a warning to those who would abandon it.

6. II JOHN

The Second Letter of John is much more like a letter than is I John. Containing only thirteen verses, it is from "the Elder" to "the chosen lady and her children" (vs. 1), probably an unidentified house church that belonged to the Johannine community.

The aim of the letter is to warn against heresies confronting the church, much the same as I John (cf. II John 7 and I John 2:18, 4:1-3; II John 9 and I John 2:23; II John 5 and I John 2:7-8).

The author commends "the chosen lady and her children" for their love and faithfulness to the truth, but he also warns them about fellowshipping with false teachers. Believers should have fellowship with God, Christ, and other believers, but they should not fellowship with false teachers.

One of the key words of II John is truth. The term occurs five times in the letter in the following order:

a. "Love in the truth" (vs. 1); b. "know the truth" (vs. 1); c. "Truth, which lives in us and will be with us forever" (vs. 2); d. Grace, mercy, and peace from God . . . will be with us in truth and love (vs. 3); and e. "Walking in the truth" (vs. 4).

This one-chapter Epistle of II John may be outlined as follows:
1. Introduction (vss. 1-3)
2. Instructions to Follow the Truth (vss. 4-6)
3. Instructions Concerning False Teachers (vss. 7-11)
4. Conclusion (vss. 12-13)

1. Introduction (vss. 1-3). The letter is addressed to a devout matron (*Kuria*-Greek) and her children—a gracious personification of a particular church. It is interesting to note the author's anonymous designation of himself simply as "the Elder." The term "the elder" is referred both to an elderly man and to the office or dignity occupied by such.[50]

2. Instructions to Follow the Truth (vss. 4-6). The author is writing to a house-church warning its members against the dangerous influence of persons who had seceded from the main Johannine community,[51] and urges them to "walk in the truth," remembering the law of love.

3. Instructions Concerning False Teachers (vss. 7-11). In verse 7 the author warns his recipients against false teachers "who do not acknowledge Jesus Christ coming in the flesh" (probably the Docetic branch of Gnosticism who denied the incarnation of Christ). Calling these heretics "deceivers and the antichrist," he cautions his readers to be on their guard, and instructs them to refuse hospitality to false teachers.

4. Conclusion (vss. 12-13). Disclosing that he has more to say than he cares to spell out on paper, the Elder promises to visit them and talk to them face to face; he closes his letter with greetings.

7. III JOHN

The Third Epistle of John is a private letter from "the Elder" to his friend Gaius. In this brief letter of fourteen verses, the Elder urges Gaius to show hospitality to some traveling missionaries led by the writer's friend, Demetrius.

The background of III John involved the refusal of one local church leader, Diatrephes, to receive the emissaries of the Elder (vss. 9-11). Whether the conflict was based on theological, church polity, or personal matters, we are not told.[52] The Elder denounces Diotrephes for withholding help from both the writer and his emissaries, for excluding them from the church, and for spreading malicious gossip about them (vss. 9-10).

The outline of III John is as follows:
1. Introduction (vs. 1)
2. Commendation of Gaius (vss. 2-8)

3. Condemnation of Diotrephes (vss. 9-11)
4. Commendation of Demetrius (vs. 12)
5. Conclusion (vss. 13-14)

1. Introduction (vs. 1). The epistolary author identifies himself here as in the introduction of II John as "the Elder."

2. Commendation of Gaius (vss. 2-8). The occasion for this brief letter is the Elder's wish to thank Gaius for the hospitality he has shown to the brothers who, in the course of their travels, sometimes sought lodging in house-churches.

3. Condemnation of Diotrephes (vss. 9-11). By contrast, one Diotrephes, a rival leader, offends the Elder by not only refusing to show hospitality to the Elder's co-laborers but by putting them out of the church. Here we see the evidence of conflict between a traveling leader, the Elder (and his emissaries), and a local church authority, Diotrephes.

4. Commendation of Demetrius (vs. 12). Demetrius, presumably an active figure in one of the deputations under discussion, may have been the bearer of the present letter. His good standing is vouched for by everyone.

5. Conclusion (vss. 13-15). The conclusion is in large part a repetition of the epilogue of II John. It closes with benediction and salutation.

8. JUDE

The Epistle of Jude is more of a tract than a letter denouncing an unidentified group of heretics.

The prescript identified the author as Jude (Judas), "the brother of James," and therefore, it has traditionally been held, of Jesus (Matt. 13:55; Mark 6:3). But, according to critical scholars, it is unlikely that Jude the brother of Jesus wrote the tract. The latter claim that the Letter of Jude is a pseudonymous work that became a New Testament book because of its presumed association with the Lord's family.[53] The author shows no personal familiarity with Jesus and cites none of his characteristic teachings.[54] Moreover, these critics contend that the phrase "brother of James" may have been an editorial addition based on inference from the Gospel lists of Jesus' brothers, or "it may represent the author's own employment of pseudonymity to gain an advantageous hearing for his message."[55]

Those biblical scholars who insist that the author of Jude was the brother of James and Jesus date the book between 67-68 A.D.[56] Others who claim that the book was composed significantly after the historical Jude's time, suggest a date between 100 and 125 A.D.[57]

Most studies deal with the Epistle of Jude before II Peter because many believe that Jude is a source used by the author of II Peter. Of Jude's twenty-five verses, nineteen are represented in II Peter. The "false teachers" referred to in II Pet. 2:1 are likely the same as Jude's "godless men, who change the grace of our God into a license for immorality and deny Jesus Christ our only Sovereign and Lord" (Jude 4). Jude's denunciations and the invective of II Peter are both directed to the Gnostics.[57]

The purpose of the Letter of Jude is to contend for the Christian faith (vs. 3) by exposing apostates (vss. 4-19) and exhorting believers to faithful life and service (vss. 20-23). The author's preoccupation is to warn against the danger of apostasy. Because of the threat from apostates, Jude urges believers to fight for the faith that had been delivered to the saints.

The outline of this brief letter is the following:
1. Introduction (vss. 1-2)
2. The False Teachers: Danger of Apostasy (vss. 3-16)
3. Building Up in "the Most Holy Faith" (vss. 17-23)
4. A Doxology (vss. 24-25)

1. Introduction (vss. 1-2). There are three aspects of the epistolary introduction-salutation of this catholic letter. First, the author refers to his family ties to identify himself. He is the brother of James. Second, he speaks of his readers as those "who have been called, who are loved by God the Father and kept by Jesus Christ." Though unknown and unnamed they share with other Christians three great experiences - *called, beloved, kept.* Third, Jude prays that three graces may be multiplied in the lives of his readers - *mercy, peace,* and *love.*[58]

2. False Teachers: Danger of Apostasy (vss. 3-16). Jude warns his readers against those who pervert the truth and under a cloak of Christianity manipulate the faith in their interests and for their own ends. These "godless men" (vs. 4) with their "immoral behavior" and "shameless deeds" have adulterated the faith. (The words "faith" and "tradition" must be understood as a fixed body of doctrines handed down from the time of the apostles.)[59]

The heretics, who have entered the Christian community in disguise, have been predestined long ago for condemnation. The punishment is underway. The author illustrates this punishment from the Old Testament by citing the plagues of Egypt (vs. 5), the fallen angels of Genesis (vs. 6), and the fiery punishment of Sodom and Gomorrah (vss. 6-7).

Jude is the only New Testament writer to go beyond the Hebrew Bible and quote directly from the *Pseudipigrapha* (a collection of religious books outside the Hebrew Bible canon that were composed in Hebrew, Aramaic, and Greek from about 200 B.C. to 200 A.D.). Jude quoted from the book of I Enoch and Assumption of Moses describing God's judgment on "the ungodly" (vss. 14-15).[60]

3. Building Up In "The Most Holy Faith" (vss. 17-23). Jude counsels his readers to stay away from these "scoffers," men "who follow their ungodly desires," and preserve the faith in the face of temptation (vss. 19-20).

4. A Doxology (vss. 24-25). To balance his vindictive tone and language, the author closes his letter with a lovely doxology.

References

1. William H. Marty, *Surveying the New Testament* (Dubuque: Kendalll/Hunt Publishing Co., 1987), p. 150.
2. Stephen L. Harris, *The New Testament: A Student's Introduction* (Mountain View, California: Mayfield Publication Co., 1988), p. 259.
3. J. Benton White, *From Adam to Armageddon*, Second Edition, (Belmont, California: Wadsworth Publishing Co., 1986), p. 176.
4. Stephen L. Harris, *Understanding the Bible*, Second Edition (Palo Alto and London: Mayfield Publishing Co., 1985), p. 346.
5. White, p. 176.
6. James L. Price, *The New Testament: Its History and Theology* (New York: Macmillan Pub. Co., 1987), pp. 398-416; Harris, *The New Testament*, pp. 259-273.
7. Henry H. Halley, *Bible Handbook: An Abbreviated Bible Commentary* (Grand Rapids: Zondervan Publishing House, 1960), pp. 592-620; Marty, pp. 150-178.
8. In the King James Version it is called, in the title, *The Epistle of Paul.*
9. White, p. 180.
10. Alexander C. Purdy, "The Epistle to the Hebrews," *The Interpreter's Bible*, Vol. XI, (New York and Nashville: Abingdon Press, 1955), pp. 591-592.
11. E. Dinkler, "Letter to the Hebrews," *The Interpreter's Dictionary of the Bible*, Vol. 2 (New York and Nashville: Abingdon Press, 1962), pp. 571-75.
12. Eusebius, *Church History*, trans. Hugh J. Lawler and John L. Oulton, (London: Society for Promoting Christian Knowledge, 1927), VI, 14, 2.
13. *Ibid.* VII, II-ff.
14. Halley, p. 592.
15. Richard L. Jeske, *New Testament: Toward a Historical Understanding* (Lawrence, Kansas: The University of Kansas, 1977), p. 151.
16. Price, p. 404.
17. Marty suggests that Hebrew seems likely; that it must have been written from Rome around 62 A.D., p. 160. Also, Halley seems to share the same view. Jeske claims that it must have been written between 81 and 96 A.D., p. 152; Harris 69-95 A.D., p. 347; Spivey and Smith maintain 80-90 A.D.
18. Robert A. Spivey and D. Moody Smith, *Anatomy of the New Testament*, Fourth Ed. (New York: Macmillan Publishing Company, 1989), p. 379.
19. Harris, *Understanding the Bible*, p. 347.
20. Robert G. Gromacki, *New Testament Survey* (Grand Rapids: Baker Book House Company, 1974), pp. 321-322.
21. Jeske, p. 152.
22. Jeske, p. 149.
23. Howard Clark Kee, *Understanding the New Testament*, 3rd Ed. (Englewood Cliffs: Prentice-Hall, 1973), pp. 283-95.
24. Norman Perrin, *The New Testament: An Introduction* (New York: Harcourt Brace Jovanovich, 1974), p. 256.
25. A.E. Barnett, "The Letter of James," *The Interpreter's Dictionary of the Bible*, Vol. 2 (New York and Nashville: Abingdon Press, 1962), pp. 795-6.
26. Joseph B. Mayer, *The Epistle of James* (Grand Rapids: Zondervan Publishing House, 1954), pp. 16-18; Marty, p. 68; Halley, p. 602.
27. Jeske, p. 150.

28. Frank Gaebelein, *The Practical Epistle of James* (New York: Doniger and Raughley, 1955), p. 8; Marty, p. 68.
29. Alexander Ross, *The Epistle of James and John* (Grand Rapids: Wm. B. Eerdmans Publishing Co., 1964), pp. 19-20.
30. Harris, *Understanding the Bible*, p. 356; Jeske, p. 150.
31. Spivey and Smith, p. 390.
32. Spivey and Smith, p. 395.
33. Jeske, p. 148.
34. Spivey and Smith, p. 395.
35. *Ibid.*
36. Harris, *Understanding the Bible*, p. 352.
37. Harris, *The New Testament*, p. 267.
38. Archipald, M. Hunter, "Introduction and Exegesis of I Peter," *The Interpreter's Bible*, Vol. XII (New York and Nashville: Abingdon Press, 1957), p. 80; White, p. 178; Harris, *The New Testament*, p. 267; Harris, *Understanding the Bible*, p. 352.
39. Harris, *The New Testament*, p. 270.
40. Harris, *Understanding the Bible*, p. 354.
41. Marty, p. 155.
42. Kenneth S. Latourette, *A History of Christianity* (New York: Harper & Brothers Publishers, 1953), pp. 112-135.
43. Albert E. Barnett, "The Second Epistle of Peter," *The Interpreter's Bible*, Vol. XII (New York and Nashville: Abingdon Press, 1957) pp. 168-69.
44. Harris, *The New Testament*, p. 270.
45. Marty, p. 170; Halley, p. 614.
46. Halley, p. 614.
47. White, pp. 190-191.
48. Kee, pp. 267-68; Jeske, p. 144.
49. Amos N. Wilder, "The First, Second, and Third Epistle of John," *The Interpreter's Bible*, Vol. XII (New York and Nashville: Abingdon Press, 1957), p. 216.
50. Wilder, pp. 302-303.
51. Price, p. 449.
52. Spivey and Smith, p. 410.
53. J.C. Becker, "The Letter of Jude," *The Interpreter's Dictionary of the Bible*, Vol. 2 (New York and Nashville: Abingdon Press, 1962), pp. 1010-11.
54. Harris, *The New Testament*, p. 268.
55. Albert E. Barnett, "The Epistle of Jude," *The Interpreter's Bible*, Vol. XII (New York and Nashville: Abingdon Press, 1957), p. 318.
56. Halley, p. 620; Marty, p. 167.
57. Spivey and Smith, p. 401.
58. Barnett, pp. 321-322.
59. Spivey and Smith, p. 403; Jeske, p. 140.
60. Harris, *The New Testament*, p. 269.

PART 5

REVELATION

The Book of Revelation belongs to the *genre* of apocalyptic literature. The term "apocalyptic" comes from the Greek word *apokalysis*, which is the Greek title of the book and means "revelation."[1] Revelation is the only apocalyptic book in the New Testament.

Because apocalyptic literature attempts to describe things beyond the human sphere and uses a language that often transcends the boundaries of spacial and temporal form of reference, it is difficult to understand and interpret. For that reason the Book of Revelation is one of the least understood and most misinterpreted books of the Bible. Moreover, it has become a happy hunting ground for self-proclaimed authorities to use its material to predict future events and the end of the world, and even the date of the end.

The general character of apocalyptic literature was well established long before the writing of Revelation; it thrived in Judaism during the intertestamental period and on into the Christian era.

We need to get a clear picture of the nature of Jewish apocalyptic literature in order to understand the Book of Revelation—the New Testament representative of that type of literature.

The Jews believed that they were chosen people and that at some time they would arrive at world supremacy, with their enemies destroyed, and then they would occupy the place of preeminence. They looked for the coming of a king of David's line who would be their shepherd-savior.

But the history of Israel did not bring that hope to fruition. After Solomon, the Hebrew kingdom split into two kingdoms. The Northern Kingdom, Israel, had its capital in Samaria. That kingdom vanished in the eighth century B.C. under the assault of the Assyrians and was never restored. This is the origin of the "Ten Lost Tribes of Israel." The Southern Kingdom, Judah, with its capital in Jerusalem, was reduced to slavery and went into exile in the sixth century B.C. It was later under the rule of the Persians, the Greeks, and the Romans. The history of Israel was a contradiction of their hope and belief.

Nevertheless the Jewish people held to their belief; they just had to readjust their thinking. They developed the idea of history divided into two ages, "the present age" and "the age to come." The present age is wholly evil, it cannot either be reformed or redeemed. It must be destroyed. The Jews waited for the end of things as they are to welcome "the age to come," which will be wholly righteous and good. It will be the golden age of God and the people of God will be vindicated.[2]

How was this to happen? It could not come by human agency or effort. It would come only by the direct invasion of history by God. The day of God's coming intervention was called "The Day of the Lord." It would be a day of terror, judgment, destruction, and the setting up of a righteous new day.[3]

Such literature is composed largely of dreams and visions and is written in cryptic style. It deals with a great deal of symbolism. It is written in code language which was understandable to the insiders but not intelligible to outsiders. This type of literature flourished in times of tyranny and oppression. A number of Jewish apocalyptic books were written including Daniel in the Hebrew Bible and a number of others in the Pseudipigrapha, such as I Enoch, Assumption of Moses, and Ascension of Isaiah.[4]

There were also a number of Christian apocalyptic books, such as the Apocalypses of James, of Paul, of Peter, and others. Only the Book of Revelation made the New Testament Canon.

The basic pattern of apocalyptic literature involves the following features and characteristics, all of which are to be found in the Book of Revelation:

a. *Special Disclosures.* The writers of apocalyptic literature provide some answers to the secrets of the hidden world by dreams, visions, and/or heavenly journeys with angelic guides (1:10-11; 4:1-2; 6:1-2; 19:9-10). These revelations are esoteric and are intended to be understood by those who understand the symbolism involved.[5]

b. *An Ethical Dualism.* Apocalypticism depicts the universe as locked in combat between two opposing camps: good and evil, God and Satan (6:2-6; 9:1-3; 12:7-9; 16:13-14).

c. *A Dualism of Ages.* In apocalypticism there is the concept of two ages: a present age dominated by evil and a future age of perfection. The present age seems almost given over to the powers of evil. Frequently, the old earth is to be replaced by a newly created earth and/or the descent of a heavenly city (21:1-5).[6]

d. *Symbolism.* The use of cryptic symbols, code words, and numbers is typical of apocalyptic literature. This symbolic language is not fully intelligible to modern readers. It employs terms and images that communicate to its intended audience but bewilder outsiders.[7] Animal symbolism is especially prominent, exhibiting bizarre features (4:6-8; 5:5-6; 9:17-19; 13:1-3). The numbers 3, 4, 6, 7, 10, and 12 and their multiples are also employed (1:4; 2:10; 11:2-3; 12:1; 21:12).

e. *Pictures of Violence and Suffering.* Apocalyptic imagery often describes the end of the world in cataclysmic terms, including the disintegration of society and a universal calamity, violence and suffering (6:3, 12-14; 7:1-3; 8:7-12; 16:2-14, 20-21).

f. *Angelology and Demonology.* Apocalypticism is often marked by the activity of angels and demons, with the angels on God's side and demons on Satan's (7:1; 8:2; 9:20; 12:7-9; 16:13-14).

g. *Messiah and Anti-Messiah.* In apocalyptic literature, there is a messiah figure who stands in opposition to an anti-messiah figure, each on the side of God and Satan respectively (9:11; 11:7; 12:4-5; 13:1-2; 19:11-16). The anti-messiah is sometimes depicted as a mythological monster or the incarnation of a demon (13:1-2).

The Book of Revelation was written by John, a Christian seer who tells us nothing about himself other than his name. From the mid-second century on, he was believed to have been the Apostle John, but there is no way to verify this tradition with certainty.

Other early Christian sources recognized that the immense differences in thought, language, and theology between Revelation and the Fourth Gospel indicate that they could not have originated with the same author.[8] There are some biblical scholars who accept the early church father Eusebius' theory about John the Elder of Ephesus.[9] Most scholars, however, simply accept the writer's own self-identification. He calls himself John, "a servant of Jesus Christ" (1:2). He claims that he was on the island of Patmos "because of the Word of God and the testimony of Jesus" (1:8). Patmos was a small, rocky, barren island in the Aegean Sea about sixty miles southwest of Ephesus.

As for the date of the book, although some have suggested an early date during the reign of the Roman emperor Nero (54-68 A.D.), the evidence favors a date near the end of the reign of Domitian (81-96). Domitian was the first emperor to demand worship while he was still living and ordered the persecution of anyone who refused to acknowledge him as god. Writing about 180 A.D., the churchman Irenaeus stated that Revelation was composed late in the reign of Domitian. Internal references to governmental persecution of Christians (1:9; 2:10; 6:9-11; 14:12; 21:4), policies then associated with Domitian's administration, support Irenaeus' assessment. Most scholars date the work about 95 or 96 A.D.[10]

In the opening verse of the Revelation, John employs three different categories for his composition:
    a. *Apocalypticism*—a branch of prophetic writing which previews the catastrophic events believed to accompany the end of time.
    b. *Letter*—New Testament letters were intended to be read during worship services (Col. 4:16), and the Revelation was written for the same purpose. It was addressed to seven local congregations in Asia Minor (1:11).
    c. *Prophecy*—John's adoption of the style of an apocalyptist in no way hinders him from thinking as a prophet. He claims that his message is "the Word of God and the testimony of Jesus" (1:2, 9; 10:10; 22:16). Prophecy includes both what God Himself purposes to do and also what God wills humans to do.

The first three chapters are in the form of letters to seven churches in Asia Minor. Because it is the number representing wholeness or completion, the number seven indicates that while the author is thinking of these congregations *per se*, he is also thinking of the entire church (1:1). Why he chose these seven and not others may be answered only tentatively in that he most likely chose those congregations that stood closest to his sphere of influence.[11]

After the letters to the seven churches, chapters 4-11 announce the coming judgment, which is imminent. Then follows a depiction of the great battle against the enemies of the Church, ending with the fall of Babylon (a symbol of Rome, 12-18). Then comes the Final Triumph (19:1-22:6). That the end is near is made clear especially in the epilogue (22:8-21).

The Book of Revelation may be outlined as follows:
1. Introduction (1:1-8)
2. Opening Vision (1:9-20)
3. The Letters to the Seven Churches (2:1-3:22)
4. The Prophetic Visions (4:1-22:50
    A. A Vision of Heaven (4:1-5:14)
    B. The Seven Seals (6:1-7:17)
    C. The Seven Trumpets (8:1-11:14)
    D. The Seven Visions of Conflict (11:15-13:18)
    E. The Seven Visions of Worshipers of the Lamb and Worshipers of the Beast (14:1-20)
    F. The Seven Bowls of the Wrath of God (15:1-16:21)
    G. The Seven Visions of the Fall of Babylon (17:1-19:10)
    H. The Seven Visions Announcing the End (19:11-22:5)
5. The Epilogue (22:6-21)

1. Introduction (1:1-8) The introduction is relatively longer than that of other biblical epistles. It gives the origin and destination of the work. The author wants his readers to know that his revelation was transmitted by Christ to his "servant" John through angelic mediation. The seven churches in the province of Asia are to be the recipients of his book.

2. Opening Visions (1:9-20). Because of his Christian witness and beliefs, John had been exiled to Patmos where Christ commissioned him to record the visions which he was about to see and to send the book to the seven churches (1:9-11). His initial vision is Christ standing in the midst of seven lampstands that represent the seven churches.

3. The Letters to the Seven Churches (2:1-3:22). This section contains the seven letters to the seven churches of Asia. John does not write seven individual letters, rather he pens one, containing seven brief letters, that was to be circulated among all the churches.

The letters follow a common literary format for the most part. They contain an address, a description of Christ, a commendation of works, a complaint, an exhortation, a warning, and an admonition to the spiritually sensitive.

a. *The first letter is addressed to the church at Ephesus* (2:1-7), the most important church in Asia Minor, one of the most important in what was then the whole of Christendom. Further, it is located in the most important city in Asia Minor. It was a powerful center of Diana worship and the temple of Artemis was one of the seven wonders of the ancient world.

The situation of the Ephesian church was a tension between correct theology and a love of others. The church had been careful to defend the faith against imposters. They opposed the Nicolaitans. They had preserved orthodoxy, but they had saved the purity of faith at the price of losing Christian love. They had kept the faith but lost the spirit. So Christ says to the Ephesians that they are to remember what Christian fellowship is about, they are to repent of what they have done to it, and they are to return to its practice.

b. *The second letter is addressed to the church in Smyrna* (2:8-11). It is one of the shortest of the letters. In it is no word of criticism. Its tone is tender, compassionate, supportive. The believers at Smyrna were facing heavy attacks from the Jewish community. The latter were spreading slanders of all kinds concerning the Christians and were constantly urging the Roman officials to take action against the Christians.

The Christians in Smyrna are encouraged in their faithfulness. The essence of the letter is "Keep up the witness."
    c. *The third letter is to the church in Pergamum* (2:12-17). Pergamum was about fifty miles north of Smyrna. It was a great cultural center. It was famous for its library of 200,000 volumes, second only to that of Alexandria.[12] Pergamum was the hotbed of emperor worship. This was the occasion of this letter. Pergamum was a very tough place to be a Christian. The Christians of the town were constantly being pressed with the choice "Worship Caesar or die."

According to the letter they had held fast under this kind of pressure, but they had not done so well in handling those succumbing to the teaching of Balaam and the Nicolaitans. So they are ordered to repent and get to work on that problem.
    d. *The fourth letter is to the church in Thyatira* (2:18-29). The letter opens with praise for their faith, service, and patient endurance. Then come the "nevertheless I have this against you: You tolerate that woman Jezebel" (2:20). Thyatira, like Pergamum, was locked in a struggle with paganism. The imagery that represents pagan syncretism is the figure of Jezebel who had sought to displace Yahwehism with Baalism in Israel (cf. I Kings 16:29-33; 19:1-2; 21:25-26). Like the Old Testament prophets, John portrays syncretistic religion as a sort of spiritual harlotry.
    e. *The fifth letter is to the church in Sardis* (3:1-6). Sardis was a city whose splendor was in decay. The church had grown comfortable and self-satisfied. It was a degenerate church in a degenerate city.[13] The command given to the church is "Wake up and repent."
    f. *The sixth letter is to the church in Philadelphia* (3:7-13). Philadelphia was the church of the open door of service opportunities. No complaint was leveled at it. Rather, it was commended for its loyalty to Christ and for its strength even though it was a little church.
    g. *The seventh letter is to the church in Laodicea* (3:14-22). This is the harshest of the letters. No praise is found among the many complaints to the church in Laodicea. It is a lukewarm and complacent church. The Laodicean Christians were neither hot nor cold about anything. Counsel was given to them rather than

direct exhortation: "I counsel you to buy from me gold in the fire, so you can become rich" (3:18). It is the church of the closed door; Christ is on the outside. If Christ is let in there can be true fellowship, for he does not force the door. It must be opened from inside (3:20).

4. The Prophetic Visions (4:1-22:7). This is the longest section of the book opening with a vision of heaven and proceeding with visions of seven seals, seven trumpets, seven conflicts, seven visions of worshipers of the Lamb and worshipers of the Beast, seven bowls of the wrath of God, seven visions of the Fall of Babylon and seven visions announcing the end.

A. *A Vision of Heaven* (4:1-5:14). From the seven churches on earth, John switches to the scene in heaven. The vision has a single theme: the God of creation is also the God of redemption, and his redemptive work is accomplished through the death of Jesus Christ. These chapters picture the heavenly court. John describes the throne of God and the momentous events taking place there, particularly the designation of the Lamb who had been slain as worthy to open the scroll. The Lamb is, of course, Christ.

B. *The Seven Seals* (6:1-7:17). The seven-sealed scroll in God's hand catches John's interest. As each seal is broken another vision is revealed, and as each seal is broken a calamity occurs. Among these are the four horses of the apocalypse—the white horse stands for conquest and invasion and its rider a conquering king; the red horse stands for war; the black horse stands for famine; the pale horse stands for death.

The fifth seal reveals the presence of martyrs in heaven crying out for divine vengeance. The sixth seal contains six events: an earthquake, the blackening of the sun, the reddening of the moon, a meteorite shower, convulsions of the planets and stars, and the displacement of mountains and islands. These events cause great consternation among the wicked inhabitants of the earth.

In the midst of these persecutions and judgments, God will seal 144,000 Israelites to be preserved from these physical calamities to serve Him. It could be that the 144,000 represent something other than Jewish bloodlines. It could mean Israel not "according to the flesh" (I Cor. 10:18) but Israel "according to the Spirit," and indeed the New Testament references in this sense are numerous. James, for instance, addressed the dispersed church as "the 12 tribes" (James 1:1).

C. *The Seven Trumpets* (8:1-11:14). When the seventh seal is broken, seven angels with seven trumpets appear, ready to sound. The trumpets serve both as a sound of judgment for God's enemies and as a sound of victory for God's people.

Like the first four seals, the first four trumpets are closely related; together they affect the natural elements of land, sea, rivers, and sky (8:7-12).

Whereas the first four trumpet judgments primarily affect the natural elements and only secondarily affect humans, the last three trumpet judgments are directed toward the rebellious human population (8:13-9:21).

Just as there was an interlude between the 6th and 7th seals, there is also an interlude between the 6th and 7th trumpet judgments. There is a scene with the description of a mighty angel who descends from heaven holding an open scroll. He announces that the cry of the martyrs is about to be answered (10:1-11).

The last part of this section deals with the measuring of the Temple. The court and the Holy City are left to be trodden under foot by the nations for forty-two months. Two witnesses prophecy in sack cloth for 1260 days.

Some scholars interpret this passage in the following way: Israel would have a temple in the tribulation and that Jerusalem would once more be controlled by Gentiles for forty-two months. In the first half of the tribulation, God will use two witnesses (Moses and Elijah) who will perform miracles and who will be divinely protected from physical harm. Then they will be martyred, but their bodies will be resurrected after three and one-half days of public display by their oppressors. Accompanying their resurrection will be an earthquake that will kill seven thousand in Jerusalem (11:1-14).[14]

Some Protestant Fundamentalist Bible students have interpreted this passage as a symbolic picture of the bloody persecution of saints by Papal Rome; the witnesses coming to life and being exalted to heaven is a symbolic picture of a purified church and God's Word again become free and prominent in the world, under the leadership of the Lutheran Reformation. Restoring God's word to the people was like a resurrection from the dead.[15]

Perhaps, the seer in the Book of Revelation had another idea: that the temple will no longer be the exclusive possession of the Jews. Rather, the temple sanctuary becomes a symbol representing Christian worship by Gentile believers demonstrating reversal of Jewish and Gentile categories. The Jewish community cannot claim an exclusive relationship to God inasmuch as the true Israel is the Israel of faith. Instead, the Jewish community which rejected Christ is represented as a city under judgment, trampled by the pagans (11:2).

D. *The Seven Visions of Conflict* (11:15-13:18). This section deals with tension between anti-God forces and the people of God. John believes that at the close of the age will be an intense persecution of the believers. He employs an internationally known mythical symbol to depict this struggle: a dragon to harm the soon-to-be-born son of a pregnant woman. This imagery is found in the mythology of ancient Greece, Mesopotamia, and Egypt.[16] The writer communicates effectively with this international symbol, drawn from not only ancient mythology but also the Hebrew Bible. The Hebrew Bible prophets pictured the people of God as a pregnant woman struggling to give birth to the messianic people and the messianic age (Is. 26:17-18; 66:7-13; Mic. 2:10).

It is against this background that the author paints the vision of the woman, the child, and the dragon in chapter 12. There are various interpretations of these symbols: The Roman Catholic view is that the woman represents the Virgin Mary, the child stands for Jesus, and the dragon imagery represents the powers of evil which sought to devour the Messiah.[17] Some Protestant scholars believe that the woman symbolizes all the people of God, Christians as well as the Old Testament believers. The Dragon is identified with the Devil, who will wage war against the believers in the last days.[18]

The Dragon will wage war against the woman's children—Christian believers who witness to Christ's sovereignty (12:13-17). The latter should not despair because this Satanic attack is a sign of the end of evil forces. Christ, who has won a decisive battle against Satan in his sacrificial death, will win the ultimate victory over all Satanic powers (12:10-12).

Then John talks about a beast coming out of the sea (13:1-4). The description of the beast is a composite of the four beasts of Daniel's vision (Dan. 7), having characteristics of a lion, a bear, a leopard, and a ten-horned monster. A great deal of discussion has accompanied the interpretation of the four beasts in Daniel 7. It would be difficult to interpret the enigmas of both Daniel and Revelation, so let it suffice to merely list two interpretations of the animal symbols in both books:

LION	Babylon	Babylon
BEAR	Medea	Medea-Persia
LEOPARD	Persia	Greece
MONSTER	Greece[19]	Rome[20]

After the beast is slain, he revives. Then a second beast emerges not from the sea but from the earth to work miracles and to enforce public worship of the first beast. The second beast is parody of Christ. He appears like a lamb (i.e., an imitation of Christ), but the content of his words betrays his allegiance to the dragon. He is called the false prophet. He allows no one to conduct business unless he bears the beast's mark. His number is that of a "Man's name," and the numerical value of its letters is 666 (13:14-18).

In attempting to decipher the meaning of the number, scholars have noted that all numbers were represented by letters of the alphabet. Thus, each letter of a person's name was also a number. By adding up the sum of all letters in a given name, we arrive at its "numerical value."[21] In both Hebrew and Greek cardinal numbers were written as letters of the alphabet (a=1; b=2; g=3, etc.).

The identification of the beast's cryptic number with a specific person has led people in every generation from John's day until ours to speculate on who might play the role of antichrist. There have been irresponsible declarations that this person was the Pope, Martin Luther, Napoleon, Hitler, Stalin, John F. Kennedy, Anwar Sadat, or Gorbachev.

Many scholars believe that in depicting the "beast" who demands his subjects' worship, John of Patmos may have had in mind one of the emperors of his day.[22] Some historians believe that the number 666 represents Nero (*Neron* in Latin) in the following way: N=50; E=6; R=500; O=60; and N=50. The sum of these numbers is 666. Supporters of this hypothesis state that the "numerical value" of the name Nero Caesar in Aramaic is 666.[23] Still other scholars suggest that John intended to imply that Nero was figuratively reborn in Domitian, who tortured Christians.[24]

E. *The Seven Visions of Worshipers of the Lamb and Worshipers of the Beast* (14:1-20). Chapter 14 provides assurance to God's people that the power of evil will be judged by God and that God's people will themselves emerge from their suffering in triumphant glory. John again has a vision of heaven (14:1-5), this time followed by a series of warnings from angels flying in heaven and the command that the heavenly Christ reap the harvest of the earth. Then follows an announcement that all image worshipers of the antichrist will suffer (14:13). The chapter ends with a symbolic description of the end in the form of a grape harvest (14:14-20).

F. *The Seven Bowls of the Wrath of God* (15:1-16:21). In this section John reviews the horrors destined to afflict the earth before the climactic Battle of Armageddon. He sees seven angels carrying the seven last plagues; in them is filled up the wrath of God. Their appearance causes the martyrs to rejoice. The seven angels then come out of the heavenly temple and receive the seven bowls of judgment. They go forth to pour out the bowls of the wrath of God upon the earth.

G. *The Seven Visions of the Fall of Babylon* (17:1-19:10). After describing the seven final plagues, John introduces a new figure with a lengthy description. He describes Babylon (Rome) in the metaphor of whoredom. In the Old Testament Israel is frequently described as God's unfaithful wife (cf. Is. 1:21; Jerem. 2:20, 3:6-10; Hos. 2:5, 3:1). Furthermore, sacred prostitution was rampant in the ancient world as referred to by the Bible.

John employs several images to describe Babylon as a prostitute (18:3, 7, 9, 11-15, 19). Like the prostitutes in Rome who wore a headband with their names, this prostitute also displays her name, a title of mystery indicating that what old Babylon was to the ancient world, this woman is to the modern world. Also this prostitute is drunk—with martyrs' blood.

Following his description of Babylon, John embarks on describing the demise and the reappearance of the beast out of the Abyss. The seven-headed, ten-horned beast then makes war with the saints.

John gives double interpretation of the seven heads of the beast: The seven heads represent seven hills; they also represent seven kings. In apocalyptic and prophetic literature seven hills is a symbol of power (cf. Dan 2:35; 11:45). Thus one interpretation maintains that the seven heads could represent seven major empires in the world: Egypt, Asyria, Babylon, Persia, Greece, Rome, and a Final Empire. This hypothesis explains the five fallen empires, the one that then was (Rome), and the one that is yet to arise, the final one being the empire of the antichrist.[24]

Another interpretation takes its cue from the number seven which denotes completeness. As such, John is not pointing out any particular empire. Rather, he is using the apocalyptic value of the number seven to describe the totality of evil political powers, wherever and however they arise.[25]

The apocalyptic imagery of ten horns is drawn from Daniel where the prophet viewed the eschatological antagonist against God as a coalition of ten kings (Dan. 2:40-44; 7:20-27). Some modern Bible students believe that these "ten kings" refer to ten nations in the European Common Market, a view especially popularized by the 1970 best seller *The Late Great Planet Earth*.[26] Other attempts at specific interpretive schemes (such as the ones occuring in the time of Napoleon or Hitler) have fallen.[27] If this prophecy is to be understood symbolically (where the number ten would denote fullness), then the horns represent the totality of nations of the world which are allied with the antichrist.[28]

The last part of chapter 17 describes the fall of the prostitute which in the final sentence is identified with Rome (17:18), even as the beast himself has been so identified earlier (17:9). While some have attempted to distinguish the prostitute and the beast as false religion and international politics, respectively, [29] such a precise delineation is not accurate since both figures represent the same thing in different metaphors.

In chapter 18, John describes the fall of Babylon. Four reasons are given for its judgment by God: it is demonic; it influences the world to participate in its sin; it affects political leaders for evil; and it uses its power for material gain (18:3-8).

Although earth mourns Babylon's destruction, heaven rejoices over its desolation as a fulfillment of a prayer of vengeance (6:9-11). A call is then extended to tribulation believers to separate from Babylon lest they receive the same physical judgments (18:1-19).

Following the description of Babylon's destruction comes the mighty chorus of the believers. The latter part of this triumphant scene introduces the bride, the antithesis of the prostitute. The bride, who is ready to celebrate her marriage, represents the body of believers who have remained faithful to their Lord (19:1-10).

H. *The Seven Visions Announcing the End* (19:11-22:5). With the fall of Babylon, John now begins his description of the last great scene, the Second Coming of Jesus Christ and the glorious union of Christ and his people.

The seven great events that will follow the Great Tribulation are now presented in rapid sequence. The imagery is no longer the Lamb. Rather, John draws his symbolism from the Old Testament ideal of Yahweh as the Man of War riding a war horse (Ex. 15:1-12). The Man of War is Jesus Christ and his armies represent the hosts of Heaven (Zech. 14:5). This is the climax of the war between God and Satan. In that day the antichrist, the kings of the earth, and their armies will be destroyed by Christ. The antichrist and his allies will be sent to the lake of fire (19:17-21).

The first six verses of chapter 20 have been the most controversial verses in the book and the most divisive in modern Christian history. In this passage, Satan is seized by a heavenly angel and is bound with a chain in the abyss for a millennium (one thousand years). There are four major views that Christians have held concerning this passage.[30] They are:

a. *Dispensational Premillennialism.* This is the view that the one thousand years are a future span of time in which the promises to Israel in the Abrahamic Covenant (Gen. 9:1-17; 12:3; 22:18) shall be literally fulfilled for Israel in Palestine. The Church will be raptured out of the world prior to the Great Tribulation.

b. *Historic Premillennialism.* This position also understands the one thousand years to be a future span of time. However, it traces its view of the millennium to the earliest centuries of the Christian Church (hence "historic") and it upholds the belief that the promises to Israel in the Old Testament are fulfilled in the Church which is the "New Israel."

c. *Amillennialism.* This view does not look for the one thousand years as a future time-span. Rather, it interprets the language of this passage as describing the realities of Satan's defeat by Christ when Jesus died and rose from the dead. The one thousand years is a symbol of the era between the Resurrection and the Second Coming of Christ.

d. *Postmillennialism.* This is the view that the millennium refers to the closing era of this present age during which the Church will evangelize the world. After the world-wide evangelization of the world Christ will return. This view looks for consummation of the Kingdom of God to occur within history rather than beyond it.

John also states that during the millennium the martyrs who resisted Satan will be resurrected to rule with Christ (20:4-6).

After the millennial reign of Christ, Satan will be released from the abyss. He will return to the earth to deceive the nations and to lead the rebels against Jerusalem. Here John draws his vocabulary from Ezekiel's prophetic drama involving Gog and Magog, symbols of Israel's enemies (Ezek. 38:12; 39:6). In this final battle, God's people are once more delivered. This time, the powers of evil are silenced forever; Satan is banished for eternity in the lake of fire (20:7-10).

With Satan banished, the wicked of all ages stand before Christ at the Judgment Throne. The present universe is purged by fire to make way for the new heaven and the new earth.

John then sees the newly created order, "the Holy City, the new Jerusalem, coming down out of heaven from God" (12:21). Several blessings of life in this new order are enumerated: the presence of God, no tears, no death, no sorrow, no crying, and no pain (21:8). God's name on each forehead (3:12; 14:1) represents the familial relationship between God and His people.

5. The Epilogue (22:6-21). In the epilogue, John emphasizes the authority of his prophecy and pronounces a blessing upon the keeper of the book's contents. Stating that his visions represent the immediate future and that the scrolls on which they are written are not to be sealed, John pronounces a curse upon those who would distort the manuscript.

Furthermore, the nearness of Christ's Second Advent is reiterated in a threefold repetition of the phrase "I am coming soon" (22:12, 17, 20).

A contrast is then made between the saved and the unsaved (22:11-15) with an invitation to the unsaved. In response to Christ's promise to return, John concludes with an appropriate prayer: "Amen. Come, Lord Jesus" (22:20). He closes his book with a benediction.

Traditionally biblical scholars have employed four major methods in interpreting apocalyptic literature in general and the Book of Revelation in particular. Based upon their theological backgrounds and presuppositions, they have adopted the following interpretation methods:

a. *Idealism.* A method allegorizing and spiritualizing the symbols. Idealism sees the Book of Revelation as describing metaphorically the spiritual conflict between God's people and the powers of evil; a view that the book has to be interpreted spiritually rather than in the context of history.

b. *Historicism.* A view that the symbols refer to personages and events in history. The beast of chapter 13, for instance, has been identified, according to the interpreter's own time, with Mohammed, the Pope, Martin Luther, Napoleon, and Hitler.[32] Particularly in the Protestant Reformation, the historicists identified the symbolism of Revelation with anti-papal struggles of the Reformers.[33]

c. *Preterism.* A view, favored by modern critical scholars, which assumes that Revelation must be understood in the context of its own time; that the book was composed for a first-century audience familiar with apocalyptic imagery. According to this method, Babylon (18:2, 10) is Rome, the beast was one of the Roman emperors, the false prophet was the cult of emperor worship, and the various plagues described are wars, famines, earthquakes, and other disasters experienced during the late first century.[34]

d. *Futurism.* A view that the book is prophetic and its prophecies are yet to be completely fulfilled. This school of thought has many branches and manifestations, such as:

— Millennialism, the belief that there will be a future Utopian age, usually thought of as 1,000 years in length.

— Pre-millennialism, the belief that the Second Advent of Christ will occur prior to an age of Utopia and that such an era will result directly from the Second Coming of Jesus.

— Post-millennialism, the belief that the Second Advent of Christ will occur after the age of Utopia which will be ushered in by the world-wide conversion to Christianity.

— Pre-tribulationism, the belief that the Church will be raptured (resurrected bodies of the believers will rise in the air to meet Christ at his Second Coming) out of the world prior to the Great Tribulation, in the 70th Week of Daniel.

— Post-tribulationism, the belief that the rapture of the Church will occur after the period of the affliction at the end of the present age.

— Dispensationalism, the view that stresses the radical difference between two peoples of God—national Israel and the Christian Church. It often divides human history in seven distinct areas.

Whatever method of interpretation a person chooses, and however he likes to interpret the symbolism and apocalyptic language of Revelation, the abiding message of the book is loud and clear: God is the Lord of history. Out of his love he has come to His creation in Jesus Christ to save it. Jesus Christ at his first advent won a decisive victory over Satan. At his Second Coming he will win the ultimate victory. Since he has the last word, there is hope for all who are on the Lord's side.

References

1. Robert A. Spivey and D. Moody Smith, *Anatomy of the New Testament*, Fourth Ed. (New York: Macmillan Publishing Co., 1989), p. 410.
2. D. Russell, *The Method and Message of Jewish Apocalyptic* (Philadelphia: Westminster Press, 1964), p. 36.
3. L. Morris, *Apocalypse* (Grand Rapids: William B. Eerdmans Publishing Co., 1972), pp. 34-35.
4. Martin Rist, "The Revelation of St. John the Divine," *The Interpreter's Bible*, Vol. XII, (New York and Nashville: Abingdon Press, 1957), pp. 347-351.
5. Russell, p. 106.
6. G. Ladd, *The Presence of the Future* (Grand Rapids: William B. Eerdmans Publishing Co., 1974), pp. 87-93.
7. Stephen L. Harris, *The New Testament: A Student's Introduction* (Mountain View, California: Mayfield Publication Co., 1988), p. 279.
8. Harris, *The New Testament*, p. 279.
9. *Ibid.*
10. George Werner Kumel, *Introduction to the New Testament*, 17th ed., (Nashville: Abingdon Press, 1975), pp. 466-69.
11. J. Benton White, *From Adam to Armageddon*, Second ed. (Belmont, California: Wadsworth Publishing Co., 1989), pp. 194-95; Harris, p. 280; Spivey and Smith, p. 410.
12. Henry H. Halley, *Bible Handbook: An Abbreviated Bible Commentary* (Grand Rapids: Zondervan Publishing House, 1960), p. 637.
13. Rist, pp. 390-391.
14. Robert G. Gromacki, *New Testament Survey* (Grand Rapids: Baker Book House, 1974), p. 406.
15. Halley, pp. 644-645.
16. M. Erickson, *Contemporary Options in Eschatology* (Grand Rapids: Baker, 1978), pp. 191-192.
17. Harris, *The New Testament*, p. 287.
18. F. Bruce, *New Testament Development of Old Testament Themes* (Grand Rapids: William B. Eerdmans Publishing Co., 1968), pp. 51-67.
19. L. Hartman and A.D. Lella, *The Book of Daniel* (Garden City: Doubleday, 1977), pp. 212-214.
20. J. Baldwin, *Daniel* (Downers Grove, Illinois: Inter-Varsity Press, 1978), pp. 161-162.
21. Harris, *The New Testament*, p. 288.
22. James L. Price, *The New Testament: Its History and Theology* (New York: Macmillan Publishing Co., 1987), pp. 425-426.
23. Daniel L. Lewis, *The Apocalypse of John* (Troy, Michigan: Diakonos, 1989), p. 62.
24. Lewis, p. 76.
25. R. Mounce, *The Book of Revelation* (Grand Rapids: William B. Eerdmans Publishing Co., 1977), pp. 315-316.
26. H. Lindsey and C. Carlson, *The Late Great Planet Earth* (Grand Rapids: Zondervan, 1970).
27. R. Wallace, *The Lord is King* (Downers Grove, Illinois: Inter-Varsity Press, 1979), pp. 130-131.

28 Lewis, p. 77.
29 Halley, pp. 664-665.
30 R. Clouse, ed., *The Meaning of the Millennium: Four Views* (Downers Grove, Illinois: Inter-Varsity Press, 1977).
31 A. Hunter, *Introducing the New Testament*, 3rd ed. (Philadelphia: Westminister, 1972), p. 194.
32 G. Ladd, *A Commentary on the Revelation of John* (Grand Rapids: William B. Eerdmans Publishing Co., 1972), p. 11.
33 Clouse, *The Meaning of the Millennium: Four Views*
34 Harris, *The New Testament*, p. 289.

Epilogue

The formation of the canon of the New Testament was one of the most important developments in the thought and practice of the early church. The canon was not the product of any one person's arbitrary judgment, nor was it set by conciliar vote. It grew out of a process of elimination of a large number of religious books written by Christians in the first and second centuries.

Besides the twenty-seven books officially accepted in the New Testament, the early Christian community produced a number of religious books, some of which carried the authority of Scripture for some segment of Christianity but never achieved broad acceptance. Some of these documents not only were held in high regard by some Christian communities, but were included in church lists of "recognized books" along with the New Testament books. Some of the earliest New Testament manuscripts contain some books which were later denied canonical status.

The most important works that appear in some New Testament lists are: The *Epistle of Barnabas*, an epistle attributed to Paul's mentor; the *Didache*, supposedly a summary of the twelve apostles' teachings; *I Clement*, a letter by the bishop of Rome to the Corinthians; *Apocalypse of Peter*, visions of heaven and hell ascribed to Peter; *The Shepherd of Hermas*, a mystical apocalyptic work.

The process of selection, and later "canonization," was a gradual one in which decisions about the inspiration and spiritual power of these early documents were significant. There were other considerations and criteria as well, such as whether a book was written by an apostle or a person closely affiliated with an apostle and whether a book was accepted by a large number of Christian communities.

In addition to works that for a time enjoyed near-canonical status, the early Christian community produced numerous other writings. These works varied in type from gospel, to letter, to apocalypse. Many of these writings were never held in high regard by most of the Christian community.

In this large body of writing are some nineteen Gospels, twenty-four Acts, seven Epistles, six Apocalypses, and fifteen other works, including some Gnostic writings. Works such as these provide some narratives about Jesus' infancy and the so-called silent years which are not preserved in the canonical Gospels. Besides these fanciful versions of Jesus' life and teachings, some of these books describe the adventures of the apostles, as well as authenticate the ideas of some unorthodox groups which had crept in the life of the early Church.

Thus, the twenty-seven books of the New Testament were selected out of many religious books and were canonized as sacred scripture toward the end of the fourth century. The canonization was the end result of a long period of development and historical process, because the second century Christians began to regard many of present New Testament books as authoritative and binding.

On the basis of their literary character, the books of the New Testament fall into four major groups: biographical, historical, epistolary, and apocalyptic. These four literary *genre* correspond to the four major parts of the twenty-seven books which are divided into four Gospels, the Book of Acts, twenty-one epistles, and the Revelation.

The grouping of these books reflects a logical rather than a chronological order. Although the Pauline letters were written first, the Gospels stand at the head of the canon. The reasoning was that the central figure, in fact, the *raison d'être*, of the Scripture was Jesus Christ himself. Without the historical life, death, and resurrection there would be neither Christian Scriptures nor a Christian Church. So, the New Testament starts with the Gospel of Matthew describing his advent and ends with the Book of Revelation, when God will bring his redemptive program to a climax.

Bibliography

Bacon, B.W. *An Introduction to the New Testament.* New York: The Macmillan Co., 1985.
Baeck, Leo. "The Phariseeism," *Pharisees and Other Essays.* New York: Schoken Books, 1966.
Baldwin, J. *Daniel.* Downers Grove, Illinois: Inter-Varsity Press, 1978.
Barclay, William. *Daily Study Bible.* Philadelphia: The Westminister Press, 1956.
Barrett, C.K. *The Gospel According to St. John: An Introduction With Commentary and Notes on the Greek Text,* 2nd Ed. Philadelphia: Westminister, 1978.
Barnett, Albert E. "The Epistle of Jude," *The Interpreter's Bible,* Vol. XII. New York and Nashville: Abingdon Press, 1957.
_____. "The Letter of James," *The Interpreter's Dictionary of the Bible,* Vol. X. New York and Nashville: Abingdon Press, 1962.
_____. "The Second Epistle of Peter," *The Interpreter's Bible,* Vol. XII. New York and Nashville: Abingdon Press, 1957.
Beare, Francis Wright. *A Commentary on the Epistle to the Philippians.* New York: Harper and Row, 1959.
_____. "Introduction and Exegesis of Ephesians," *The Interpreter's Bible,* Vol. XI. New York and Nashville: Abingdon Press, 1953.
_____. "The Epistle to the Colossians," *The Interpreter's Bible,* Vol. II. New York and Nashville: Abingdon Press, 1955.
_____. "The Letter to the Romans," *The Interpreter's Dictionary of the Bible,* Vol. IV. New York and Nashville: Abingdon Press, 1962.
Becker, J.C. "The Letter of Jude," *The Interpreter's Dictionary of the Bible,* Vol. II. New York and Nashville: Abingdon Press, 1962.
Betz, O. "Dead Sea Scrolls," *The Interpreter's Dictionary of the Bible,* Supplementary Volume. Nashville: Abingdon Press, 1955.
Briggs, R.C. *Interpreting the New Testament Today,* Nashville: Abingdon Press, 1973.
Brown, Raymond E. *The Gospel According to John,* Vol. I. Garden City, New York Doubleday, 1966, 1970.
Bruce, Frederick Fyvie. *Paul: Apostle of the Heart Set Free.* Exeter: Paternoster, 1977.
_____. *New Testament Development of Old Testament Themes.* Grand Rapids: William B. Eerdmans Publishing Co., 1968.
_____. *New Testament History.* Garden City, New York: Doubleday & Co., Inc., 1980.
_____. *The New Testament.* Garden City, New York: Doubleday & Co., Inc., 1969.
Buechner, Frederick. *Peculiar Treasures.* New York: Harper & Row, 1979.
Bultmann, Rudolf. *The Gospel of John.* Philadelphia: Westminister Press, 1971.
Burrows, Millar. *The Dead Sea Scrolls.* New York: Viking Press, 1955.
Buttrick, George A. "The Gospel According to St. Matthew," *The Interpreter's Bible,* Vol. VII. New York, Abingdon Press, 1954.
Cadbury, J.H. *The Making of Luke-Acts.* New York: The Macmillan Co., 1927.
_____. "The New Testament and Early Christian Literature," *The Interpreter's Bible,* Vol. VII. New York: Abingdon Press, 1962.
Cadoux, A.T. *The Parables of Jesus.* New York: The Macmillan Co., 1931.
Chamberlin and Feldman. Ed. *The Dartmouth Bible.* Boston: Houghton Mifflin Co., 1961.

Charlesworth, James H. Ed. *The Old Testament Pseudipigrapha*. Garden City, New York: Doubleday, 1983.

Clouse R. Ed. *The Meaning of the Millennium: Four Views*. Downers Grove, Illinois: Inter-Varsity Press, 1977.

Cragg, Gerald R. "The Epistle to the Romans," *The Interpreter's Bible*, Vol. IX. New York and Nashville: Abingdon Press, 1954.

Craig, Clarence R. "The First Epistle to the Corinthians," *The Interpreter's Bible*, Vol. X. New York and Nashville: Abingdon Press, 1954.

Cullman, Oscar. *The New Testament: An Introduction to the General Reader*. Philadelphia: Westminister Press, 1966.

Daling, Dennis C. *Jesus Christ Through History*. New York: Harcourt Brace Jovanovich, Inc. 1979.

Dibelius, Martin. *From Tradition to Gospel*, Trans. by G.L. Woolf. Philadelphia: Westminister Press, 1935.

_____. *Studies in the Acts of the Apostles*. Edited by H. Greeven. Translated by M. Ling. New York: Charles Scribner's Sons, 1956.

Dinkler, E. "Letter to the Hebrews," *The Interpreter's Dictionary of the Bible*, Vol. II. New York and Nashville: Abingdon Press, 1962.

Dodd, C.H. *The Epistle of Paul to the Romans*. London: Hodder and Stoughton, 1932.

_____. *The Interpretation of the Fourth Gospel*. New York: Cambridge University Press, 1953.

Drower, E.L. *The Mandeans of Iraq and Iran*. Leiden: Brill, 1962.

Duncan, George Steward. *St. Paul's Ephesian Ministry: A Reconstruction With Special Reference to the Ephesian Origin of the Imprisonment Epistles*. London: Hodder and Stroughton, 1929.

Easton, Burton Scott. *The Pastoral Epistles: Introduction, Commentary and World Studies*. New York: Charles Scribner's Sons. 1947.

Erickson, M. *Contemporary Options in Eschatology*. Grand Rapids: Baker, 1976.

Eusebius, *Church History*. Trans. by High J. Lawler and John L. Oulton, London: Society for Promoting Christian Knowledge, 1927.

Fee, Gordon D. and Stuart, Douglas. *How to Read the Bible for All its Worth*. Grand Rapids: Zondervan Publishing House, 1982.

Filson, Floyd N. "The Second Epistle to the Corinthians," *The Interpreter's Bible*, Vol. X. New York and Nashville: Abingdon Press, 1954.

Gabel, John B. and Charles B. Wheeler, *The Bible as Literature*. Oxford: Oxford University Press, 1986.

Gaebelien, Frank. *The Practical Epistle of James*. New York: Doniger and Roughly, 1955.

Gealy, Fred D. "The First and Second Epistles to Timothy and the Epistle to Titus, *The Interpreter's Bible*, Vol. XI. New York and Nashville: Abingdon Press, 1955.

Goguel, Maurice. *Jesus and the Origins of Christianity*, 2 Vols., trans. by Olive Wyon. New York: Harper and Brothers, Torchbooks, 1960.

Gilmour, S.M. "The Gospel According to St. Luke, Introduction and Exegesis," *The Interpreter's Bible*, Vol. VIII. New York and Nashville: Abingdon Press, 1954.

Goodspeed, Edgar J. *The Introduction to the New Testament*. Chicago: University of Chicago Press, 1938.

_____. *The Meaning of Ephesians*. Chicago: University of Chicago Press, 1933.

Grant, Frederick C. and Luccock, Halford E. "The Gospel According to Mark," *The Interpreter's Bible*, Vol. VII. New York: Abingdon Press, 1962.

Grant, Frederick. *The Growth of the Gospels.* New York: Abingdon Press, 1933.
Gromacki, Robert G. *New Testament Survey.* Grand Rapids: Baker Book House, 1974.
Guignebert, Charles. *The Jewish World in the Time of Jesus*, Trans. by S.H. Hooks, Book IV, ch. 2, "The Judeao-Pagan Syncretism." London: Keegan Paul, Trench, Trubner and Co., 1939.
Halley, Henry H. *Bible Handbook: An Abbreviated Bible Commentary.* Grand Rapids: Zondervan Publishing House, 1960.
Harris, Stephen L. *Understanding the Bible.* Palo Alto and London: California State University, 1986.
_____. *The New Testament: A Student's Introduction.* Mountain View, California: Mayfield Publications Co., 1988.
Harrison, P.N. *The Problem of Pastoral Epistles.* London: Oxford University Press, 1821.
Hartman, L., and Lella, A.D. *The Book of Daniel.* Garden City: Doubleday, 1977.
Howard, W.F. "Introduction and Exegesis to the Gospel of John," *Interpreter's Bible*, Vol. VIII. New York and Nashville: Abingdon Press, 1954.
Hunter, M. Archipald. *Introducing the New Testament*, 3rd Ed. Philadelphia: Westminister, 1972.
_____. "Introduction and Exegesis of I Peter," *The Interpreter's Bible*, Vol. 12. New York and Nashville: Abingdon Press, 1957.
Jackson, F.J.F. and Lake, Kirsopp, eds. *The Beginning of Christianity*, Vol. XXV. London: Macmillan & Co., 1920-33.
Jeremias, J. *Jerusalem in the Time of Jesus.* Philadelphia: Fortress, 1967.
Jeske, L. Richard, *New Testament: Toward a Historical Understanding.* Lawrence, Kansas: University of Kansas, 1988.
Jewett, Robert. *Jesus Against the Rapture.* Philadelphia: The Westminister Press, 1979.
Johnston, G. "Letter to the Ephesians," *The Interpreter's Dictionary of the Bible*, Vol. X. Nashville: Abingdon Press, 1962.
Josephus, Flavius. *Antiquities of the Jews.* Loeb edition, Vol. IX, trans. by L.H. Feldmann. Cambridge, Massachusetts: Harvard University Press, 1965.
_____. *The Jewish War.* Loeb edition, trans. by L.H. Feldmann. Cambridge, Massachusetts: Harvard University Press, 1965.
Kasemann, Ernst, *The New Testament: A Study of the Gospel of John in Light of Chapter 17.* Trans. by G. Krodel. Philadelphia: Fortress Press, 1968.
Kee, Howard Clark. *Understanding the New Testament.* 3rd Ed. Englewood Cliffs: Prentice Hall, 1973.
_____. *The Origins of Christianity: Sources and Documents.* Englewood Cliffs: Prentice-Hall, 1973.
Keyes, Nelson Beecher. *The Story of the Bible.* Pleasantville: The Reader's Digest Association, 1962.
Klasner, Joseph. *Jesus of Nazareth: His Life, Times, and Teaching.* Trans. Herbert Danby. Boston: Beacon Press, 1964.
Knox, John. "The Epistle to Philemon," *The Interpreter's Bible*, Vol. II. New York and Nashville: Abingdon Press, 1955.
_____. "The Gospel According to St. Luke," *The Interpreter's Bible*, New York: Abingdon Press, 1955.
Kumel, George Werner. *Introduction to the New Testament.* 17th Ed. Nashville: Abingdon Press, 1975.

Kysar, R. *The Fourth Evangelist and His Gospel.* Minneapolis: Augsburg, 1975.
Ladd, G. *A Commentary on the Revelation of John.* Grand Rapids: William B. Eerdmanns Publishing Co., 1972.
_____. *The Presence of the Future.* Grand Rapids: William B. Eerdmanns Publishing Co., 1974.
Latourette, Kenneth S. *A History of Christianity.* New York: Harper and Brothers Publishers, 1953.
Lewis, Daniel L. *The Apocalypse of John.* Troy, Michigan: Diakonos, 1989.
Lindsey, H. and Carlson, C. *The Late Great Planet Earth.* Grand Rapids: Zondervan, 1970.
Loescher, Vernon A. *The Gospel of Luke.* New York: F.C.C. Press, 1975.
Lohse, Eduard. *Colossians and Philemon.* Philadelphia: Fortress Press, 1971.
Macgregor, G.H.C. "Introduction and Exegesis of Acts," *The Interpreter's Bible*, Vol. IX. New York and Nashville, Abingdon Press, 1954.
Magee, David. *Roman Rule in Asia Minor to the End of the Third Century After Christ*, Vol. I. Princeton: Princeton University Press, 1950.
Manson, T.W. "Background to the Ministry of Jesus," *The Bible Today.* New York: Harper & Brothers, 1955.
Martin, Hugh. *The Parables of the Gospels.* New York: The Abingdon Press, 1937.
Marty, William H. *Surveying the New Testament.* Dubuque, Iowa: Kendall/Hunt Publishing Co., 1987.
_____. *The New Testament.* Dubuque, Iowa: Kendall/Hunt Publishing Co., 1987.
Mayer, Joseph B. *The Epistle of James.* Grand Rapids: Zondervan Publishing House, 1954.
Metzger, Manning Bruce. *The New Testament: Its Background, Growth, and Content.* Nashville and New York: Abingdon Press, 1965.
Morris, L. *Apocalypse.* Grand Rapids: William B. Eerdmans Publishing Co., 1972.
Mounce, R. *The Book of Revelation.* Grand Rapids: William B. Eerdmans Publishing Co., 1977.
Neusner, Jacob. *From Politics to Piety: The Emergence of Pharisaic Judaism.* Englewood Cliffs, New Jersey: Prentice-Hall, 1973.
Nigosian, Solomon. *Judaism: The Way of Holiness.* Great Britain: Crucible, The Aquarian Press, 1986.
Parry, R.S. John. *The Pastoral Epistles.* Cambridge: Cambridge University Press, 1920.
Perkins, Pheme. *Reading the New Testament.* New York: Paulist Press, 1977.
Perrin, Norman. *The New Testament: An Introduction.* New York: Harcourt Brace Jovanovich, 1974.
_____. *What is Redaction Criticism?* Philadelphia: Fortress Press, 1969.
Price, James L. *The New Testament: Its History and Theology.* New York: Macmillan Publishing Co., 1987.
Purdy, Alexander C. "The Epistle to the Hebrews," *The Interpreter's Bible*, Vol XI. New York and Nashville: Abingdon Press, 1955.
Radford, Lewis Bostock. *The Epistle to the Colossians and the Epistle to Philemon.* London: Methuen & Co., 1931.
Rall, Harris Franklin. *New Testament History.* New York and Nashville: Abingdon Press, 1929.
Ramsay, W.M. *St. Paul the Traveler and the Roman Citizen.* London: Hodder and Staughton, 1896.

Ringren, Helmer. *The Faith of Qumran*. Philadelphia: Fortress Press, 1961.
Rist, Martin. "The Revelation of St. John the Divine," *The Interpreter's Bible*, Vol. XII. New York and Nashville: Abingdon Press, 1957.
Ross, Alexander. *The Epistle of James and John*. Grand Rapids: William B. Eerdmans Publishing Co., 1964.
Russell, D. *The Method and Message of Jewish Apocalyptic*. Philadelphia: Westminister Press, 1964.
Scott, Ernest F. "The Epistle to the Philippians," *The Interpreter's Bible*. Vol. XXI. New York and Nashville: Abingdon Press, 1955.
_____. *The Fourth Gospel*, 2nd Ed. Edinburgh: T. & T. Clark, 1908.
_____. *The Pastoral Epistles*. New York: Harper and Brothers, 1936.
Simon, Marcel. *Jewish Sects at the Time of Jesus*. Philadelphia: Fortress Press, 1967.
Smith, Dwight Moody. "Gospel of John," *Interpreter's Dictionary of the Bible*. Supplementary Volume. Nashville: Abingdon Press, 1976.
Spivey, Robert A. and Smith, E. Moody. *Anatomy of the New Testament*. 4th Ed. New York: Macmillan Publishing Co., 1989.
Stamm, Raymond T. "The Epistle to the Galatians," *The Interpreter's Bible*, Vol. X. New York and Nashville: Abingdon Press, 1954.
Stewart, James S. *The Life and Teaching of Jesus Christ*. New York: Abingdon Press, n.d.
Streeter, B.H. *The Four Gospels: A Study of Origins*. London: Macmillan & Co., 1930.
Strobe, Donald. *Secretary to St. Peter*. Knoxville: Seven Worlds Publishing, 1989.
Tenney, C. Merrill. *New Testament Survey*. Grand Rapids: William B. Eerdmans Publishing Co., 1967.
The People of Promise: A Survey of the Old Testament. Dallas: Gold Label Publications, 1982.
Toombs, Lawrence, E. *The Threshold of Christianity*. Philadelphia: Westminister Press, 1960.
Tootikian, Vahan H. *A Survey of the Hebrew Bible*. Southfield, Michigan: Armenian Heritage Committee, 1990.
Wallace, R. *The Lord is King*. Downers Grove, Illinois: Inter-Varsity Press, 1979.
Walker, W.O., Ed. *The Relationship Among the Gospels*. San Antonio: Trinity University Press, 1978.
White, J. Benton. *From Adam to Armageddon*. 2nd Ed. Belmont, California: Wadsworth Publishing Co., 1986.
Wikgren, Allen. "The English Bible," *The Interpreter's Bible*, Vol. 1. New York and Nashville, Abingdon Press, 1956.
Williamson, Lamar. Mark, *"Interpretations."* Atlanta: John Knox Press, 1983.
Wilder, Amos N. "The First, Second, and Third Epistle of John," *The Interpreter's Bible*, Vol. XII. New York and Nashville: Abingdon Press, 1957.

Index

A *Manual of Discipline,* 30
Aaron (High Priest), 237-238
Abba (father), 76
Abraham, 43, 44, 48, 49, 84, 161, 186, 189, 190, 238
Abrahamic Covenant, 277
Abyss, the, 274, 275, 276, 277
Acts, Book of, 129-155
Adam, 48, 49, 80, 84, 87, 161, 178
Agape (love), 177
Agrippa, 106, 142
Alexander the Great, 21, 27, 29, 197
American Revised Version, 17, 235
Amillenialism, 277
Andrew, 65, 66, 113
Angelology, 265
Anna, the prophetess, 82, 87
Annas, 121
Antichrist, 254, 256, 265, 275
Antioch (in Syria), 41, 43, 46, 80, 107 130, 131, 132, 141, 142, 188, 236
Antiochus Epiphanes IV, 21, 22
Antipas, Herod, 64, 83, 102
Aphrodite (Venus), 168
Apocalyptic Gospel, 46-47
Apocalyptic Literature, 263-266
Apocalyptic Predictions of Jesus, 55-56, 72, 74-75
Apocalypse of Peter, 11, 282
Apocrypha, 22, 29, 30, 36, 282
Apollos, 170, 235
Apphia, 215, 216
Aquila (and Priscilla), 147, 148, 168
Arabia, 140
Aramaic, 12, 37, 43, 245, 259
Archippus, 203, 215, 216
Areopagus (Hill of Mars), 147
Arimathea, Joseph of, 58, 75, 77, 122
Aristarchus, 203
Armenia, 132
Aristotle, 52
Armageddon (Battle of), 274
Artemis (Diana), 148, 193, 268
Ascension of Isaiah, 264
Assumption of Moses, 259, 264

Assyria(ns), 275
Athanasius, 19
  Easter Letter, 12
Athens, 147, 148
Augustine (Saint), 158
Augustus Caesar, 19, 23, 86

Baalism, 269
Babylon, 246, 267, 274, 275
Baptism, 162
  See Jesus, baptism of;
  John the Baptist, 50-51, 64, 86-87, 111-113
Baptist, the. See John the Baptist.
Barabbas, 77
Barnabas, 59, 139-140, 142, 143, 144, 145, 235
Bartholomew, 66
Beast, the, 273-274
Beatitudes, 51, 58, 82
Bede, Venerable, 15
Beelzebub, 53, 92
Benedictus, the, 84
Bethany, 72, 73, 75, 92, 114
Bethlehem, 18, 49, 86
Bethsaida, 68, 70, 108, 114
Bible
  Authorized (see King James), 16, 17
  American Standard Version, 17, 235
  Bishop(s), 16
  Coverdale, 16
  Geneva, 16
  Great, 16
  Hebrew, 9, 10, 29, 44, 46, 104, 122, 144, 185, 222, 264, 272
  James Moffatt, 17
  Jerusalem, 18
  King James, 16, 17, 190, 235
  J.B. Phillips, 17
  Reims Douay, 16
  Revised Standard Version, 17
Bithynia, 35, 132, 246

291

Caesar (Julius), 73, 121, 168, 269
Caesarea, 130, 141, 150, 152, 153
Caesarea Philippi, 45, 68
Caiaphas, 115, 121
Calvin, John, 235
Cana, Jesus' miracle at, 113, 116
Capernaum, 61, 66, 68, 88, 113, 114, 116
Catholic (General) Epistles, 233-259
Chloe (household), 169
Cilicia, 136, 138
Circumcision, 143, 201, 203, 224
Party, 141, 166, 189
Paul's arguments against, 187, 189 190
Claudius, 36, 147
Clement of Alexandria, 203, 235
Clement of Rome, 235
Cleopas, 103
Codex Alexandrinus, 11, 14
Codex Bezae, 14
Codex Sinaiticus, 14
Codex Vitacanus, 13
Colossians, 202-208
Conduct of Women (in church), 174
Constantine I, 13
Corinth, 147, 148
Corinthians,
First, 167-178
Second, 179-185
Cornelius, 141
Council of Trent, 236
"Courage in Ministry Passage," 181
Coverdale, Myles, 16
Crete, 132, 230, 231
Cross, 57, 58, 75, 206, 223
Crucifixion, the. 55, 57, 75, 102-103 120
See Jesus, Crucifixion of,
Cyprus, 139, 141, 143

Dalmanutha, 68
Damascus, 137, 139, 151, 178, 188
Daniel, Book of, 46, 264, 273, 279
David (King), 44, 46, 49, 50, 55, 63, 72, 263
Deacon(s), 135, 136
Dead Sea Scrolls, 25, 29
Decapolis, 68
Derbe, 143, 186
Diana (Artemis), 148, 193, 268

Demetrius (the Elder's friend), 256, 257
Demetrius (silversmith), 193
Demonology, 68, 265
Devil. See Satan.
Didache, the, 282
Diotrephes, 256
Dispensationalism, 279
Dispensational Premillennialism, 277
Divorce, 71
Docetism, 122, 250, 256
Domitian, 19, 212, 236, 266, 274
Dorcas, 140
Dragon, 272, 273
Druscilla, 152

Ecclesia, 45, 54, 192
Egypt, 44, 45, 50, 132, 272
"Ecumenical Gospel," 45-46
Elder, the, 252, 254, 255, 266
Elijah, 31, 71, 77, 88, 112, 271
Elizabeth, 50, 82
Emmaus, 84, 104
English Revised Version, 17
Eunuch, Ethiopian, 137-138
Epaphras, 203, 204, 205, 206
Epaphroditus, 197, 201
Ephesians, Epistle of, 191-196
Ephesus, 106, 107, 148, 149, 167, 191, 193, 196, 218, 219, 268
Episltes, 157-263
Epistle of Barnabas, 235
Erasmus, Desiderius, 14, 235
Eusebius, 43, 60, 154
Eschatology, 74-75, 98, 160
Essenes, the, 25-26, 29
Estienne, Robert, 14
Euodia, 202
Eutychus, 149
Exeguus, Dionysius, 49
Exorcism, 91-92
Ezekiel, 24, 277

Faith,
Paul's doctrine of, 161-162, 189-190
Felix, 80, 152
Festus, 152
First Clement, 282
First Enoch, 259, 264
Form Criticism, *Formsgeschichte,* 39

292

Freedom, Christian, 173-174, 190, 202
"Freedom Passage," the, 181
Futurism, 279

Gadarene, 52
Gaius, 256, 257
Galatia Theory, 186
Galatians (Epistle), 185-191
Galilee,
 in John, 109, 113, 122
 in Luke, 87-89, 100
 in Mark, 61, 63, 68, 69
 in Matthew, 51-54
Galilee, Sea of (Tiberius), 63, 64, 68, 123
Gallio, 148
Gamaliel, 134, 138
Gaza, 137, 138
Gerizim (Mount), 27, 116
Genealogy, of Jesus, 43, 86
Gerasene, 68
Gethsemane, 57, 75, 76, 101-102, 108
Gloria in Excelsis, 84
Glossolalia (Speaking in tongues)
 Paul's view on, 176
 at Pentecost, 133
Gnostic(ism), 40, 110, 204, 222, 223, 249, 253, 256, 258, 283
Gog of Magog, 277
Golden Rule, the, 52
Golgotha, 57, 77
Good Samaritan, the, 90-91
Gospels, the
 Synoptic, 42-105
 See also Mark, Matthew, Luke, Gospels of.
Great Bible, 16
Greece, 131
Gregorian Calendar, 49
Great Commission, 58-59
Guttenberg, Johann, 16

Hagar, 190
Hanukkah, 22
Hasmanean, Dynasty, 22
Hebrews, Book of, 234-240
Herod Agrippa I, 106, 142
Herod Agrippa II, 152
Herod Antipas, 64, 69, 83, 101, 102
Herod Archelaus, 23

Herod the Great, 19, 22, 23, 49
High Priest, Jesus as, 237-238
Historic Premillennialism, 277
Historicism, 278
Holy Family, 50
Holy Spirit, the
 in Acts, 131, 132, 133, 176
 in John, 118-119, 123
 in Luke, 84, 85, 86, 87, 104
 in Mark, 64, 73
 in Matthew, 51
 in Paul's letters, 163, 176, 181, 185, 186, 189, 190, 191, 195, 196
 See also Paraclete.
Homosexuality, 160
Horsemen of the Apocalypse, 275-276
Husbands and wives (Pauline letters), 196, 207, 248
Hymns
 in Luke, 84
"Hymn to Agape," the, 177
Hyrcanus, John, 27

"I Am" statements
 in Gospel of John, 117
Iconium, 143, 186
Idealism (in Revelation), 278
Idumea, 19, 22
Ignatius, 218, 219, 224
"Immortality Passage," the 181
Intercessory Prayer (Jesus'), 120
Irenaeus, 203, 266
Isaac, 190
Isaiah, 85, 86, 164
Ishmael, 190

Jairus, 52, 68, 89, 115
James (Jesus' brother), 67, 69, 241, 257
 relations with Paul, 144, 151
James, Letter of, 240-244
James (son of Alphaeus), 66, 241
James (son of Zebedee), 19, 65, 66, 71, 142, 234, 241
Jason, 209
Jericho, 50
Jerome, 15
Jerusalem,
 Apostolic conference in, 143-145, 187

293

Christian community, 134-135, 234
Collection for church in, 178, 183, 184
in Acts, 131, 132, 135, 138, 142, 151
in John, 108
in Luke, 90-104
in Mark, 72-78, 79
in Matthew, 55-58
Jerusalem, heavenly, 278
Jerusalem Bible, the, 18
Jesus,
in Apocryphal Gospels, 282
ascension of, 82, 132
baptism of, 50-51, 64, 86-87, 111-113
birth story, 49-50, 86-87
crucifixion of, 55, 57, 75, 77, 102-3
incarnation, 50, 86, 112
miracles, 52, 66, 68, 69-70, 91, 98, 113-115
parables, 53-54, 55, 56, 67, 90, 93-97, 98
post-Resurrection appearances, 58, 104, 123-124
Resurrection, 58, 103, 122, 123
temptations, 51, 64, 87
Virginal Conception, 49, 86
"Jewish Gospel" (Matthew), 44-45
Joanna, 83, 123
Johannine community (School), 253
John, Gospel of, 105-124
John, Letters of, 252-257
John Mark, 41, 59, 139, 142, 144
John, son of Zebedee, 65, 66, 71, 106, 107, 130, 134, 234, 252
John of Patmos, 19, 266, 268
John the Baptist, 19
in Acts, 148
in John, 108, 112-113
in Luke, 82
in Mark, 61, 64, 69, 73
in Matthew, 50
John the Elder (Presbyter), 107
Jonah, 92
Joppa, 140
Joseph (husband of Mary), 19, 48, 50, 69, 86
Joseph (Joses, Jesus' brother), 67, 69
Joseph of Arimathea, 58, 75, 77, 122
Josephus, Flavius, 23, 36

Judaizers, 143, 144, 186, 187, 189, 190
Judas Barsabbas, 144
Judas (Jude, Jesus' brother), 67, 69, 234, 259
Judas Iscariot, 56, 66, 76, 118, 121, 133
Judas Maccabeus, 22
Jude, the Letter of, 257-259
Judea, (Judah), 21, 25, 51, 131, 133, 135-136
Judgment Day (Final), the, 211
Justification by Faith, 162, 189
Justus, Titius, 147
Kerygma, 133, 134
Kingdom of God, 53, 64-65, 73, 92, 96, 108, 158
Koine (Greek), 12, 13, 15, 29

"L" Source, 41, 79
Laodicea, 269, 270
Last Supper (Lord's Supper; Eucharist), 75-76, 101, 104, 108, 109, 116, 118, 174-175
Latin Vulgate, 15
Law. See Torah.
Lazarus (brother of Mary and Martha), 108, 110, 114-115
Lazarus, in Luke's parable, 82, 95, 96
Letter(s),
of Paul, 157-221
Levi (Matthew), 43, 66, 67
Levite(s), 91
Logos, 42, 105, 107, 109, 110
Lord's Prayer, the, 91
"Lovely Letter," the, 198
Luke (companion of Paul), 79-80
Luke, Gospel of, 78-105
Luther, Martin, 16, 235, 243, 278
Lydia, 197
Lystra, 143, 145, 186, 224

"M" Source, 44
Maccabean Revolt, 22
Macedonia, 131, 146, 149, 167, 180, 183, 209
Magi, the, 46, 50
Magnificat, 84
Marcion, 10-11, 222
Mark, Gospel of, 59-78

Marriage, 71, 73-74, 196
Martha (sister of Mary), 91
Mary (Mother of Jesus), 19, 49, 50, 69, 82, 86
Mary (sister of Martha), 91
Mary Magdalene, 58, 83, 122, 123
Matthias, 132, 133
Mattathias, 22
Matthew, 43, 66
Matthew, Gospel of, 42-59
Melchizedek, and Christ, 238
Mercury (Hermes), 143
Mesopotamia, 13, 132, 272
Messiah, 30, 45
  Jesus as King, 38-47, 50, 63, 108
  Jesus as Priestly, 30-31, 38
  Jesus as Prophet, 90
"Messianic Secret," 63, 70
Millennium, 276, 277, 278, 279
Mishnah, 23, 92
Moses, 31, 44, 45, 71, 136, 237, 271
Muratorian Canon, 11, 203, 223, 235, 242

Nain, widow of, 89, 115
Nathanael, 113
Nazareth, 50, 66, 68-69, 87-88
Nebuchadnezzar, 21
Nero, 19, 60, 148, 154, 236, 245, 266, 274
"Neutral Text," 14
New American Bible (NAB), 17
New International Version (NIV), 18
Nicodemus, 115, 122
Nicolaus, 135
Nicholaitans, 268, 269
Nunc Dimittis, 84, 87

Obedience to (State), 165, 231-232
Onesimus, 203, 204, 208, 215, 216-219
Origen, 154
Orthodoxy
  in the Catholic epistles, 239, 251, 259
  in the Pastoral epistles, 206, 224, 226, 228

"Painful Letter" (Severe Letter) to Corinth, 179, 180
Papius, 60

Parables, 53-54, 55, 56, 67, 90, 93-97, 98
Paraclete, 118-119
Parents and Children, 196, 207-208
Parousia, 38, 40, 47, 55, 56, 74, 78, 99, 100-101, 211, 212, 213, 214, 229, 251
Passion, of Jesus,
  in John, 120-122
  in Luke, 101-103
  in Mark, 70, 71, 74, 75-77
  in Matthew, 56-58
Passover and Last Supper, 56, 76
Pastor, the, 222, 226, 228, 230
Pastoral Epistles, the 222-232
Pastoral Qualificatons, 228-229, 231
Patmos, 266, 268
Paul (Saul), 19, 32, 59, 79, 80, 234, 235, 249
  in Acts, 130, 136, 138-139, 140, 141, 142-154
  Apostolic Status, 170, 179, 182, 188, 205
  imprisonment, 150-154, 199
  letters of, 157-221
  ministry in Rome, 154
  Missionary Journeys, 142-150
  opposition to the law, 161-162
  "Sermon on the Mount," 165
  voyage to Rome, 152-153
Paulus, Sergius, 143
Pentecost, 132, 140, 149, 230
Perea, 23, 69, 71
Perean Ministry, 71-72
Perga, 59, 143
Pergamum, 269
"Perpetual Virginity," 67
"Persecution Literature," 245
Peter,
  First, 245-248
  Second, 248-252
Peter, Apocalypse, 11, 282
Peter, Simon (Cephas), 45, 48, 52, 54, 57, 60, 64, 65, 66, 70, 75, 88, 102, 113, 123, 130, 133, 134, 140, 141, 170, 234, 245, 248
Pharisees, 23-24, 53, 55, 58, 82, 88, 92, 94, 95, 97, 115, 117-118, 138, 151, 201
Philadelphia, 269
Philemon, Letter of, 215-219

Philip (Apostle), 66, 113
Philip (King), 197
Philip (the Evangelist), 130, 131, 136, 137-138, 236
Philippi, 68, 146, 149, 196, 209
Philippians, Letter of, 196-202
Phoebe, 159, 166
Pilate, Pontius, 23, 48, 58, 65, 75, 76, 81, 102, 120, 121
Pisidia, 143, 151
Pisidian Antioch, 186
Pompey (General), 19, 22, 27
Postmillennialism, 277, 279
Preterism, 274
Priesthood, Royal 247
"Prison Letters," 196, 216
Prodigal Son, parable of, 82, 94-95
Prostitution, 172-173
Prostitute, the (in Revelations), 275-276
Pseudepigrapha, 29, 259, 264
Pseudonymity, 212, 224, 246, 257, 258
Ptolemy, 21

Q *(Quelle)* Document, 39, 41, 79
Qumran (Scrolls), 29, 30, 183, 214

Reconciliation, Letter of, 179, 181-182
Resurrection, of the dead, 177, 178
Resurrection, of Jesus
  in John, 122-123
  in Luke, 103-104
  in Mark, 78
  in Matthew, 58-59
  Paul's teaching on, 177-178, 211, 214
Resurrection (of Lazarus), 114-115
Revelation, Book of, 263-279
Revised Standard Version (RSV), 17, 190
Rich Fool, the, 92-93
Riches
  James' criticism of, 244
  Luke's criticism of, 95-96
Roman Empire, 79, 81, 130, 149, 157, 159, 168
Romans, Epistle of, 158-166
Rome, 61, 65, 67, 129, 130, 131, 132, 152, 153, 154, 158-159, 214
Royal Priesthood, 247

Sabbath, 53, 58, 67, 78, 93, 116
Sacrifice, Book of, 120-123
Sadducees, 24-25, 73, 74, 134, 151
Samaria, 90, 131, 132, 133, 135-136, 137, 140, 263, 264
Samaritan, parable of, 27
Samaritans, the, 27, 90, 96, 115, 131, 136
Samaritan woman, the, 108, 110, 115, 116
Sanctification, 163
Sanhedrin, the, 25, 57, 58, 63, 76, 100, 102, 114, 115, 121, 136
Sarah, 190
Sardis, 269
Satan, (Devil), 51, 64, 107, 265, 272, 273, 275, 276
Saturnalia, 49
Saul of Tarsus, 138-139
  See also Paul.
Sayings, 43
Scribes, 88, 92, 94, 95
Second Coming (Parousia), 47, 55, 65, 93, 99, 218
  Paul's views on, 211-212, 214-215
  in II Peter, 245-251
  in Revelation, 276-279
Septuagint, 29, 37
Sermon on the Mount, the, 43, 44, 47, 48, 51, 52, 91, 240
Service, Book of, 117-120
Seven, numerical use in Revelation, 270, 271, 273, 274, 276
"Severe Letter" (Painful Letter), 179, 180
Sexual Misconduct, 171-172, 195, 207
Shepherd of Hermas, 11, 282
Sidon, 68
Signs, Book of, 113, 117
Silas, (Silvanus,), 144, 145, 146, 209, 213, 236
Simeon, 83, 86
Simon (brother of Jesus), 67, 68
Simon Magus, 137
Simon of Cyrene, 57, 77, 122
Simon Peter. See Peter (Cephas).
Sirach, 240
Six-hundred sixty-six, 273-274
Slavery, Paul's attitude toward, 196, 208, 217-218
Smyrna, 268, 269

Spain, 154, 166, 216
Spiritual Gifts, use of, 175-177
Stephen, 130, 131, 135, 136-137
Syncretism, 204, 207
Synoptic Gospels, *(Synoptics)*, 38, 41, 61, 70, 106
  relationship of, 38-39, 41-42
  relationship to John, 107-109
Syntyche, 202
Syria, 131, 140, 142, 149
Syrophoenician (woman), 69, 70

Tabernacles, Feast of, 114, 116
Tabitha, 140
Tacitus, 36
Tarsus, 138
Tax collector (publican), 82, 97
Temptations of Jesus, 51
Ten Lost Tribes of Israel, the, 264
Tertullian, 137, 203, 235
Thaddaeus, 66
The People of the Land, Am Haaretz, 26-27
The Thankful Letter, 184
Theophilus, 80, 129
Thessalonians
  First, 208-212
  Second, 212-215
Thessalonica (Salonica), 146, 209
Thomas, 66, 123
Thyatira, 269
Tiberius, 19
Timothy 145, 201, 209, 210, 222, 225
  First, 225-227
  Second, 227-229
Titus (emperor), 19
Titus (Paul's companion), 180, 222, 225
Tongue control, 244
Torah, (the Law), 44
  in Acts, 141, 145, 161
  in Galatians, 185-186, 189-190
  in Hebrews, 237, 238, 239
  in James, 242
  in Luke, 90
  in Mark, 74
  Matthew's views on, 48, 51, 52
  Paul's attitude toward, 161-163, 201-202
Trajan, 35, 246, 252
Transfiguration, the, 63, 72, 248
Triumphal Entry, 47, 72, 99-100
Troas, (Troy), 80, 146, 149
Twelve, the,
  in Luke, 86, 89, 90
  in Mark, 65, 66, 69
  in Matthew, 53
Twelve tribes of Israel, 65, 271
Tychicus, 191, 204
Tyndale, William, 16
Tyrannus (Lecture Hall), 149
Tyre, 68

Unity, Christian, 120, 134, 170-171, 194-195

Versions of the Bible, 15-17
Virgin, the, 50, 272
Vulgate (Bible), 15
  See also Latin Vulgate.

"Warning" ("Danger") Passages," 237, 238, 239
Wescott and Hort, standard Greek text of 14, 15
Widow's mite, the, 74
Wise Men, the, 46, 50
  See Magi, the.
Word (Logos), 42, 105, 107, 109, 110
Wycliffe, John, 15

Ximenes (Bishop), 14

Yahweh, 24, 32, 67, 112, 276

Zaccheaus, 82, 98
Zadok, 24
Zealots, the, 26
Zebedee,
  sons of, 65, 71, 142
Zechariah (father of John the Baptist), 50
Zechariah (prophet), 46, 56, 86, 99
Zeus (Jupiter), 21, 143

About the Author

Vahan H. Tootikian is the pastor of the Armenian Congregational Church of Greater Detroit and President of the Armenian Evangelical World Council. He is also a lecturer in the humanities department of Lawrence Technological University since 1976. His courses include: The Bible as Literature, History of Christian Thought, World Religions, Contemporary Christian Thought, and Western Armenian.

Minister, lecturer, writer, administrator, world traveler, Dr. Tootikian received his college education in the American University of Beirut, and his theological training in the Near East School of Theology. He did his graduate work in Hartford Seminary Foundation, Harvard University, and Andover Newton Theological Seminary.

Dr. Tootikian has been an active member of several Armenian and non-Armenian religious, educational, philanthropic, and cultural organizations, and a recipient of many awards.

He is the author of nine books, and literary contributor to various papers and magazines.

BOOKS BY
VAHAN H. TOOTIKIAN

REFLECTIONS OF AN ARMENIAN / KHOHK YEV KHOSK
(Los Angeles, 1980)

THE ARMENIAN EVANGELICAL CHURCH
(Los Angeles, 1982)

**ARMENIAN CONGREGATIONALISM:
FROM MISSION TO MEMBERSHIP**
(Cambridge, 1985)

ESSAYS
(Los Angeles, 1986)

FROM A MINISTER'S DESK / KHOHER YEV HOOSHER
(Los Angeles, 1987)

MY VANTAGE POINT / PANK YEV HOOSHK
(Los Angeles, 1988)

PERSPECTIVES: RELIGIOUS, LITERARY, AND ARMENIAN
(Los Angeles, 1989)

A SURVEY OF THE HEBREW BIBLE
(Detroit, 1990)

UNDERSTANDING THE NEW TESTAMENT
(Detroit, 1991)

TRANSLATION

DEMOS SHAKARIAN:

THE HAPPIEST PEOPLE ON EARTH (1985)

BS
2330.2
.T66
1991